Wednesday and
it was s[...]
meet you a[...]
Valle I - and to have y[...]
as part of the forum
on this book. Already
I know that you have
the same passion, vision,

Lessons from an Activist Intellectual

Teaching, Research, and Organizing for Social Change

Edited by
José Zapata Calderón

and practice that
we try to exemplify
in the lessons
that are in this
book.

University Press of America,® Inc.
Lanham • Boulder • New York • Toronto • Plymouth, UK

Library of Congress Control Number: 2015935962
ISBN: 978-0-7618-6588-9 (pbk : alk. paper)

Cover photo by Jorge de la Torre *depicting the Author, José Zapata Calderón*, helping to lead a seven-mile march from Ontario, CA, to Pomona, CA, in protest of immigration raids in the region. La Opinión newspaper estimated 10,000 participants, calling it the largest demonstration in the history of the Inland Valley region. See Chapter 13: "Immigration Raids in the Inland Empire: A Historical Pattern And Its Responses."

∞™ The paper used in this publication meets the minimum requirements of American National Standard for Information Sciences Permanence of Paper for Printed Library Materials, ANSI/NISO Z39.48-1992.

Contents

Acknowledgments

I want to thank my family for pushing me forward to publish this anthology of articles. I had posted them on my blog but my wife Rose and sons Joaquin, Jose Luis, and Chris thought that there were important lessons from my work as a professor and organizer that could be shared with others through a book. Without my family, including my father Juaquin and mother Maria (who have both passed away), I would not be who I am today. I especially want to thank my son, Jose Luiz, who took the time to format every article according to the publisher's specifications. I also want to especially thank UCLA Emeritus Professor in Sociology John Horton who worked with me on the early articles on Monterey Park that allowed me to complete a dissertation and to ultimately land a professor position at Pitzer College.

There are so many people to acknowledge in the course of my organizing, teaching, and research that this would be a book in itself. In general, I do want to thank all the individuals, communities, and organizations that have played a role in helping me to make the connections between theory and practice, academia and community, and between community-based organizing and research.

Introduction

This book is an anthology of articles that provide examples of how an academician can combine the roles of teacher, researcher, and activist with a critical democratic pedagogy approach in implementing community-based social change projects. It is about how finding one's passion in one's lived experience can serve as a foundation for overcoming obstacles in academia and how the application of an interactive, intercultural, and interdisciplinary approach can involve students and community participants in community-based teaching, research, and learning experiences for social change. This style of pedagogy has a particular salience for historically excluded individuals from diverse racial, class, gender, and sexual orientation backgrounds, for whom the educational experience can be both an alienating and empowering experience.

Drawing on my history as an immigrant, student, faculty member, community organizer, ethnographer, and activist, the articles in this anthology provide examples of campus/community partnerships that are moving beyond the traditional "charity" models to social change practices that are empowering the participants, building capacities in community organizations, and advancing collaborative participatory action approaches between faculty, students, and community-based individuals/organizations.

Chapter One

Inclusion or Exclusion

*One Immigrant's Experience of Cultural
and Structural Barriers to Power Sharing and Unity* [1]

José Zapata Calderón

This narrative looks at the dialectic of inclusion and exclusion as tied to my experiences as a first-generation immigrant of Mexican origin. In this context, it is about being stigmatized and marginalized by a dominant group who has benefited from forced migration and colonization. It is about coming to this country in search of a better life but being forced to accept the dominant group's agenda of what it takes to succeed in this society. It is about power relations and the forces that shape identities in their own image through public institutions and through the visual and printed media. It is about the meaning of being an immigrant in a society where a dominant group imposes its language, values, culture, and institutions. As much as it is about this author's life, it is also about the life of the Mexican-origin people in the United States and their struggles for social justice and democratic rights.

There has been a tendency for some social theorists to view the issues of social justice and democratic rights in the context of the assimilation of all racial and ethnic groups (Park, 1950; Gordon, 1964). The term implies that Chicanos and other people of color are like European immigrants and that if they only follow their same road, they too will receive the fruits that the society has to give. The assimilationist view "blames the victim," and basically says that our problems are related to our culture, to our family ties, to our lack of accepting the American way. What the assimilationist view fails to point out is that we have a different history than European immigrants. Like Asian Pacific, African, and Native Americans, we were not voluntary immigrants to this country (Steinberg, 1981). The reality is that we were a

1

people dispossessed of our land and forced to become wageworkers in the mines, on the railroads, on ranches, and in farm fields.

For Chicanos, the historical roots of these trends are found in two early historical developments: (1) the United States' annexation of the Southwest in 1848, and (2) the penetration of Mexico by U.S. capitalist interests.

The Treaty of Guadalupe Hidalgo was supposed to protect privileges that came from customs, languages, law, and culture. Property rights were also guaranteed (Acuna, 2000). However, after 1848 the treaty was broken and the Chicano people were faced with discrimination and oppression in all spheres of life, including loss of land and democratic rights. Hence, although the Chicano/Mexican people will constitute a majority in the Southwest and be part of a Latino population that now numbers 35 million people in the United States, and although the estimated 20.6 million Chicano/Mexican people living in the United States have made gains in some areas, they are still faced with historical factors that make them poorer, more prone to unemployment, and faced with generally less opportunity than the rest of the population. [2]

While we are a multicultural and multiracial country, the issue in this debate is the issue of power and who has it. Although stratified in the lower levels of the economic ladder, we have had a long history of resistance. This has been a tradition among the Chicano/Mexican people and will continue until the issues of denial of land, cultural, and democratic rights are resolved.

Our lives and their intersections are rooted in the past, guide our actions in the present, and help provide a vision for the future. It has been this way with my life: a lived experience influenced by the past and present history of the Chicano/Latino people.

EXCLUSION AS LIVED EXPERIENCE

I was born in Madera, Chihuahua, Mexico, and migrated with my grandparents (whom I called Madre y Padre) to the United States as a 6-year-old in 1954. We moved into a one-room house in a small farm community of northern Colorado called Ault. We lived on the east side of the tracks in a farm worker barrio that was close knit and where everyone knew and cared for one another. Our neighbors paid no attention to having someone come over and ask for salt or tortillas. This was the norm. If someone was sick or someone passed away, the entire barrio would know about it.

There were aspects that were related to the two cultural worlds that we were now living in. On the one hand, as a family in a lower socioeconomic level, we were beholden to the institutions that surrounded us. As a day laborer, my father had to sell his labor to the farmer for whatever wage they decided to pay him. There were years when my father did not earn over

$2,000 in one year. In order to survive, my father had to negotiate a charge account with the nearby grocery store.

On Saturdays, my father got paid by the farmer he worked for. We would always wait until he brought the check home and then we would walk to Johnson's Grocery Store together and do the weekly shopping. Actually, my mom would do the entire shopping. I would tag along with my mother while my father waited outside until we were done. When we were finished, I would go get him and he would come and sign his check.

After bringing the groceries home, my father would go and play pool with some of his friends in one of the bars downtown. He would stay all day and often return somewhat drunk after midnight. My mother would stay up and wait for him while I fell asleep. As soon as he arrived, she would jump up, help him inside the house, take off his shoes, and put him to bed.

There was a traditional gender division of labor in our home that had some of the characteristics brought over from Mexico but that also fit into some of the norms of U.S. culture. My mother carried out all the household chores. She would cook, wash and iron our clothes, sweep the floors, and make the beds.

Since we had a wood stove, I was expected to do most of the wood chopping. Now and then, some of the area farmers would drop off huge tree trunks in our yard and I would spend days helping my father saw them into manageable logs.

At the same time, I grew up in a distinct cultural pluralist environment of two worlds: the world at home with its roots in Mexican culture and the world at school that stressed learning the ways of the dominant Anglo culture. At home, with my parents, I spoke only Spanish, prayed to the patron saint of the poor, San Martin de Porres, listened to *corridos* (Mexican ballads) on the radio, and celebrated Mexican holidays (such as Mexican Independence Day and Dia de los Muertos). Although our home was within the city limits, we raised chickens, rabbits, and pigs. We also grew a garden that included corn, beans, vegetables, and chiles (lots of very hot chiles). All these products helped to get us through the cold winters. In addition to canning the products from the garden, my mother used the natural foods from the garden to make enchiladas, tamales, chile rellenos, and refried beans. Hence, a lot of our diet was based on natural foods.

The world at school demanded English only. Since I couldn't understand a word that my first-grade teacher taught, I turned to ditching school and playing in a nearby feedlot. A friend of my parents, Mel Martinez, would always find me and take me back. The next day I would hide once again. This went on for six months until a teacher, Mrs. Elder, realized that there was nothing wrong with my speech patterns and began to tutor me after school. We negotiated the idea that she would learn to speak Spanish and that I would learn to speak English. She stayed after school pointing to the window, the desk, the door, the wall, and whatever was around us. I repeated after her: "window, table, door, wall." I would follow the same pattern by asking her to repeat the words "ventana, mesa, puerta, pared." By the time I was in sixth grade, I had learned English so well that I placed second in the county spelling contest. Looking back on this experience, I credit my knowledge of the Spanish language in helping me to sound out words that I did not know. Although I was one of the lucky ones who learned English, some of my other classmates from the barrio weren't as fortunate. Six other Mexican students dropped out before the sixth grade.

"Making it" in U.S. society, I later discovered, meant that one had to give up being part of oneself. I did not know it then but the world at school, much like the larger society, was shaping my identity and knowledge of who I was.

I remember being laughed at by white students who looked down on me for speaking Spanish at school. There was an unwritten law not to speak it. When I brought my mother's burritos to lunch, my classmates made fun of them. Although I laughed alongside of them, I decided to never bring my lunch again. On snowy days, I went without eating.

Language became a powerful tool of cultural and structural oppression in our history. The English language was not only used as a tool to enact racist treaties and policies, it also allowed for the writing of a history that excluded our Chicano people.

I remember the games that I played with my friends in the barrio after school. We would pretend that broomsticks were horses. We were as brown as the ground, as Indian-looking as you could be, but we fought over who would be Tonto and the Lone Ranger. The meaning of who we were was already being shaped by television. Everyone wanted to ride the big white horse and wear the big white hat. Everyone wanted to play the part of Kemo Sabe and resisted the idea of being called Tonto. For my barrio friends, the word *sabe* implied a person who was smart or "knowing." What the television never taught us is how the "all-American cowboy" actually had its roots back with the cattle raising vaqueros of the 1800s. Many of the techniques, tools, language, styles, and methods that were used to describe the American cowboy were actually appropriated from the Mexican vaquero (McWilliams, 1968:144–156). Some of the earliest "American cowboys" were ex-slaves with African roots (Porter, 1994:158–167).

I remember that there were no brown faces on television. No, I take that back. On all the Western programs of the late 1950s and early '60s, we were portrayed as drunkards, murderers, and robbers—dozens of us shot down by one cowboy with a six-gun that never ran out of bullets. The TV programs also decided the meaning of "beauty" for us. We never saw a Latina in any of the facial advertisements. It was always a rich blonde in a Mercedes-Benz with push-button windows selling us pimple cream.

The books in the classroom were no different. We learned about Spot, Dick, Jane, and the all-time hero, Tom Sawyer. We never heard the names of Juan, Maria, Jose, or Patricia. If these names appeared in a class roster, they were quickly changed. The name on my birth certificate read "José Guillermo Zapata Calderón." By the time that I graduated from high school, it had been changed to "Joe William Calderon." I am sure that they would have changed the name "Zapata" also, but it did not sound right to call me "Shoes" Calderon.

When we did hear about our people, it was in a bad sense. We were told that the Mexicans outnumbered the "heroes" in the Alamo ten to one and that is why the Mexicans won. We were supposed to feel sorry for Davy Crocket, Daniel Boone, and some of the others who helped "develop" this land: Billy the Kid, Kit Carson, and General Custer. The Mexican heroes, such as Pancho Villa and Emiliano Zapata, were merely portrayed on television as "frito" bandidos (bandits who always stole the chips and ran).

We were taught that the United States "bought" from Mexico nearly one-third of its territory from Mexican president Santa Ana and that we have been a downtrodden people with little social mobility ever since.

They didn't tell us about the many that resisted lynching, murders, theft of land, and resources. They didn't tell us about Joaquin Murrieta who, in 1850, fought the land takeovers resulting in his death and that of his wife (Gonzalez, 1999). They didn't tell us about Juan "Cheno" Cortina, who organized to defend the rights of Mexicans guaranteed by the Treaty of Guadalupe Hidalgo (Acuna, 2000:72–74).

The history books left out the role of Chicana women altogether. They were merely portrayed as "the malinche" who passively sold out her people. They didn't tell us about women leaders in the Mexican revolution such as Dolores Jimenez y Muro and Carmen Serdan, two women who joined the war against the dictatorship of Porfirio Diaz.

We were told that our people were lazy, not willing to work, and without any incentive to go to school. I knew otherwise. As I moved from elementary to high school, I learned how hard my parents worked by working alongside of them in the fields. We would work from sunup to sundown, like squirrels, in order to save for the winter. My mother would be up before the sunlight to start the fire in the stove and to cook breakfast. Then she would be with us working the same long hours and come home at sundown to cook dinner and wash the dishes. When I tried to help my mother by washing the dishes or making tortillas, my father would call me a *maricon*.

I didn't know that this was a derogatory term that was later used against anyone labeled as being from a different sexual orientation. All I knew was that this type of work was something that I was not supposed to do. I became a professional at chopping wood, vaccinating sheep, thinning beets, weeding onions, and stacking hay. But I didn't know a thing about sewing, washing clothes, or cooking. These tasks were considered "women's work" and men were not supposed to do them. Anyone who went outside these roles was considered different.

In the summer we worked, and in the fall I would cross the tracks to the west side of Ault, back to school, and back to learning.

The books in school never mentioned that in the 1900s, together with Chinese and Irish workers, we helped build the railroads, recruited by the thousands, making up a majority of the workforce on the western railway lines (Takaki, 1993). When the railroad companies were through exploiting our labor, they left us living in old railroad cars on the east side of the tracks (the birth of the barrio).

We worked in the mines all over the Southwest and created billions of dollars in profits but we remained excluded from union organizing by the copper and silver barons (Acuna, 2000:127–129). They didn't tell us about the leaders who organized to change these conditions, as in San Antonio when thousands of Mexican workers went on strike protesting their wages of $1.50 for a 54-hour week in the pecan industry (Acuna, 2000:243–245). We were never taught that the leader of that organized strike was a woman named Emma Tenayuca.

Our payment in the 1920s was "immigration population control" and Americanization activities. The norm for success became assimilation with standardized IQ and achievement tests used to measure our success. English oral proficiency became a requirement for immigration as did English literacy for voting. Segregated Mexican schools were maintained (Estrada, Garcia, Macias, & Maldonado, 1981).

Although the school I attended wasn't openly segregated, it was evident that many of the Mexican students from the east side of the tracks didn't fare well in the school system. When I was a senior at the University of Colorado, I went back to find many of the Mexican students who had started in the first grade with me. I kept asking, "Why I had been able to graduate and go on to college while six others from the east side had dropped out?" After interviewing them, I realized that the school system had turned them away because they could not "fit in" to the dominant culture and because of their lack of understanding English. As I learned English and got involved in sports, I was much more accepted by the teachers and other students. The price for this "acceptance," however was immense. Through my four years of high school basketball, my parents never showed up to the annual "parent's honor night" sponsored by the school. At halftime of an important game, each one of the players was introduced alongside their parents. My parents refused to go, always excusing themselves by sharing that they did not have the proper clothes for the occasion and that they did not know anyone there.

Through the four years of high school, I excelled in football, basketball, and track. In my sophomore year, I also lettered in baseball. During these years, my father did not have to worry about employment in the winter. For the first time, we were not in debt and we were able to save a little money. However, once I graduated and went to a junior college, the farmers quit coming around in the winter months. For a while, I blamed it on the hard winters and the economy. I even helped my father buy a pickup truck so that he could travel to the farmer's houses to ask for jobs, but nothing changed. My father went back to accepting the conditions that existed before my four years in high school: a day laborer finding few jobs in the winter. Slowly, I came to the conclusion that my contributions to the sports teams were rewarded through jobs in the winter for my father.

What was consistent throughout the life of my father was the constant harassment by immigration officials. Although my father was born in Los Angeles, his parents took him to Chihuahua when he was five years old. He didn't return to the United States until the 1950s as a farm laborer. Since he never learned English, INS officials always mistook him for an undocumented worker. They would pick him up at the bars or at his work. I remember waking up many times late at night to find my mother rummaging through suitcases to find my grandfather's legal papers. On two different occasions, my father came very close to being deported.

In the history of the Mexican-origin people in the United States, the threat of deportation was always used as another means of domination. This was especially true when the economy went downward and our labor was not needed. At least half a million of our people, including U.S. citizens, were put on trains during the Depression and deported back to Mexico (Acuna, 2000:220–225; Gonzales, 1999:146–149). In the early years of the Depression, any Mexican-origin person who applied for welfare, unemployment, or any type of social services was forced to leave the country under the U.S. government category of "voluntary repatriation." Approximately half of those deported were U.S. citizens, a clear violation of both their civil and human rights.

When the economy got better and the United States entered World War II, the doors at the border were opened once again. The *bracero*, or Emergency Labor program was established in 1942, as a bilateral agreement between Mexico and the United States, to meet U.S. labor shortages in agriculture (Acuna, 2000:285–289; Takaki, 1993:391–392). The program was extended after the war as Public Law 78 and was justified as a means of meeting labor shortages caused by the Korean War. The program ended in 1964 with five million Mexicans used in the peak years between 1954 and 1962. With the establishment of a regulated labor pool, the United States Immigration and Naturalization Service began a massive drive known as Operation Wetback to deport undocumented immigrants to Mexico. Operation Wetback grossly violated the civil rights of many Mexican-origin people, as did the repatriation project of the 1930s (Barrera, 1979:116–130). Hundreds of Chicanos were arrested and harassed. They were threatened and forced to produce "proof" of their citizenship. Only a few of the thousands of those deported had formal hearings. When the project ended, more than a million persons had been deported to Mexico.

We were present in World War II when half a million of us served in the Pacific, North Africa, and Europe. We won twelve Congressional Medals of Honor but, after the war, we were met back home with hostility, attacked as "pachucos," as zoot suitors, and not allowed to bury our dead in cemeteries labeled "White Only" (Gonzales, 1999:161–164; Acuna, 2000:268–273, 280).

As I moved from junior college to the University of Colorado, I became aware of the war in Viet Nam and the draft. I learned that we were not only wanted for our cheap labor but that we were also wanted for the military service. Because I was in college, I was not drafted. Two of my best friends, Louis Renteria and Mauro Martinez, were not as lucky. I met Mauro when I was a freshman in high school. My track coach took me to the state track meet and told me to watch this "Mexican boy." I noticed that he didn't have any track shoes or a uniform like the other runners. I watched him as he ran the first 880 yards of the mile run. He was not impressive to me until the last 440 yards, when he took off running as though it were the hundred-yard dash and won the race. In the next three years until he graduated, Mauro broke the state record and held it until he was drafted into the military. Similarly, I had the opportunity of speaking with Louis Renteria after he returned from boot camp and a few days before he was sent to Viet Nam. When he came to visit me, I was working at an all-night gas station. He stayed there all night reminiscing about his family, childhood, and high school memories. Before leaving, he raised doubts about whether he would return alive, and I consoled him with visions of how he would return to attend college. Twenty-five days before his nineteenth birthday, on October 28, 1966, Louis was killed in combat. Louis and Mauro returned, like many of our young people who fought in previous wars, to be buried, and later to be forgotten. Although comprising only 11 percent of the population according to the 1960s census figures, they disproportionately represented 20 percent of those who died on the frontlines in Viet Nam (Gonzales, 1999:211–213).

ORGANIZING FOR INCLUSION

In the 1960s, our communities benefited from struggles to obtain lost land in New Mexico, voting rights through La Raza Unida Party and the Southwest Voter Registration and Education Project, and union rights in the fields of Delano, California. There were walkouts in the schools to protest the lack of

Latino teachers, principals, bilingual education, and Chicano studies in the curriculum.

Because of the gains made from those movements, I was not shut out like others previously and was able to go to college. At the University of Colorado, I became more politicized through my involvement in student government and in protests against the war in Viet Nam. As a leader in student government, I helped lead a strike of 10,000 students to protest U.S. war policies and the unjust killing of four college students at Kent State by the National Guard. We shut the campus down.

After graduating from the University of Colorado, I had planned to go to law school. Instead, the course of my life was changed when I learned that the Nixon administration, in 1969, had ordered the Defense Department to increase their purchase of California table grapes. The Defense Department eventually purchased ten thousand tons of grapes and sent more than two thousand of those tons to Viet Nam (Del Castillo & Garcia, 1995:92). When I learned about this, I felt angry because I knew that the farm workers were simply asking for better wages, clean drinking water, and bathrooms in the fields. I remembered the years of working in the fields without proper drinking water or sanitation. I remembered the long sugar beet rows and the culture of turning our heads when someone had to "go" in the fields. I thought about how 40 percent of those dying on the front lines in Viet Nam were disproportionately black and Latino and how many of these soldiers were probably the sons of striking farm workers. Like other young Chicanos from farm worker backgrounds, I began to question the meaning of fighting for justice abroad when the U.S. government was supporting the denial of basic rights for farm workers in the fields.

It was from this questioning that, with only $57 in my pocket, I caught a bus that took me to experience the organizing efforts of the United Farm Workers' Union in Delano, California. Upon arriving at the UFW national headquarters, called "40 acres," I heard a speech by Cesar Chavez that influenced the rest of my life. In that speech, Cesar Chavez said:

> There is only one thing for sure in life—and that is that we will one day die. In that space between now and when we die, we have the choice of throwing away our lives or to fully use them by sacrificing in the service of others. Because life is so precious—every minute, second, hour, week, month, and year truly count. You can easily throw your life away on drugs, alcohol, and selfishness or you can use your life in service to others. Those who truly use their lives and minds, when compared to the average human being in this country, may live the equivalent of a thousand years.

A combination of my experiences with the farm workers and Cesar Chavez's words led me to return to northern Colorado in 1971 to organize farm workers, undocumented workers, students, welfare mothers, and migrants as part of an emerging movement for democratic rights. This movement had various trends that, up until the present, have affected my life and have continued to affect the development of the Chicano/Latino people and their position in U.S. society.

First is the "democratic rights" trend. I remember that the early Chicano struggles were focused on issues having to do with bilingual education, community control, welfare rights, Chicano studies, and demands for Chicano teachers and principals in the schools. Although many Chicana women were involved in those early struggles, I remember that they were primarily assigned the roles of doing the typing, making food for fundraisers, making leaflets, and organizing day care. The men were usually the leaders who made the speeches, held the press conferences, or carried out the security for demonstrations. I remember conferences where some Chicana women were criticized for espousing any kind of feminism on the basis that it was related to the middleclass white women's liberation movement. During this period, tensions between women and men were hardly addressed. "Adelita," from the revolution in Mexico, was played up as the model for women. However, she was usually portrayed in the image of supporting the Mexican men in battle.

The second trend involved finding the commonality of class and gender. I found the significance of class through various experiences revolving around a workers' strike at a meatpacking plant. With other community organizers, I remember making the mistake of primarily organizing Chicano meatpackers in a strike for better working conditions. The bosses used this strategy to divide the Chicano workers from the white workers. The strike was lost. I learned that all workers have the commonality of owning their hands and their minds and having to sell that ownership as labor for wages to survive.

I also began to understand the deep significance of chauvinism. In 1976, I married a Chicana whom I had met in the course of various campus and community educational struggles. It was during this period that I had to confront my own chauvinism as it related to roles in the household. I was running around organizing all over the state and attending conferences in various parts of the nation. Rose would attend some of these conferences with me. However, when we had our first child, I tried to maintain the same schedule, but Rose was left with primary responsibilities in the household. At a certain point she argued, "If this is what the movement is all about, I want no part of it." Eventually, as our sons grew up, we developed a culture of holding family meetings and dividing up all the household work. Our sons grew up helping with everything from cooking to dusting, washing dishes, sweeping, and getting on their hands and knees to clean the toilets.

In addition to the family roles, our community organizing efforts were also tied to the family. When we first moved to California, we developed a parents' club in the day care our son attended. Subsequently, the parents' club played a role in helping to elect the day care director to our local school board. As our sons grew older, Rose and I helped to form various multi-ethnic coalitions that united parents around common issues in the high schools and in city hall.[3]

I learned, though, that just being involved together or creating a division of labor in the household is not enough. In our family, there are daily contra-dictions that arise and that we work through. There is still the larger system out there and a dominant culture that promotes male dominance, that treats women as sexual objects and advances those images to our children, that tracks children into specified gender roles, and that promotes sexism and homophobia. Our sons sometimes bring some of these tendencies home with them from school, from friends, or from the mass media influence. To deal with these issues that arise, we have learned to communicate about them. We have learned to talk about sexism and homophobia when we see it on the tube or when we see it in practice. Certainly, writers such as Gloria Anzaldua have taken the lead in critiquing both the sexism in the dominant culture as well as in the Chicano/ Latino culture. Her refusal to "glorify those aspects of my culture which have injured me and which have injured me in the name of protecting *me* signals a new agenda for our communities" (Anzaldua, 1987).

The third trend has been finding the commonality that we have as Latinos. The fastest-growing segment of the U.S. population today is the Latino popu-lation, increasing from 35.3 million on April I, 2000, to 38.8 million on July 1, 2002 (U.S. Bureau of the Census, 2003). The emergent "narrow trend" has tended to divide Mexican-origin Chicanos and Latinos from other peoples of Latin America. However, we have a lot of commonalities with Puerto Ri-cans, for example, who also find themselves living primarily in segregated communities. Their historical experience of subordination has also largely been determined by the colonial relationship between the United States and the island of Puerto Rico. It was the creation of a one-crop agricultural society dominated by U.S. sugar companies that originally created a large group of agricultural workers seeking other work. With the later industrial-ization of Puerto Rico, under the auspices of large multinational firms, many Puerto Rican workers became part of a growing surplus labor population, one that was forced to migrate from the countryside to the cities and from the island to the U.S. mainland (Gonzalez, 2000:246–267).

In recent years, there have been some concrete examples of Latino unity. For example, a conservative campaign to require a constitutional amendment was largely defeated by the coalition efforts of Latino groups throughout the States. Similar campaigns have been waged to fight various anti-immigrant initiatives, including Propositions 187, 209, and 227. The various Latino groups were also able to fight historical gerrymandering and elect Gloria Molina, the first Chicana Los Angeles county supervisor in history. They had to go all the way to the Supreme Court to prove that the county supervisors had historically and consciously drawn districts in such a way as to divide the Latino vote.

INCLUSION FOR A MULTICULTURAL SOCIETY

This brings me to a contemporary fourth trend. Every country in the world, right now, is being faced with the question of whether they can raise the level of technology and production to the highest levels possible without destroying the world. For destruction not to happen, it will take the types of values that give more weight to the quality of human life than to the quantity of profit, greed, and exploitation.

If we are to survive, we must be able to harness the great advances that have been made in many social, political, and economic fields and combine them with values and interests that are committed to empowering our communities and ourselves. Unfortunately, there is a vacuum of leadership on a global scale. Hence, there is a rise of racism, protectionism, and chauvinism.

The fourth trend espouses an appreciation of our diverse historical experiences. However, there is no getting around that U.S. history had its origins in laws and ideologies that were used to justify the varied stratification of different groups through conquest, slavery, and exploitation (Almaguer, 1994; Omi & Winant, 1994; Steinberg, 1981; Takaki, 1993). If we don't absorb and appreciate this aspect in all its manifestations, there is the danger of our accepting an ideology that simply blames the victim.

For example, there are the myths that immigrants, and particularly Latino immigrants, come to this country and steal jobs and social services. The reality is that the labor force participation rate for Latino immigrants is much higher than for native-born Americans, that immigrants in this country contribute to U.S. society in taxes and Social Security, and that the undocumented have actually improved local economies. Because of their willingness to work for lower wages, it has rejuvenated the profitability of ailing industries and prevented further job losses in many localities.

Another myth is the one propagated by some of our political leaders that Asian Pacific Americans are succeeding at the expense of Latinos, African Americans, and other groups. This is particularly prevalent in southern California, where the Latino and Asian Pacific groups are becoming a majority in various cities. While Asian Pacific Americans have achieved in the realms of education, there is a tendency to categorize this achievement as that of being a "model minority" example that others can follow. The "model minority" myth is used to place tremendous pressure on those groups that are having difficulties in our schools. If Latinos do not perform to the standards prescribed, the tendency is to think that something is wrong with them. This becomes a real problem for both Asian and Latino immigrants who cannot speak English and for those who find that English laws have been aimed at them. The use of this myth by the state, by growers, and by white workers afraid of losing their privilege has resulted in the existence of a divided and weak working class in this country. Every time there has been the potential of workers from diverse backgrounds to unite, the "model minority" myth has been raised. Recent studies, instead, have shown that while there are some Asian Pacific American successes in respect to education, income, and employment, African Americans and Latinos are equally successful and that the Asian community has a large poverty pool with high levels of disenfranchisement (Blackwell, Kwoh, & Pastor, 2002:86–115; Daniels, 1997; Bing, 1997; Ong & Hee, 1994).

Today, the "model minority" myth is used to cover the significance of race. What is proposed is that if Asian Americans "can do it," other groups can too. With this type of thinking, the issue of race is not seen as an obstacle. All one has to do to achieve the American dream is to work hard, abandon one's old cultural ways, and learn to speak good English. For those categorized into a "model minority category," it becomes a no-win situation when they are criticized for not assimilating to the dominant culture but condemned when they are viewed as being too successful.

This aspect of the "model minority myth" does not apply simply to Asian Pacific Islander groups; it also applies to Latinos and other people of color. A good example occurred in the city of Pomona, California. Similar to the demographic changes taking place in Los Angeles, Pomona's overall population has grown from 131,723 in 1990 to 149,473 in the year 2000, a 13.5 percent change (U.S. Bureau of the Census, 1990, 2000). The population changes between 1990 and 2000 have resulted in Pomona, like many other cities throughout southern California, being a "minority" majority city with Latinos, Asian Pacific Islanders, and African Americans now in the majority. In this city, even the mayor, Eddie Cortez, like many other Latinos (regardless of their class background), could not sweep away the results of racism and racial profiling. In an effort to improve his health, Mayor Cortez began a daily program of running in his exercise clothes through the streets of Pomona. Thinking that Cortez was just another Mexican running from the law, the Immigration and Naturalization Service stopped him—and because he did not have proper identification, picked him up and almost deported him.

While scapegoating and the model minority myth have served to divide us, it is important to point out some concrete historical examples of how groups have been able to overcome the use of race and divisive myths and teachings to build effective and strong coalitions. In the early 1900s, hundreds of Japanese American and Mexican American agricultural workers joined forces to protest the working conditions in the agricultural fields of California. They formed a union, the Japanese-Mexican Labor Association (JMLA), in which meetings were conducted in Japanese and Spanish. Unfortunately, denied support by the American Federation of Labor, this union only lasted a few years (Takaki, 1993:187–189). It did demonstrate, however, the possibilities for overcoming the pitting of one group over another by the growers and the state to build interracial coalitions. Another example, in the late 1960s and early '70s, occurred when Filipino and Mexican workers united under the banner of the United Farm Workers union and made gains to improve the lives of agricultural workers (Griswold Del Castillo & Garcia, 1995).

A good example of collaboration that beat back the "divisive myths" took place in the city of Monterey Park, where coalitions developed around language and growth issues. The multi-ethnic Coalition for Harmony in Monterey Park (CHAMP) successfully defeated an English Only ordinance in 1987 and laid the groundwork for a trend that advocated citizen input into city planning decisions and the appreciation of diverse cultures (Horton et al., 1995). These types of concerns have united African Americans, Latinos, Asians, and working-class people of all colors around numerous power-sharing efforts (Calderón, 1990; Horton et al., 1995; Pardo, 1998; Regalado & Martinez, 1991; Saito, 1993, 1998; Sonenshein, 1993). Such coalitions have been effective in winning political reapportionment and mutual empowerment battles throughout the country. In Chicago, for example, such political coalitions emerged to preserve black wards and to increase the number of Latino wards.

Another example that I have recently been involved in is with the development of a day labor center in Pomona. When the city of Pomona passed an ordinance to stop day laborers from looking for jobs on street corners, students and community leaders from diverse backgrounds organized to develop a community organization and center that could empower the workers through the establishment of employment training programs, language classes, health referral networks, immigration rights counseling, and biweekly leadership meetings.

A recent conference led by the Latino Round Table brought together over a hundred leaders in the San Gabriel and Inland Valleys of Los Angeles County to develop a long-term plan on issues having to do with education, immigrant rights, politics, labor, and art. The conference was a catalyst for community-building and power-sharing initiatives in the region that are having an effect in changing institutions and in electing political representatives accountable to the community. These coalitions have had the distinction of advancing a new style of leadership that is challenging the traditional dominant power hierarchy and giving more weight to quality-of-life issues.

A genuine multiracial society based on power sharing will strike at the heart of gender, race, class, and sexual inequalities. It will be inclusive of the contributions of women, Chicanos and Latinos, African Americans, Asian Pacific Americans, Native Americans, gay and lesbians, and working people of all colors. Most important, it will build unity and power through focusing on the larger structural issues that are causing our institutions to decay.

While struggles in this decade have revolved around basic rights issues such as language rights, cultural rights, and the right to political representation, the struggles today are also grappling with the larger structural issues involving the need for educational reform and curriculum transformation; the need for access to the public health system; and the need for greater government investment in housing, education, and job development. In this trend, it is not enough to be in support of multiculturalism or multiracial unity. While the calls for multiculturalism and multiracial unity are an advancement on the politics that advance nativism, they can also be used as conflicting strategies to obtain differing goals. The underlying economic class issues can be camouflaged by the state with token acts promoting superficial power and unity. That is why multiracial unity has to go beyond the rubbing of shoulders by different ethnic/immigrant groups to a unity that brings the various ethnic groups together around the larger structural issues that are dividing them.

The larger structural issues facing our communities go beyond appreciating cultures and even beyond local municipalities. With state and federal funding cuts, local governments are raising taxes and reducing social services. The challenge for community leaders, as well as others, is to find creative new sources of revenue without, at the same time, relying on unbridled development and racial scapegoating as responses to these problems. Solutions to the larger structural issues are going to take a style of leadership that understands the interdependent character of a globalized economy; that seeks regional cooperation between policy makers; that pushes forward the process of empowering the community as a whole; and that advances the full and diverse participation of all ethnic/racial groups in the decision-making process. This means not just training people in the tools of leadership but building unity and power through collaborative initiatives aimed at advancing structural change.

What stands out in my research of the contemporary history of southern California is the importance of leadership in taking multiracial coalescing from a level of cultural and social interaction to one that involves all ethnic/racial groups in the process of creating structural change. From my experiences, the politics of exclusion can be replaced with the politics of inclusion by (1) combining the practice of participatory democracy at the grassroots neighborhood arena with policy making at the local and national governance levels, and (2) taking into consideration the particular history of each oppressed group in the United States while simultaneously building coalitions that focus on the underlying structural issues affecting all groups.

NOTES

1. Copyright Acknowledgement: This chapter was previously published in the following: *Minority Voices: Linking Personal Ethnic History and the Sociological Imagination.* Ed. John Myers. Boston: Allyn & Bacon, 2004: 106–20.

2. U.S. Department of Commerce estimates released on March 8, 2000, showed that nearly twothirds (20.6 million) of Latinos were of Mexican origin; 14 percent (4.5 million) were of Central American and South American origin; 10 percent (3 million) were of Puerto Rican origin; 7 percent (2 million) were from Caribbean and other countries, and 4 percent (1.4 million) were of Cuban origin.

3. See *Politics of Diversity* by John Horton, which illustrates some of our family's involvement in the building of coalitions in the city of Monterey Park.

REFERENCES

Acuna, Rodolfo. 2000. *Occupied America: A History of Chicanos.* 4th ed. Menlo Park, CA: Longman.

Almaguer, Tomas. 1994. Racial Fault Lines: *The Historical Origins of White Supremacy in California.* Berkeley: University of California Press.

Anzaldua, Gloria. 1987. *Borderland/La Frontera: The New Mestiza.* San Francisco: Spinsters/ Aunt LuteBook Company.

Barrera, Mario. 1979. *Race and Class in the Southwest: A Theory of Racial Inequality.* Notre Dame, IN: University of Notre Dame Press.

Blackwell, Angela Glover, Stewart Kwoh, & Manuel Pastor. 2002. *Searching for the Uncommon Common Ground: New Dimensions on Race in America.* New York: W. W. Norton & Co.

Calderón, José. 1990. "Latinos and Ethnic Conflict in Suburbia: The Case of Monterey Park." *Latino Studies Journal.* 1, 2: 23–32.

Calderón, José. Fall 1998. "Sources of Inter-Community Conflict and Models of Collaboration." *Journal of California Politics and Policy.* Edmund G. "Pat" Brown Institute of Public Affairs, California State University, Los Angeles.

Daniels, Roger. 1997. "United States Policy Toward Asian Immigrants." In *New American Destinies: Reader in Contemporary Asian and Latino Immigration,* Darrell Y. Hamamoto & Rodolfo D. Torres, eds. New York: Routledge, pp. 73–90.

Estrada, Leobardo F., Chris Garcia, Reynaldo Flores Macias, & Lionel Maldonado. Spring 1981. "Chicanos in the United States: A History of Exploitation and Resistance." *Daedalus* 110, 1.

Gonzales, Manuel G. 1999. *Mexicanos: A History of Mexicans in the U.S.* Bloomington: Indiana University Press.

Gonzalez, Juan. 2000. *Harvest of Empire: A History of Latinos in America.* New York: Penguin Books.

Gordon, Milton M. 1964. *Assimilation in American Life.* New York: Oxford University Press.

Griswold Del Castillo, Richard, & Richard A. Garcia. 1995. *Cesar Chavez: A Triumph of Spirit.* Norman: University of Oklahoma Press.

Hing, Bill Ong. 1997. "Immigration Policy: Making and Remaking Asian Pacific America." In *New American Destinies: Reader in Contemporary Asian and Latino Immigration,* Darrell Y. Hamamoto & Rodolfo D. Torres, eds. New York: Routledge, pp. 315–323.

Horton, John, with José Calderón, Mary Pardo, Leland Saito, Linda Shaw, & Yen-Fen Tseng. 1995. *The Politics of Diversity.* Philadelphia: Temple University Press.

McWilliams, Carey. 1968. *North From Mexico: The Spanish-Speaking People of the United States.* New York: Greenwood Press.

Omi, Michael, & Howard Winant. 1994. *Racial Formation in the United States: From the 1960-1980's.* New York: Routeledge and Kegan Paul.

Ong, Paul, & Suzanne J. Hee. 1994. "Economic Diversity." In *The State of Asian Pacific America: Economic Diversity, Issues, and Policies*, Paul Ong, ed. Los Angeles: Leadership Education for Asian Pacifics, Asian Pacific American Public Policy Institute, UCLA Asian American Studies Center.

Pardo, Mary. 1998. *Mexican American Women Activists: Identity and Resistance in Two Los Angeles Communities*. Philadelphia: Temple University Press.

Park, Robert E. 1950. *Race and Culture*. Glencoe, IL: Free Press.

Porter, Kenneth W. 1994. "African Americans in the Cattle Industry, 1860's–1880's." In *Peoples of Color in the American West*, Sucheng Chan, Douglas Henry Daniels, Mario T. Garcia, & Terry P. Wilson, eds. Lexington, MA: D. C. Heath and Company, pp. 158–167.

Regalado, James A., & Gloria Martinez. 1991. "Reapportionment and Coalition Building: A Case Study of informal Barriers to Latino Empowerment in Los Angeles County." In *Latinos and Political Coalitions: Political Empowerment for the 1990's*, Roberto E. Villareal & Norma G. Hernandez, eds. New York: Praeger, pp. 126–143.

Saito, Leland. 1993. "Asian Americans and Latinos in San Gabriel Valley, California: Ethnic Political Cooperation and Redistricting, 1990–92." *American Journal* 19: 55–68.

Saito, Leland. 1998. *Race and Politics: Asian Americans, Latinos, and Whites in a Los Angeles Suburb*. Urbana and Chicago: University of Illinois Press.

Sonenshein, Raphael J. 1993. *Politics in Black and White: Race and Power in Los Angeles*. Princeton, NJ: Princeton University Press.

Steinberg, Stephen. 1981. *The Ethnic Myth: Race, Ethnicity, and Class in America*. Boston: Beacon Press.

Takaki, Ronald. 1993. A Different Mirror: *A History of Multicultural America*. Boston: Little, Brown, and Company.

U.S. Bureau of the Census. 1990. *Population Statistics*. Washington, DC: U.S. Government Printing Office.

U.S. Bureau of the Census. 2000. *Population Statistics*. Washington, DC: U.S. Government Printing Office.

U.S. Bureau of the Census. 2003. "Hispanic Report." Washington, DC, June 18.

Chapter Two

Lessons from an Activist Intellectual

*Participatory Research, Teaching,
and Learning for Social Change*[1]

José Zapata Calderón

As a professor with a history in various social movements, I have often asked myself, "How do I justify my teaching and research objectives without losing my commitment to progressive social change? How do I carry out research that does not belittle or hurt our communities? Is it possible to be a critical activist, a researcher, a committed teacher, and a dedicated learner?" Opposing the positivist view that academicians should remain neutral in the classroom and in their research, I suggest that connections can be made between teaching, research, and action.

My research and teaching correspond with aspects of the participatory action approach, particularly the explicit connections that approach makes between social research and action (Maurasse, 2001; Zlotkowski, 1998; Nyden et al., 1997; Ostrow, Hesser, and Enos, 1999; Fals-Borda and Rahman, 1991; Whyte, 1991; Greenwood and Levin, 1998). Coming from an activist background, I have had to find a way of combining the roles of teacher, researcher, and activist. In the area of research, I have had to resolve the issue that my data were collected in the dual roles of researcher and participant, where one is involved in the process of social change while simultaneously describing the world of the participants through their eyes. In the area of teaching, I have implemented a style of critical pedagogy that involves the students both inside and outside the classroom.

The "banking" concept of pedagogy is still widely accepted in the college classroom. Teaching according to this method is based on the premise that the teacher "educates" while the students "memorize" and feed back to the

19

teacher the information they absorb. With this type of pedagogy, there is little room for interaction among the students and between the students and the teacher. An alternative pedagogy involves participatory learning and research that fosters classroom collaboration and draws connections between lived experience and academic theories. (Aparicio and Jose-Kampfner, 1995; Cantor, 1995; Jacoby, 1996; Buroway, 2000; Darder, 2002).

BACKGROUND

I have been part of various movements to create social change by combining participation, research, and action. Through the Coalition for Harmony in Monterey Park, I was involved in an effort to overturn an English-only resolution of the city council and in a larger movement opposing anti-immigrant and progrowth sentiment in the city.[2] As president of the San Gabriel Valley Chapter of the League of United Latin American Citizens (LULAC), I helped promote more visibility of Latinos in all aspects of city and county government. As a co-chair of the Multi-Ethnic Task Force and chair of the Alhambra School District Human Relations Advisory Committee, I helped advance coalition-building efforts aimed at the establishment of multicultural and conflict-resolution programs in the local high schools. In 1988 and 1990 I complemented this activity with work as a researcher with John Horton of the UCLA Department of Sociology in the community of Monterey Park. Over the next two years, our research was variously funded and supported by the Institute of American Cultures and the Ford Foundation's Changing Relations Project. In 1989, in conjunction with the Ford Foundation project, I became a member of a seven-member local research team charged with studying political relations between newcomer immigrants and established community residents. Our research was part of a national study of the impact of immigration on everyday life in six communities: Miami, Houston, Philadelphia, Chicago, Monterey Park, and Garden City, Kansas. This national project emphasized the use of critical ethnography as a means of determining how day-to-day interaction was related to class and power. To avoid assuming static ethnic entities, we focused on the formation of political agendas through intergroup relations (Horton et al., 1995). I incorporated these concerns into my own research by observing sites that were part of my everyday life in the city, including the neighborhood I lived in, the sports clubs in which my sons participated, and the community organizations and coalitions that I helped to organize. My observations were complemented by formal and informal interviews and consultation of work that grounds theory in data collected by participant observation, interviewing, the writing and coding of field notes, and analysis (Emerson, Fretz, and Shaw, 1995; Lofland and Lofland, 1995; Stauss and Corbin, 1990).

My work did not, however, entirely follow the grounded-theory approach, because I was more than a participant observer in the process. My prior involvement as a leader in various community neighborhood and civic groups made it impossible for me to be a neutral observer. Gathering data in the dual roles of researcher and activist gave me special insight into activities and trends in the community, but it opened my work to criticism from some who disagree with my public positions. For example, the former mayor of Monterey Park, Barry Hatch, said in a *Los Angeles Times* article that the Changing Communities project would be biased because I was part of it (Hudson, 1988).

LINKING ACTION AND RESEARCH

The participants in the coalitions that I was involved in were less concerned about bias than about finding solutions to the many problems that they confronted in the community and the schools. I was considered an "insider" by these coalitions, since I lived with my family in the community and had children in the district schools. They also knew that I was a researcher from my having told them or from having read about it in the local newspapers. What we had in common was the desire to find solutions to problems of ethnic/racial conflict in the community. When an all-white city council passed a resolution calling for the use of English only in city literature, I was part of a group of multiethnic residents that formed the Coalition for Harmony in Monterey Park (CHAMP). Together, we were able to defeat the ordinance and eventually vote out of office its main proponents. Further, we were able to elect candidates who called for planned development without casting the issue of "growth" in anti-immigrant terms. By working actively in these coalitions, I was able to develop an ongoing dialogue with the participants that allowed me to serve as both active participant and researcher. In this dialogue we not only engaged in analysis and reflection but also challenged each other and began to develop theories and strategies for dealing with the emerging ethnic/racial divisions in the city.

As conflict moved from the city hall level to the schools, I was able to join in other coalition-building efforts. A series of fights between Latino and Chinese students at Mark Keppel High School led to the formation of two coalitions of parents. The Asian Coalition, led by the Chinese American Parents and Teachers Association of Southern California, included 21 Asian groups composed primarily of Chinese professionals, including teachers, teacher's aides, and bilingual social service workers. The other coalition, the Coalition for Equality, was predominantly Latino, with a handful of white parents. At first these coalitions were unable to work together for what members of both coalitions pointed to as reasons of cultural and class difference.

After numerous meetings between their leaders, they were able to overcome these differences to form one coalition, the Multi-Cultural Community Association.

Pressure by the association on school administrators led to the establishment of an official advisory group to the school board, the Alhambra School District Human Relations Advisory Committee. This 30-member committee included representatives of groups including the Multi-Cultural Community Association, the Parent-Teacher Association, the teachers' union, school staff and administrators, and student representatives from the district's three high schools.

I served as committee chair and worked alongside the community representatives to produce concrete evidence of ethnic/racial conflict in the school district.[3] Together we carried out a survey of 1,500 students and 300 limited-English-speaking students in English as a Second Language programs. The results showed that 86 percent of the English-speaking students at Mark Keppel High School and a majority of the students at all three high schools perceived racial tensions as an important problem.

We also examined school district reports to establish that Latinos had a disproportionate percentage of student expulsions and that they were being guided into the lower-level noncollege-track courses. With this research in hand, the Multi-Cultural Community Association was able to rally the various ethnic groups around a ten-point plan that included the abolition of the tracking system.

Further, the committee wrote and the school board adopted a policy for dealing with hate-motivated behavior. This policy required principals to develop plans for creating an environment that would allow all persons "to realize their full individual potential through understanding and appreciation of society's diversity of race, ethnic background, national origin, religious belief, sex, age, disability, or sexual orientation." As part of this policy, the school district institutionalized conflict-resolution classes and gave students the option of mediation as an alternative to expulsion (Calderón, 1995).

In these examples, the coalition leaders and researchers developed concrete theories through "co-generative dialogue" to develop "empowering" plans of action (Eldin and Levin, 1991). In both the Monterey Park and the Alhambra school district coalition efforts, participants went beyond cultural differences to seek the structural foundations of the problems. Thus the "insiders" were not just sources of data but active participants in gathering the data and utilizing it to produce institutional change.

At the same time, as both a participant and researcher in the process, I clearly influenced the process, the content of the research, and the outcomes.

CRITICAL PEDAGOGY

When I began my academic career, I implemented a pedagogy that, similar to my research methodology, aimed at connecting the classroom with participatory and lived experience. To advance a culture of action and participation, I practiced what Ira Shor, in his book *Empowering Education* (1992), calls "critical-democratic pedagogy." This technique seeks to place the readings and classroom activities in the context of the lived experience of the students. In creating dialogue on the subject matter, I have used generative themes that "grow out of student culture and express problematic conditions in daily life that are useful for generating critical discussion"(Shor, 1992: 55) in addition to themes emerging from readings and research.

In my class on race and ethnic relations I have the students read sections from Paulo Freire's *Pedagogy of the Oppressed* (1993) to emphasize that we are all students and teachers who have the capacity to create culture. I then challenge the students to learn from each other, to share knowledge, and to consider where their experience fits in with that of the literature. I use a combination of readings that promote a comprehensive and critical study of the significant concepts and issues in the field: *Racial Formations in the United States* (Omi and Winant, 1994), *Racial and Ethnic Relations* (Feagin and Feagin, 2003), *A Different Mirror* (Takaki, 1993), *Racial Fault Lines* (Almaguer, 1994), *Race, Class, and Gender* (Andersen and Collins, 2003), and *Searching for the Uncommon Common Ground* (Blackwell, Kwoh, and Pastor, 2002). With the use of these readings as a foundation, I fashion this class as a society, purposely dividing the students into various types of "cultural" discussion groups. One type is randomly selected and usually multiethnic. Another is divided in terms of a series of novels dealing with the everyday lives of individuals who face obstacles of racial, class, gender, or sexual inequality.

The discussion groups focusing on the novels are required to identify major themes, relate them to course concepts, and develop class presentations that creatively use multicultural media. One group, focusing on Toni Morrison's *The Bluest Eye* (1972), combined original poetry, rap, and video to express its idea that "race is a pigment of our imagination." The video included interviews of shoppers at a nearby mall. After being shown pictures of various individuals representing different racial/ethnic groups, shoppers were asked to point out the one that they thought best represented their conception of "beauty." The results of this creative exercise sparked a dialogue on the role of society in the formation of ideas regarding race, class, gender, and sexual orientation. Another group, utilizing Sandra Cisneros's description of a barrio in *The House on Mano Street* (1991), presented a video comparing a nearby "Latino barrio" with the more affluent area of Los Angeles. Students in another group utilized John Okada's *No No Boy* (1976) in a play about the troubles that Japanese-Americans face in the aftermath of Pearl Harbor. Yet another group, after reading Louise Erdrich's *Love Medicine* (1989), used poetry, film, and music to describe the relocation of Native Americans and the obstacles that they confront when they leave behind the familiarity of the reservation for the alienation of the city. A group of students from varied backgrounds read Maya Angelou's *I Know Why the Caged Bird Sings* (1996) and applied its content to various theories of stratification. In the process of deepening their understanding of these theories, they found connections to their own lived experience and shared this collective interpretation through a mural. As they worked on the project, it became apparent that students of different ethnic and class backgrounds and genders could collaborate to produce a masterpiece. Other novels that students have used in their presentations include Amy Tan's *The Joy Luck Club* (1989), Alex Haley's *Malcolm X* (1965), Leslie Marmon Silko's *Ceremony* (1986), T. Coraghessan Boyle's *The Tortilla Curtain* (1995), Hector Tobar's *The Tattooed Soldier* (1998), and Luis Rodriguez's *Always Running* (1993).

The grading for this exercise requires students to write a paper connecting the concepts outlined in the texts to the main themes of the novels. A group grade for the class presentations is based on the cohesiveness of the presentation, the connection of novel themes with class concepts, and the effectiveness of the use of the creative media.

The final research paper for this class requires students to utilize the ideas of Freire in examining whether a chosen site (institution, group, movement, or community) is advancing a process of "liberation" or merely a process of "domestication."

PARTNERSHIP WITH THE UNITED FARM WORKERS' UNION

Although the readings and exercises in my classes relate to the lived experiences of the teacher and students, this classroom learning pales by comparison with the type of learning that involves students outside the classroom. Having come from a farm worker background and worked with the United Farm Workers in the early 1970s, I was moved to develop a class that could create dialogue on new-social-movements theory as applied to the farm workers' movement.[4] Utilizing union contacts from my early organizing efforts, I worked with them to develop a participatory action class that is now in its ninth year.

In that class called "Rural and Urban Social Movements," we spend the first half of the semester studying social movement theories and the historical foundation of farm workers' unions in the United States (Barger and Reza, 1994; Weber, 1994; Wells, 1996; Broyles-Gonzales, 1994; Del Castillo and Garcia, 1995; Buss, 1993; Edid, 1994; Ross, 1989; Scharlin and Villanueva,

1994; Rose, 1990). Then, during the spring break, I take the students to the central headquarters of the United Farm Workers in La Paz to observe and experience firsthand how the union works. In return for the union's hospitality and shared knowledge, the students contribute their skills and abilities with the various segments of the farm worker community. Since 1995 the students have worked in various offices of the union, doing data entry, archive filing, legal research, union by-laws collating, and advocacy planning. In addition, they have joined in organizing actions in nearby cities to support the contract efforts of the union. On the last day of the visit, the students present skits regarding their service-learning experiences. One skit, for example, compared a spring break in Tijuana with the UFW alternative spring break. The Tijuana spring break depicted students lying on the beach, drinking beer, and partying. The UFW alternative chronicled the student experience in cleaning up after a flood, working in the UFW offices, and planting roses at Cesar Chavez's grave. Students returning from La Paz have organized a campus commemoration of Cesar Chavez on his birthday that has included the students' skits presented at La Paz, speeches by representatives from the United Farm Workers, mariachi music, community *teatro*, and *ballet folklórico*.

Nine years ago, students organized a fast to boycott grapes in the college's cafeteria. Eighty-one-year-old Pete Velasco, one of the original Filipino strikers in the grape fields, joined the students in their negotiations with the Marriott Corporation, the college's food provider.[5] With the president of the college supporting the fast, the corporation agreed to stop serving grapes in the cafeteria. When Brother Pete passed away in the fall of 1995, the union acknowledged the depth of the relations that had developed between the union and the students by inviting various Pitzer students to attend the funeral, to help carry his casket in a union procession, and to take turns holding UFW flags at an all-night vigil.

The collaboration between Pitzer College students and the UFW is now a year-round activity. In the spring of 2000, the Pitzer College United Farm Workers' student organization drew over 300 supporters to a speech by UFW cofounder Dolores Huerta. In response to a UFW campaign in the strawberry fields, students negotiated the removal of strawberries from the college's cafeteria. Several students committed themselves to the UFW's strawberry campaign through a "Union Summer" project and are now working full-time for the union. While some of the students have gone on to make presentations in local high schools about their experiences, others have written research papers for academic conferences motivated by their work with the union (McGouhan, 2000; Camacho, 1995; Espinosa, 1999).

PARTICIPATORY ACTION RESEARCH
IN A DAY-LABOR CENTER

A participatory style of activism and research has also been the foundation for the development of a day-labor center in the city of Pomona, California. [6]

In July 1997, the city passed an ordinance that prohibited "the solicitation of or for work on any street or highway, public area, or non-residential parking area" (Tresaugue, 1997). The penalty for violation of the ordinance was a $1,000 fine and up to six months in jail.

At the time I happened to have a group of students, part of a class called "Restructuring Communities," working with various community activists to study day laborers. To protest the city ordinance, we worked with these activists to organize the day laborers on various street corners and to pack city hall. When city officials defended their action by claiming that all day laborers were undocumented, the students were able to present evidence from their research that permanent residents were also among those who solicited work on the street. The student researchers visited models of day-labor centers organized by the Coalition for Humane Immigration Rights of Los Angeles. With the help of this research, a funding proposal was written and a nonprofit organization, the Pomona Economic Opportunity Center, was formed. Subsequently, the city council allocated $50,000 to this nonprofit organization for the purpose of developing a day-labor center. They also appointed a board of directors that included city commission members and representatives from the community.

Because of the involvement of our class, I was appointed to the board and so were various students. Fabian Nuñez, also a student at the time and now a state assemblyman, was elected president.

From the very beginning, two distinct philosophies emerged on the board. One view, backed by some city officials and consultants from a national hardware supply company, supported the ordinance and proposed using the police to get day laborers off the streets and into the center. Another view, which I supported along with Nuñez, the students, [7] the day laborers, and a community activist lawyer, opposed the ordinance while supporting the development of a day-labor center. Rather than relying on the police to force the day laborers into the center, we proposed making the center a place that could help empower them through the establishment of employment rights counseling, biweekly organizational meetings, and worker representation on the board.

In addition to holding language and computer classes every morning, the students have been instrumental in ensuring worker representation on the organization's board. Rather than allowing city officials or consultants to control the decision-making process, we have organized biweekly meetings to build the "voice" of the workers in running the center.

When the city council decided to provide some funding for the day-labor center, we employed surveys, questionnaires, and focus groups to determine how the resources of the day laborers could be maximized.[8] Our collaborative research has resulted in the acquisition of several grants from area foundations. One grant, in addition to helping pay the rent for the center, has allowed us to develop a health referral program for the day laborers and their families. Another has helped support language, computer, and job training programs.

MOVING BEYOND "CHARITY" MODELS

The examples presented here have the commonality of using critical pedagogy, participatory action research, and service learning as a means of bringing students and faculty together with community-based organizations to work on common issues and to effect social chance. These collaborative efforts are examples of policy-making models that go beyond charity and dependence on "experts" to "get at the root causes of problems, and focus directly or indirectly on politically empowering the powerless" (Morton, 1995: 23). These participatory action learning and research models require the faculty and students to immerse themselves alongside community participants collectively to develop theories and strategies and pursue common objectives. An essential component of this style of learning and research is its commitment to equality of interest between academicians and community participants. Participating students and faculty collaborate to "intentionally promote social learning processes that can develop the organizational, analytical, and communication skills of local leaders and their community-based organizations" (Reardon, 1998: 59).

It is essential for faculty members to make a long-term commitment to the sites and communities in which they have placed their students. Although students can only make a commitment for a semester or until graduation, faculty participants are in a better position to sustain campus-community partnerships. An example of this type of community-based partnering is the Center for California Cultural and Social Issues, created in 1999 at Pitzer College. This center, in addition to supporting research and education projects, has developed a number of core partnerships that at the minimum require a faculty member to make a four-year commitment to a community-based organization.[9] As these long-term campus-community partnerships are developed, students and faculty can become a political force in their communities. No longer limited to the role of visitors, they can see themselves as participants with a stake in the decisions being made.

Finally, in the participatory learning and research promoted here it is important to define "community." The "community," as ordinarily understood, is made up of many competing interests. Those who are corporate growers, developers, and polluters call themselves part of the "community" even though their profit-making interests often place them in conflict with its "quality-of-life" initiatives. In contrast, "community" referred to in this chapter is a geographical, political, and spiritual body that is confronting inequality or trying to improve its quality of life. The research and learning described here focus on the sources of inequality and what can be done about it. The dominant understanding of inequality tends to blame individuals for their inadequacies. Instead, the practices described here focus on the historical and systemic foundations of inequality and challenge students and faculty to find common ground with community institutions, unions, organizations, and neighborhood leaders to arouse social consciousness and effect long-term structural change.

Although it is considered outside the "objective" mainstream of social science, critical and participatory action research, teaching, and learning are gaining in acceptance (Maurasse, 2001; Nyden et al., 1997; Greenwood and Levin, 1998; Richardson, 1990). This type of approach takes the academic beyond the traditional bounds of "community service" to a level at which students and faculty join community members in using research, teaching, and learning to bring about fundamental social change. Jim Thomas summarizes this distinction as follows (1993: 4):

> Conventional ethnographers study culture for the purpose of describing it; critical ethnographers do so to change it. Conventional ethnographers recognize the impossibility, even undesirability, of research free of normative and other biases, but believe that these biases are to be repressed. Critical ethnographers instead celebrate their normative and political position as a means of invoking social consciousness and societal change.

CONCLUSION

Participatory research, teaching, and learning constitute a viable alternative to the traditional "banking" concept of knowledge that connects abstract theoretical concepts to lived experience and community engagement; provides a practical means for promoting positive social relations by building bridges between students, faculty, and community participants from diverse backgrounds; and moves beyond top-down charity and project development models to models based on collaborative action for social change.

NOTES

1. Copyright Acknowledgement: This chapter was previously published in the following: *Latin American Perspectives*, Vol. 31, No. 1, Jan., 2004.

2. At the time I began living in the city with my family, it had just received the national designation of "All-America City," reflecting its volunteer and innovative programs in dealing with new Chinese immigrants. Concurrently, an organized backlash against the unbridled growth policies of the city council had also begun. A primary target of the "no-growth" movement came to be the city's growing Chinese population. Up until 1960, Monterey Park's population had been 85 percent Anglo, 3 percent Asian, and 12 percent Latino. By the 1990 census the Anglo population had dropped to 11.7 percent, while the Asian Pacific population had grown to 56 percent and the Latino to 31.3 percent. In the preliminary 2000 census, these rapid changes have continued, with Anglo numbers decreasing to 8.2 percent and the Latino to 26 percent while the Asian Pacific population increased to 63.7 percent.

3. School officials had vehemently denied that the source of the student conflicts was ethnic/racial tensions. One principal blamed the fighting between ethnic groups on "machismo," while another explained to the press that it was the "hormones" of the teenagers that were responsible for the conflicts

4. For new-social-movement theory I used selected readings from Michael Buroway's *Ethnography Unbound* (1991) and *Global Ethnography* (2000) and *New Social Movements: From Ideology to Identity*, edited by Enrique Larana, Hank Johnston, and Joseph R. Gusfield (1994).

5. Brother Pete had developed a close relationship with Pitzer students during the alternative spring break in 1994. Upon learning that he had terminal cancer, the students had invited him to speak on the campus and to help in the negotiations with the Marriott Corporation.

6. Pomona, 30 miles east of Los Angeles and with a population of 149,473, is 64.5 percent Latino, 17 percent white, 9.3 percent African American, 7.2 percent Asian Pacific Islander, and 0.3 percent American Indian.

7. Two of these students (now alumni), Suzanne Foster and Silvia Rodriguez, and I have produced an article, "Organizing Immigrant Workers: Action Research and Strategies in the Pomona Day Labor Center," that is scheduled to appear in a book edited by Enrique and Gilda Ochoa.

8. Six students wrote their senior theses on the day-labor center while others made presentations at the National Association of Chicana and Chicano Studies (NACCS), the American Sociological Association, the American Association of Higher Education, and the Pitzer College Undergraduate Research Conference.

9. In its three years of operation, the CCCSI has given over 100 awards including community-based summer projects and internships, academic-year course-enhancement and senior-year projects, and urban and community fellowships to students, faculty, and members of the community.

REFERENCES

Almaguer, Tomas. 1994. *Racial Fault Lines*. Berkeley: University of California Press.

Anderson, Margaret L. and Patricia Hill Collins. 2003. *Race, Class, and Gender*. 5th edition. Belmont, CA: Wadsworth.

Angelou, Maya. 1996. *I Know Why the Caged Bird Sings*. New York: Chelsea House Publishers.

Aparicio, Frances R. and Christina Jose-Kampfner. 1995. "Language, culture, and violence in the educational crisis of U.S. Latino/as: two courses for intervention." *Michigan Journal of Community Service Learning* 3 (Fall):128–138.

Barger, W.K. and Ernesto M. Reza. 1994. *The Farm Labor Movement in the Midwest: Social Change and Adaptation Among Migrant Farm Workers*. Austin: University of Texas Press.

Blackwell, Angela Glover, Stewart Kwoh, and Manuel Pastor. 2002. *Searching for the Uncommon Common Ground*. New York: W.W. Norton.

Boyle, T. Coraghessan. 1995. *The Tortilla Curtain*. New York: Penguin Books.

Broyles-Gonzales, Yolanda. 1994. *El Teatro Campesino: Theater in the Chicano Movement*. Austin: University of Texas Press.

Buroway, Michael. 1991. *Ethnography Unbound.* Berkeley: University of California Press. 2000. *Global Ethnography.* Berkeley: University of California Press.

Buss, Fran Leeper. 1993. *Forged Under the Sun/ Forjado Bajo del Sol: The Life of María Elena Lucas.* Anne Arbor: University of Michigan Press.

Calderón, José. 1995. "Multi-ethnic coalition-building in a diverse school district." *Critical Sociology* 21 (Spring): 101–111.

Camacho, Patricia. 1995 "An interpersonal process: redefining traditional and nontraditional roles of women supporters and leaders in the UFW." Senior thesis, Pitzer College.

Camacho, Jeffrey A. 1995. *Experiential Learning in Higher Education: Linking Classroom and Community.* George Washington University Report 7.

Cisneros, Sandra. 1991. *The House on Mango Street.* New York: Vintage Books.

Darder, Antonia. 2002. *Reinventing Paulo Freire*: A Pedagogy of Love. Boulder, CO: Westview Press.

Del Castillo, Richard Griswold and Richard A. Garcia. 1995. *Cesar Chavez: A Triumph of Spirit.* Norman: University of Oklahoma Press.

Edid, Marilyn. 1994. *Farm Labor Organizing: Trends and Prospects.* Ithaca, NY: ILR Press.

Eldin, Max and Morton Levin. 1991. "Cogenerative learning: bringing participation into action research," pp. 127–142 in William Foote Whyte (ed.), *Participatory Action Research.* Newbury Park, CA: Sage.

Emerson, Robert M. Rachel I. Fretz, and Linda L. Shaw. 1995. *Writing Ethnographic Fieldnotes.* Chicago: University of Chicago Press.

Erdrich, Louise. 1989. *Love Medicine.* New York: Bantam Books.

Espinosa, Alex. 1999. "The development of critical consciousness through a praxis of reflection and involvement." Senior thesis, Pitzer College.

Fals-Borda, Orlando and Mohammed Anisur Rahman. 1991. *Action and Knowledge: Breaking the Monopoly with Participatory Action Research.* New York: Apex Press.

Feagin, Jose R. and Clairece Booth Feagin. 2003 *Racial and Ethnic Relations.* 7th Edition. Englewood Cliffs, NJ: Prentice-Hall.

Freire, Paulo. 1993. *Pedagogy of the Oppressed.* New revised 20th-century edition. New York: Continuum.

Greenwood, Davydd J. and Morten Levin. 1998. *Introduction to Action Research: Social Research for Social Change.* Thousand Oaks, CA: Sage.

Haley, Alex. 1996. *Malcolm X.* New York: Ballantine Books.

Horton, John, with José Calderón, Mary Pardo, Leland Saito, Linda Shaw, and Yen-Fen Tseng. 1995. *Politics of Diversity.* Philadelphia: Temple University Press.

Hudson, Berkeley 1988. "Monterey Park's mix lures researchers." *Los Angeles Times*, October 23.

Jacoby, Barbara. 1996. *Service Learning in Higher Education.* San Francisco: Jossey-Bass.

Larana, Enrique, Hank Johnston, and Joseph R. Gusfield. 1994. *New Social Movements: From Ideology to Identity.* Philadelphia: Temple University Press.

Lofland, John and Lyn Lofland. 1995. *Analyzing Social Settings: A Guide to Qualitative Observation and Analysis.* Belmont, CA: Wadsworth.

Maurasse, David J. 2001. *Beyond the Campus: How Colleges and Universities Form Partnerships with Their Communities.* New York: Routledge.

McGougan, Jill. 2000. "The internal and external factors impacting a day labor center as part of a social movement." Senior thesis, Pitzer College.

Morrison, Toni. 1972. *The Bluest Eye.* New York: Washington Square Press.

Morton, Keith. 1995. "The irony of service: charity, project, and social change in service-learning." *Michigan Journal of Community Service Learning* 2: 19–32.

Nyden, Philip, Anne Figert, Mark Shibley, and Daryl Burrows. 1997. *Building Community: Social Science in Action.* Thousand Oaks, CA: Pine Forge Press.

Okada, John. 1976. *No No Boy.* Rutland, VT: C. E. Tuttle.

Omi, Michael and Howard Winant. 1994. *Racial Formations in the United States: From the 1960s to the 1990s.* 2nd edition. New York: Routledge.

Ostrow, James, Gary Hesser, and Sandra Enos. 1999. *Cultivating the Sociological Imagination: Concepts and Models for Service-Learning in Sociology.* Washington, DC: American Association of Higher Education.

Reardon, Kenneth M. 1998. "Participatory action research as service learning." *New Directions for Teaching and Learning* 73 (Spring): 57–64.

Richardson, Laurel. 1990. "Narrative and sociology." *Journal of Contemporary Ethnography* 19 (1): 116–135.

Rodriguez, Luis. 1993. *Always Running:* La Vida Loca, *Gang Days in L.A.* Willimantic, CT: Curbstone Press.

Rose, Margaret. 1990. "Traditional and nontraditional patterns of female activism in the United Farm Workers of America, 1962 to 1980." *Frontiers* 11 (1): 25–32.

Ross, Fred. 1989. *Conquering Goliath: Cesar Chavez at the Beginning.* Keene, CA: Taller Gráfico.

Scharlin, Craig and Lilia V. Villanueva. 1994. *Philip Vera Cruz: A Personal History of Filipino Immigrants and the Farmworkers' Movement.* Los Angeles: UCLA Labor Center and Asian American Studies Center.

Shor, Ira. 1992. *Empowering Education: Critical Teaching for Social Change.* Chicago: University of Chicago Press.

Silko, Leslie Marmon. 1986. *Ceremony.* New York: Penguin Books.

Strauss, Anselm and Juliet Corbin. 1990. *Basics of Qualitative Research.* Newbury Park, CA: Sage.

Takaki, Ronald. 1993. *A Different Mirror.* Boston: Little, Brown.

Tan, Amy. 1989. *The Joy Luck Club.* New York: Delphinium Books.

Tresaugue, Matthew. 1997. "Pomona Oks labor center." *Daily Bulletin,* July 31.

Weber, Devra. 1994. *Dark Sweat, White Gold: California Farm Workers, Cotton, and the New Deal.* Berkeley: University of California Press.

Wells, Miriam J. 1996. *Strawberry Fields: Politics, Class, and Work in California Agriculture.* Ithaca, NY: Cornell University Press.

Whyte, William Foote. 1991. *Participatory Action Research.* Newbury Park, CA: Sage.

Zlotkowski, Edward (ed.). 1998. *Successful Service-Learning Programs.* Bolton, MA: Anker.

Chapter Three

Latinos and Ethnic Conflict in Suburbia

The Case of Monterey Park[1]

José Zapata Calderón

As the U.S. Latino population has evolved into a largely urban population, with a growing middle class, it has had to confront new obstacles and questions which affect its relations with other ethnic groups. With the continued increase in the proportion of new immigrants into areas where Latinos have resided, there have emerged new and evolving relationships between Latinos, old residents and new immigrants. These relationships are creating an ambivalence in the Latino community forcing it to make choices between ethnic and class alliances and between conflict and accommodation.

This chapter, as part of a larger study of "Changing Communities," is a beginning case study of how urban restructuring is affecting the Latino population in a multi-ethnic middle-class suburb, the city of Monterey Park.

The beginning research, presented here, is based on an analysis of newspaper articles, ethnographic observations, and interviews with community leaders.

Up until 1960, Monterey Park's population consisted of 85% Anglo, 3% Asian, and 12% Latino. In the 1970's, however, there were a number of external changes which deeply affected the city. Briefly, these included the federal government's recognition of mainland China and the exclusion of Taiwan from official diplomatic status; the emergence of the Pacific Rim as an interrelated economy; a dissatisfaction of incoming immigrant Asian families with the conditions in older and nearby Los Angeles ethnic neighborhoods; and a significant increase in the Mexican/Latina population in the city. By the 1980 census, Monterey Park's population had radically changed to 40% Asian, 37% Latino, and 20% Anglo.

These changes have, on the one hand, created an internationally-diverse community but, on the other, have resulted in conflicts between the Latino, Anglo, and Asian populations. As the economic situation has deteriorated in the United States, the competition for resources has increased. Consequently, the capacity for scapegoating groups for the ills of the economy has also increased. In Monterey Park, tension between the old white residents and new incoming immigrants has increased but it has also increased amongst the Latino population.

CONFLICT BETWEEN ASIAN AND LATINO POPULATION

The conflict between the Asian and Latino populations is rooted in their differing origins and unequal access to resources.

Many Latinos of Mexican nationality, in Monterey Park, have expressed that they "were here first" and that their origins in the Southwest predate Columbus. Now, in addition to having lost their land to the Anglo, they see a large influx of Asian immigrants setting up shop in "their backyard" and succeeding in areas where they have been excluded. In particular, the Chinese who are moving into Monterey Park are overall well-educated and have the available resources to develop small and medium-sized businesses. Latinos, on the other hand, have few businesses in the city and are primarily situated in the service sector or as professionals in the city of Los Angeles.

Many Latinos react negatively to the numerous Chinese businesses, signs, and restaurants. Like the Anglo population, they carry on shopping primarily outside the city in places like the mall in Montebello.

Further, like the Anglo population, they also complain about the mannerisms and culture of the Chinese. The Chinese are seen as cold, indifferent, bad drivers, cutting into lines at supermarkets, and isolating themselves in their own civic groups and religious institutions.

These differences spill over into the schools where there have been numerous fights between Latino and Asian students. In 1986, one fight led to the stabbing of a Chinese youngster at Mark Keppel High School. In response, the Alhambra school district has established a series of cultural "harmony" retreats designed to sensitize students to the diverse cultures in the area. According to Alhambra School District Board Member, Dora Padilla, these programs have eased the tension in the student population. However, some Latino parents have expressed indignation at the Asian students' ability to win a good share of the Academic honors.

Resentment has also been heightened by the influx of Asians into areas of the city where Latinos once dominated. The Latino population, in Monterey

Park, grew from 12% in 1960 to 38% in 1980. This sharp increase can be attributed to the development of a middle class in the area. After World War II, many returning Latino soldiers utilized some of the benefits from the G. I. bill to buy housing in the city. The population of Latinos began to grow although the residents had attempted to exclude "Mexicans" from living there and in the nearby city of Montebello (Compeán, 1983).

As the 1960's civil rights movements opened up new possibilities for Chicanos, many moved away from nearby neighborhoods in East Los Angeles to the more-suburban atmosphere of Monterey Park. Consequently, by 1980, Monterey Park had three and one-half times more professionals than North East Los Angeles and Chicanos in North East Los Angeles lagged four years behind Monterey Park residents in median of education (Compeán, 1983).

Others, who came as professionals from other states and worked in the inner-city, liked the lower crime rate and quality schools. Some were made residents of Monterey Park when the city annexed part of census tract 5304 which is partially in East Los Angeles and includes East Los Angeles College. This may account for the large number of Mexican immigrants in the city. According to the 1980 census, there are 4,778 foreign-born Mexicans in the city with 3,116 not naturalized (or 15% of the total population).

While the overall population of Monterey Park grew from 54,338 in 1980 to 62,877 in 1987, it also grew in the minority population within the city.[2] However, while the Latino population experienced a 275% increase from 1960 to 1970 and a 27.9% increase from 1970 to 1980, it dropped 11.3% from1980 to 1986. Overall, the Latino population went from being 37% of the city in 1980 to 30.5% in 1986. Meanwhile, the Asian population experienced a 568% growth rate from 1960 to 1970, 156% from 1970 to 1980, and 65.2% from 1980 to 1986 (Census, 1986). According to the 1980 census, the majority of the Latino population resided primarily in census tracts 4817.02 and 4822 in the northeast section of the city and census tracts 4827 and 4828 on the city's southern border.

In 1980, the pairs of census tracts, showed two contrasting Latino populations when compared according to family income. Census tracts 4817.02 and 4822 were among the lowest levels of mean family income in the city with incomes of $17,149 and $15,909 respectively while census tracts 4827 and 4828 had incomes of 21,753 and 23,023 respectively. Census tract 4820.01, which showed the lowest concentration of Latinos in the city at 12.8% of the total Latino population, averaged an income of $41,449 amongst Latinos. This compared with a median income of $22,586 overall in the city. The 1980 census showed that Monterey Park is indeed becoming a more affluent area. While there were 3,767 families (or 20%) who were considered low and moderate income families in 1980, this was actually a 40% decline from the 1970 level.

While there are no income figures, in the 1986 special census, there are figures on the growth or non-growth of population in the areas. The figures show that in the three census tracts in the northeast section of Monterey Park which had the majority of the Latino population in 1980, the population of Latinos dropped. Census tract 4817.01 went from 3,443 Latinos in 1980 to 2,406 in 1986. Similarly, census tract 4817.02 went from 1,199 to 1,782 and census tract 4828 went from 2,198 to 1, 981. At the same time, the Asian population grew dramatically in census tracts 4817.01 (from 1,528 in 1980 to 5,043 in 1986) and 4817.02 (from 998 in 1980 to 2,825 in 1986). Census tract 4828 showed a moderate increase from 1,151 in 1980 to 1,493 in 1986.

The comparison of these census tracts does show a "flight" of Latinos from the areas which have the low incomes. Further, it shows that the Asian population is moving into these same areas in large numbers. What needs to be further studied is whether the Asian population is buying-out the owners of this housing. Since incomes are so low for Latinos in these census tracts, it is very possible that they are being forced to move either as renters or as individuals whose houses are being bought out from under them. Either way, there is a basis here for increased resentment from the Latino population.

In terms of the two census tracts which also have large Latino populations, but are more in keeping with the median income of the city, they too show a decrease in the Latino population. However, it is a more moderate decrease. Census tract 4827 went from 3,377 in 1980 to 3,325 in 1986 and census tract 4828 went from 2,198 in 1980 to 1,981 in 1986.

Some reasons for the decrease of the Latino population include: the lack of affordable housing, high rents, the buying-out of property by developers offering lucrative payments, and the wish of some Latinos to move to areas where the Latino culture is more evident. In addition, the cost of housing would have to be counted as a factor. In 1970, 97.2% of housing units were valued at less than $50,000. In 1980, only 8.3% of the owner occupied housing units were valued at less than $50,000 (Census, 1986). A typical house, now sells for $140,000 to $150,000 (Tanzer, 1985).

CONFLICT BETWEEN THE LATINO AND ANGLO POPULATIONS

The Latino population in Monterey Park is very diverse and fits into the categories of first, second, and third generations. Since Monterey Park is considered a city of upward mobility for Chicano/Mexican people leaving East Los Angeles, it has a higher percentage of middle-class or middle-income Chicanos. Even so, only a handful make incomes in the $40,000 range (census tract 4820.01, 1980). Seven, of the twelve census tracts in which Latinos reside have incomes primarily in the $20,000 range while four are between $15,000 and $18,500 (Census, 1980). With so few Latino businesses evident in Monterey Park, it is likely that Latinos are primarily employed outside the city in service or professional jobs.

In terms of empowerment, the Latino community, until recently, has not had any visible Latino organization in Monterey Park. Latinos are primarily organized through established or institution-related social and civic groups. The recognized Latino city leaders, in the city, emerge out of these groups. What is more, since the Latino community has not had any visible political organization, there has been little political activity around Latino issues. They have not been very visible in community-wide issues such as community development. However, their interest in elections when Latino candidates are running was exemplified by the high voter registration and voter turn-out rates in the 1986 city council elections. In that election, there were 8,178 Latinos registered (or 38% of the Latino population in the city). Of these, 32% turned out to vote as compared to 40% Caucasian, 13% Chinese, and 14% Japanese.

There is an "ethnic sentiment" amongst Latinos in Monterey Park which, in relation to issues or candidates which affect them, can be galvanized. According to the 1980 census, there is a significant Latino immigrant population in the city which adds to this sentiment: 4,778 foreign-born Latinos with 3,116 not naturalized (or 15% of the total Latino population).

Consequently, ethnic antagonism in Monterey Park has not all been targeted at the Asian population. After two Latino city councilmen and one Chinese councilwoman were voted out of office in 1985, the elected Anglo council members led the passage of a resolution (9004) which, in addition to calling for supporting English as the Official Language, called for the police to cooperate with the Immigration and Naturalization Services in deporting so-called "illegal aliens," called for non-support to cities who advocate sanctuary, and called for Congress to close the borders.

Council-members Barry Hatch and Pat Reichenberger went as far as to blame immigrants for a long list of ills including crime, disease, and the use of government services that "might otherwise go to citizens" (Gottlieb, 1986:A-10). In claiming that immigrants were taking cheap housing and jobs from senior citizens and college students, Councilwoman Reichenberger was quoted in the August 10th issue of the Los Angeles Herald-Examiner as saying: "When my kids go out to get jobs it's your little Mexicans, very rarely Chinese, who are there."

These statements, together with an English Only movement inside Monterey Park and throughout the state which attacked bilingualism, fueled divisions between some Latino residents and old-time Anglo residents. Many Latino residents, subsequently, joined the efforts of a multi-racial coalition of residents, the Coalition for Harmony in Monterey Park (CHAMP), to rescind the "English Only" resolution 9004. After gathering over 5,000 signatures against the resolution (with a large part of them being Latino and Asian signatures), the resolution was rescinded by the city council in a 5–3 vote on October 27, 1986.

This coalition was able to bring together Asian, Latino, and progressive Anglo leaders together in fighting the resolution. The coalition also included some developers who later sought a recall of the city council members who had supported the resolution.

ROLE OF THE DEVELOPERS AND RAMP IN THE CONFLICT

The developer's interests in Monterey Park have primarily focused on the issues of "racism" in Monterey Park while the anti-growth forces, concentrated in an organization called RAMP (the Resident's Association of Monterey Park), have focused on limits in new construction.

These interests followed-up the success of the CHAMP coalition (in defeating the English Only resolution) by organizing their own group, called the Association for Better Cityhood, to recall council-members Reichenberger and Hatch. This association, primarily made up of contributors listing their occupations as "trading" or "investments," sought to take the multiracial CHAMP coalition in the direction of recalling the council-members on the basis of their "racism" (Lemann, 1988). However, the CHAMP coalition decided against the recall on the basis that the English Only resolution had already been rescinded and that the charges of "racism" were not enough to win a recall.

Unable to build a momentum around their pro-growth policies, the ABC coalition tried to build unity amongst the Asian and Latino populations by appealing to issues of nativism and racism. Utilizing various quotes of council-members Reichenberger and Hatch which were derogatory toward the Latino/Asian people, the ABC coalition gathered enough signatures for a special recall election. Although there was a high voter turn-out by Latinos, the recall was soundly defeated by a 62–38 margin. Just as impressive as the plurality was the voter turn-out numbering 23,396 or 36.5 percent of all registered voters (Danielson, 1987).

These events shows how class interests can override ethnic differences while, at the same time, ethnic factors can be utilized to promote class interests.

The CHAMP coalition was able to build a broad coalition and defeat the English Only resolution by showing how the implementation of such a resolution would hurt all residents regardless of color. As a result, CHAMP was able to involve residents of all nationalities, forces from the anti-growth sector (including some from RAMP), and even some with developer interests. Essentially, the coalition was multi-class (in terms of interests) and multi-ethnic.

The ABC coalition also was able to organize multi-ethnically but its class interests were different. The coalition served business and developer interests which included Anglo, Latino and Asian individuals. In order to try and build broad support, the coalition was forced to hide behind the issues of how "racism" affected the Latino/Asian people. According to the leaders of the ABC coalition, the effort was successful in particularly drawing-out Latino voters. However, there were also many Latinos who saw through the tactics of the coalition and voted against the recall. Other Latinos reacted to the ABC literature which raised the specter of the city council moving to deport resident Mexican-Americans in Monterey Park. According to the January issue of the *Atlantic Monthly* magazine, this tactic backfired since, as legal residents, they knew "that there was no chance of this happening, and finding themselves challenged implicitly to choose sides between immigrants and native-born Americans, they picked the native-born side, because that's what they are" (Lemann, 1988:61).

The RAMP coalition, made up primarily of older white residents, has been in the forefront of fighting the developer interests. While they have been able to unite solidly around anti-growth environmental issues, they have split on issues such as English Only. However, in the 1986 city council elections, RAMP was able to unite around and elect three white city council candidates (two of who were strong English Only supporters). Thrown out of office were two Latinos and one Chinese councilwoman who were accused by RAMP of defending developer interests.

While the RAMP coalition cannot be considered a homogeneous group, there is a sector of the membership which looks at the cause of the growth problems, in Monterey Park, as being due to the large influx of Chinese into the community. Consequently, the RAMP coalition overall de-emphasizes the question of ethnic conflict in the city and primarily places the blame for such conflict as being initiated by the developer's interests. Due to its varied character, though, (and as shown by the struggle around English Only) it is possible that sectors of the RAMP membership will join other ethnic groups, in the city, in fighting for ethnic harmony and against discrimination. It is also possible for RAMP to unite with sectors of the Latino community. Like RAMP, the Latino community includes those who are genuinely concerned about the quality of development for all people in the city, regardless of their national origin, and there are also those who blame the Chinese.

CITY COUNCIL ELECTION TRENDS

In the April 12, 1986 city council elections, all these trends came into play. The RAMP coalition ran two candidates, Betty Couch and George Ristic, on a no-growth stop-the-developers platform. Another candidate, Marie Purvis, a business owner and former president of the local chamber of commerce, ran on a similar platform.

The developer interests primarily supported the Latino candidate, Fred Balderrama, (an associate of one of the Asian leaders of the ABC recall coalition) and incumbent councilman Cam Briglio.

Once again, both class and ethnic factors were involved. The RAMP coalition depended primarily on its support in the established white community to pull it through. However, it also reached-out to those sectors of the Latino community who are either disenchanted with the developers or with the large influx of Asians into the city. With this approach, it appealed to the way Monterey Park "used to be" while slighting the importance of ethnic factors in the conflict.

The developer interests, once again, advanced a multiracial character in being represented by the Latino candidate Balderrama, the Anglo councilman Briglio, and the influence and money of various Chinese businessmen. While Briglio ran primarily on the defense of his past record, Balderrama hardly had a program. This unnamed, but assumed, coalition based its hopes on pulling enough votes from the incumbency of Briglio, the Latino name of Balderrama, and Chinese business circles. Once again, as in the recall campaign, the class interests of the developers were able to unify over and above the differences in their ethnicity. However, ethnicity played a major factor in relation to the base they were trying to pull-out for the election: the primarily-white supporters of Briglio, the Latino supporters of Balderrama, and the Chinese developer circles.

The other candidate for city council, Garvey School Board member and college professor Judy Chu, was able to bridge the most progressive aspects of a program for the city's development without slighting the existence of conflict between the various ethnic groups comprising the city. She was able to do this in such a way as to not accept developer interest money while, at the same time, calling for citizen input in all facets of the city's decision-making process. Her campaign, while aimed at appealing to all the groups, included key leaders from all the ethnic groups in the community.

Like the ABC coalition, and unlike the RAMP coalition, the Chu campaign was multi-racial. Unlike both coalitions, however, the Chu campaign had differing interests. The ABC coalition primarily defended the class interests of developers and a continued program of growth. The RAMP coalition focused on the older white residents who (sought to "go back to the way it was") and their traditional values while ignoring the reality that their community now also belonged to an 80% ethnic population. The Chu campaign neither denied the need for planned development nor the necessity of citizen input in solidifying a multi-cultural, multi-ethnic community.

In the April election, Latinos supported this emerging trend in the city. While the majority of Latino voters (63%) supported the Latino candidate

Balderrama, thirty-five per cent cast their vote for Judy Chu who subsequently won the election. Further, almost half (46% of the Balderrama supporters cast their second vote for Chu (Southwest Voter Research Notes, 1988:3).

Many Latinos, as shown by an exit poll carried out by the Southwest Voter Research Institute and the Asian Pacific American Voter Registration Project, had to go beyond simply supporting a candidate on the basis of ethnicity to supporting a candidate who was Chinese but represented some of their common interests of planned development and ethnic unity. In this election, at least, Latinos were able to see through the hidden interests of the Balderrama campaign, go outside of narrow ethnic sentiment, and vote on the basis of the issues before them. For, neither the interests of the RAMP coalition nor the interests of the ABC coalition, in the long-term, could serve the interests of the Latino community.

CONCLUSION

This chapter has described the politics of ethnic conflict which Latinos are facing in a middle-class, multi-racial suburb that is undergoing rapid demographic changes.

It shows how class and ethnic issues can intersect in the struggle over how a community is to develop. Slow-growth movements laid the basis for a united struggle against the interests of large developers. However, the large influx of Asian immigrants into the community brought on the added dimension of racism which both divided and united old and new residents. On the surface, both the Anglo and Latino populations appear to resent the growth of Asian businesses and influence in the city. One a deeper level, the real culprits of unplanned development in the city are the large developers who are made up of representatives of all ethnic groups. At issue, has been the question of whether the various ethnic groups in Monterey Park are able to look beyond the issues of ethnicity to uncover the class interests of the developers.

The April 12, 1986 Monterey Park city council election showed how Latinos, through cross-ethnic voting, can put aside ethnic conflict to unite with other ethnic groups and elect a candidate which is more in keeping with their common interests.

Overall, Latinos in Monterey Park will continue to be a dwindling group while the Asian population will continue to grow. However, the proximity of Monterey Park to East Los Angeles and to the business sector of downtown Los Angeles, will allow for a good percentage of the Latino population to remain in the city. In the interim, they are still a potentially powerful political force. Primarily organized through social and civic groups, they have shown the capacity to move beyond the simple need for Latino representation, take a stand against developer interests, and unite with other groups to support a program which calls for more long-term community-controlled planning.

NOTES

1. Copyright Acknowledgement: This chapter was previously published in the following: *Estudios Chicanos and the Politics of Community: Selected Proceedings National Association for Chicano Studies.* Editors: Mary Romero and Cordelia Candelaria. Boulder, CO: NACCS, 1988.

2. Monterey Park experienced a steady growth in minority population from 1960 to 1986. Hispanic population experienced a 275% increase from 1960 to 1970 and 27.9% increase from 1970 to 1980. However, the Hispanic population dropped 11.3% from 1980 to 1986. The Asian population segment has shown steady growth since 1960 and is now the largest portion of the City population at 51.4%. This segment experienced a 568% growth rate from 1960 to 1970, 156% from 1970 to 1980, and 65.2% from 1980 to 1986. Black population experienced 909% growth rate from 1960 to 1970, a 495% rate from 1970 to 1980, and 77.6% from 1980 to 1986. Although the black population segment has experienced the fastest growth rate in the City, it still comprises the smallest portion of total population at 1.9%.

REFERENCES

Compeán, Guadalupe. 1983. *The Los Angeles Corporate Center: Its Probable Impact On North East Los Angeles.* UCLA: School Of Architecture and Urban Planning, 1983.

Danielson, Candy. 1987. "Monterey Park Recall Election Unlikely to Resolve The Issues." *Los Angeles Herald-Examiner.* June 24: Part A, 2.

Gottlieb, Jeff. 1987. "Temperatures Rising In Monterey Park's Melting Pot." *Los Angeles Herald-Examiner.* June 24: Part A, 2.

Lemann, Nicholas. 1988. "Growing Pains." *The Atlantic Monthly.* (January): 58.

Tanzer, Andrew. "Little Taipei." *Forbes.* (May 6): 71.

Southwest Voter Research Notes. 1988. "The Politics of Growth in L A.'s Suburban China-town" (June): 3.

U.S. Bureau of the Census. 1980. Statistical Abstract. Washington, D.C.: U.S. Government Printing Office.

U.S. Bureau of the Census. 1986. Statistical Abstract. Washington, D.C.: U.S. Government Printing Office.

Chapter Four

Language Struggles
in a Changing California Community[1]

José Zapata Calderón and John Horton

The rise of the Official English movement in the United States could well signal a growing nativism and anti-immigrant backlash. Like the nativist movements of the late nineteenth and early twentieth centuries, the campaign for Official English coincides historically with a period of massive immigration. During the 1980s about 6 million immigrants and refugees, overwhelmingly from Asia and Latin America, entered the country legally and an undetermined number came without documents. California has been a primary destination. By 1983 its foreign-born population was already estimated to be about 20 percent.[2] In this state dramatically transformed by newcomers, voters have approved Official English measures by wide margins.

Will the broad consensus behind Official English translate automatically into strong support for the restrictive legislation being proposed by the movement's leaders? Recent electoral studies show significant pockets of opposition behind the dominant consensus: mainstream media and public officials, liberals, the highly educated, Latinos, and (to a lesser extent) Asian Americans. Can the rest of the population—the apparent supporters—be dismissed as xenophobic, racist, or right-wing? Electoral statistics cannot provide all the answers because they touch only the surface of complex and unexamined social processes. In order to assess the significance of the Official English movement, and to locate its roots of support and opposition, we need to tap the lived experience of established residents and immigrants in their communities. We need detailed ethnographic case studies of how the forces for and against language restrictions are played out—how they are formed, reinforced, or transformed in the course of actual political struggle.

What follows is a report on one such study of politics and language in Monterey Park, California, the city widely proclaimed, and frequently denounced, as the first suburban Chinatown in the United States: "Little Taipei" or the "Chinese Beverly Hills." We trace the language struggle from an abortive attempt to declare Official English in 1986 to electoral support for Proposition 63, the state's Official English amendment later in the same year, to compromises on city codes regulating the use of Chinese business signs in 1989. It is a story of initial polarization and conflict, followed by a lessening of language struggles and accommodation to the realities of a multiethnic community.[3]

A city of 62,000 residents located just east of Los Angeles in the populous San Gabriel Valley, Monterey Park exemplifies the kinds of economic, demographic, and political changes that could fuel nativistic reactions to immigration. In 1960 the town's population was 85 percent Anglo (non-Hispanic white), 12 percent Latino, and 3 percent Asian. By 1980 the accelerated arrival of second-and third-generation Chicanos (Americans of Mexican descent), Nisei (second-generation Japanese Americans), and Asian immigrants had changed the ethnic makeup of the city to 25 percent Anglo, 39 percent Latino, and 35 percent Asian. During the 1980s these proportions continued to change dramatically in response to increased Chinese immigration from Taiwan, Hong Kong, and Southeast Asia. According to the 1986 Special Test Census, between 1980 and 1986 the number of Asian residents in the city increased by 70.6 percent to become a 51 percent majority; Anglos made up 15.8 percent, Latinos 30.5 percent, and blacks 1.9 percent. If current trends continue, Asians may reach 70 percent of the population in the 1990s.

Today, Monterey Park is a town in transition from a middle-American, racially mixed suburban bedroom community to a financial and service center for a growing regional Chinese and Asian population. Chinese signs and businesses line the major commercial streets, and longtime citizens complain about having to go outside of town to find "American" stores. Mandarin is spoken downtown in most offices, banks, and shops. Just seconds away, English is the language of city hall, where every other Monday the five-person city council hotly debates the issues of the day. Monterey Park is precisely the kind of community where one expects to find a backlash against change by established residents. Throughout the 1980s city politics were dominated by battles over growth, as developers and proponents of "slow growth" fought for control over land use, mini-malls, condominiums, high-rise apartments, and traffic.

In this city where economic development has an Asian face, a related conflict developed over the questions of language and immigration. In 1985 Monterey Park received a national award for its cross-cultural programs. But a year later, after intense debate, the city council enacted an ordinance requiring signs to include an English-language description of a firm's business. In

1986 Monterey Park became the second California city (after Fillmore) to pass an ordinance declaring English its official language. The measure also denounced the concept of sanctuary and encouraged local police to cooperate with the U.S. Immigration and Naturalization Service in apprehending undocumented immigrants. It was introduced by Councilman Barry Hatch, an outspoken advocate for restrictions on language and immigration. Even before the ordinance was passed, two Anglo residents and their supporters had collected three thousand signatures of registered voters—with Asians, Latinos, and Anglos equally represented, the organizers claimed[4]—on a petition to place an Official English referendum on the ballot.

The Official English law was immediately challenged by a new group, the Coalition for Harmony in Monterey Park (CHAMP), uneasy interethnic coalition of business people and civil libertarians. Targeting the major "American" and several Chinese supermarkets, CHAMP volunteers collected five thousand signatures on a counter-petition requesting the city council to rescind the ordinance.[5] This challenge was temporarily successful. One council member of the three who had supported Official English changed his vote, and the measure was rescinded. However, when the voters had the opportunity to express their own opinions, they demonstrated their divided support for the idea. In November 1986 the citizens of Monterey Park voted 53 percent to 47 percent for Proposition 63, the statewide Official English initiative. Nevertheless, the margin was much closer than in neighboring cities in the San Gabriel Valley, with an average 73 percent "yes" vote.

The clash between opponents and proponents of Official English was not over. Several powerful Anglo and Chinese developers formed a new organization, Americans for Better Cityhood (A.B.C.), to mount an attack against the "racism" of leaders of the Official English and slow-growth movements. Mobilizing its considerable financial resources, A.B.C. collected enough signatures to hold a special election to recall two council members, Barry Hatch and Pat Reichenberger, who had strongly supported Official English legislation. But in April 1987 the Monterey Park voters rejected the recall by 62 percent—an apparent victory for both slow-growth and Official English advocates, who denied the charges of racism. The outcome, however, can also be attributed to the tactics of A.B.C., which hired Spanish speakers to try to persuade middle-class, assimilated, and English-speaking Latino residents that the city council was out to deport them to Mexico.

After the defeat of the recall movement, the stage seemed to be set for a resurgence of defensive and xenophobic politics. In the April 1988 council elections, the pro-growth candidates were defeated, attesting to the continuing strength of the slow-growth forces. But at the same time, the voters defeated an extreme advocate of language and immigration restrictions and elected a Chinese American, Judy Chu, along with Betty Couch, one of two candidates endorsed by the slow-growth movement. Chu introduced a new tendency in local politics which would have a profound impact on the course of language struggles. She combined the implicit promise of Asian representation with the explicit promise of support for managed growth within a framework of appreciation for diversity. This formula has usually prevailed over the politics of language restrictionism.

As predicted, Councilman Hatch, the city's most vocal proponent of Official English, revived his campaign on the language issue. In 1988 he introduced an ordinance to require two-thirds English on all business signs, led a move to fire the city's independent and progressive library board, and used his office to complain about the increasing number of Chinese books in the library. In many speeches and media appearances, Hatch has advocated a temporary moratorium on all immigration. But ultimately, none of Hatch's campaigns was successful. The city's Planning Commission and Design and Review Board recommended no action on signs, and in the end a compromise ordinance was passed, requiring only slightly more English signage.[6] A federal court ordered the reinstatement of the library board, and the library continues to receive Chinese books and to cater to Chinese patrons.

The most devastating blow to Hatch and his political agenda, however, was his defeat in the April 1990 city council election, in which he received the lowest vote among six candidates. The winners for the three open seats were, in order of vote size: Samuel Kiang, a political newcomer, Chinese immigrant, engineer, and lawyer; Fred Balderrama, a Latino and president of the Monterey Park Chamber of Commerce; and Marie Purvis, an Anglo businesswoman and longtime resident. It would be wrong to attribute Hatch's defeat solely to his anti-immigrant politics. No doubt he was also a victim of the local tendency to sweep incumbents out of office and to blame them for the city's many ills. Nevertheless, voters were clearly dissatisfied with Hatch's particular brand of politics. Onetime political allies in the slow-growth movement did not endorse his candidacy. Ideological supporters of Official English told us that he was "divisive," "against everything," and that he did not "propose positive solutions to anything." These sentiments translated into a lack of electoral support. Hatch not only received the fewest votes; according to our exit poll, he was the last choice among voters of every ethnic group. Kiang, the largest vote-getter, was the first choice among Chinese voters, the third choice among Latinos, and the fifth choice among Anglos.

Monterey Park now has a less white and more ethnically diverse city council—one Chinese immigrant, a Chinese American (the current mayor), two Anglos, and a Latino. Nobody on the council talks about language restrictions; everyone at least gives lip service to the more important goal of managed growth. The composition of the council reflects a voter reaction against ethnically divisive politics and in favor of addressing shared problems like overdevelopment, traffic, a crumbling dam, earthquakes, and malathion spraying. While neither of these tendencies can be interpreted as a victory for tolerance over nativism, two important facts suggest that the local battle about immigration and language has died down. First, the city's most visible supporter of Official English lost his reelection (as did Reichenberger, who finished next to last). Second, at least for the moment, political discourse is colored by the language of "cultural diversity" rather than by charges against immigrants and countercharges of racism.

The story of the rise and apparent decline of language conflict in Monterey Park can be reconstructed from day-to-day political struggles wherein contradictions are exposed. It is a story of the gradual emergence of cross-ethnic politics. There is no question that the first round of language struggle was extremely divisive. The call to English language unity targeted Asians for linguistic and economic discrimination and polarized the community between established residents and new immigrants. But the actual course of battle revealed class, political, and ethnic contradictions within both groups. The Official English movement drew support from slow-growth Democrats and fiscal-conservative Republicans and contained two political currents: a populist concern with community control and planning and a reactionary attempt to restrict the cultural and political influence of new immigrants. Out of the struggle between these factions, within and across both movements, emerged a new political alliance that undercut racial polarization and pushed both developers and Official English leaders into more isolated positions.

Early in the battle, the slow-growth and Official English currents tended to coincide at the level of leadership and also probably in the minds of many Monterey Park residents. Thus Barry Hatch got slow-growth support for his election in 1986 because he spoke out strongly for community control over development. He got the same kind of support during the unsuccessful recall in 1987, when developers lumped together slow growth with Official English and labeled both as racist. It was the fight against racism that also united a disparate coalition of business people and liberals. But out of the struggle surrounding racism, Americanism, language, immigration, and land use grew an altogether new political force that cut across the old nativism/slow growth and diversity/development divisions by combining the populist issue of community control over development with a new emphasis on ethnic harmony. This realignment weakened both developers and Official English forces.

In 1988 the old opposition coalition, CHAMP, split along class lines. Local business people who opposed slow-growth restrictions on the rapid development of homes and commercial areas in Monterey Park ran their own minority and pro-business candidate, a Latino for city council. Those within CHAMP who supported controlled growth and steps towards ethnic harmony supported Judy Chu, who refused developer contributions. The developer candidate was defeated, while Chu led the field of seven candidates, with massive support from Chinese and Japanese Americans and significant support from Latino and Anglo voters. The rise of the controlled-growth/harmony tendency also prompted slow-growth leaders to begin backing away from the Official English campaign and to stress the primacy of economic rather than language issues. Lacking non-Anglo leadership in their movement, they were beginning to see the political virtues of an alliance with progressive Asian and Latino forces on issues of controlled development. Although these former supporters of Barry Hatch stopped short of denouncing him as a racist, they began to say: "He is going too far," "He is too extreme." One leader of the Residents Association of Monterey Park (RAMP), the major slow-growth group, put this changing perspective very clearly:

> The problem with Barry is that he divides the community into "newcomers/ bad guys" and "us good-old Americans." His pressing the point on these social issues and taking advantage of being mayor to gain national notoriety is harmful. We need peaceful reconciliation on all fronts. [7]

In sum, there are three reasons why ethnic polarization seems to have subsided from the moment in Monterey Park. First, the language struggle and continual charges of racism hinder the goals of the strong slow-growth movement. Second, the reality of demographic change requires established residents to come to terms with Asians. Third, the emergence of a politics of diversity and controlled growth opens up a middle ground for uniting moderates and progressives around demands for representation and diversity in the struggle for controlled development.

In Monterey Park, as elsewhere in the United States, the Official English movement has been divisive and xenophobic. It pits longtime residents against newcomers, particularly Asians and Latinos. Its declarations, written into law, seem to give legal justification for depriving immigrants of the tools they need for empowerment and mobility, while blaming them for all the complex problems brought by rapid economic and demographic change. The major lesson of our case study, however, is that this movement can be challenged and defused through political struggle around issues that cut across divisions between established residents and immigrants.

Activists interested in explaining and resisting this movement have two tasks. First, they must carefully distinguish between leaders and followers of the movement and not dismiss both as racists. There is the racism which is built into the very structure of capitalist exploitation, the racism of white supremacists who can be found in the leadership of Official English, and the scapegoating of immigrants by established residents in the working and middle class who fear competition and displacement in increasingly internationalized workplaces and neighborhoods. Second, activists must expose the xenophobia of leaders of the Official English movement, while addressing the structural causes of ethnic conflict within a framework of genuine ethnic and cultural diversity. The followers of Official English cannot be won over through charges that they are racist or through bland sermons about respect for diversity that fail to address the genuine problems behind the current wave of nativism—economic dislocations, and the alienation of ordinary people from the process of social planning.

For many Anglos and assimilated minorities, restrictive language legislation has offered a concrete response to insecurities cause by the rapid restructuring of community life, and especially those brought on by immigration. The nativistic reaction in Monterey Park was reinforced by the arrival of (real or imagined) high-status Asian immigrants with assets as entrepreneurs or educated professionals. Another factor in the rise of nativism has been the economic context of the new immigration. It comes at a time of uncertainty for the United States in an increasingly competitive world economy and of cutbacks in domestic social services and wages, a lack of affordable housing, and a general decline in the quality of life. While these forces most severely affect the working classes, they also extend to the middle class, as the case of Monterey Park demonstrates.

Paradoxically, the same historical conditions that breed nativism and racism open up opportunities for greater ethnic and cultural diversity and for the emergence of ideologies that undermine the assumption that the United States will be saved through policies of linguistic and cultural subordination. The domination of English in this country has historically depended on Anglo political superiority and the weakness of ethnic communities. Today, this power balance is shifting, with the territorial and political growth of non-white minorities in the United States and with the rapid integration of the United States into a world economy. Under these new conditions, the appeals for popular control over community development within a framework of cultural and linguistic diversity, as expressed at the grass roots in Monterey Park, are not pie-in-the-sky idealism, but reasonable responses to local and international realities that can only be addressed through interethnic alliances.

NOTES

1. Copyright Acknowledgement: This chapter was previously published in the following: *Source Book on Official English*, (With John Horton) edited by Jim Crawford, University of Chicago Press, 1990.

2. Thomas Muller and Thomas J. Eppenshade, *The Fourth Wave: California's Newest Immigrants* (Washington, D.C.: Urban Institute, 1985), p. 40; Alejandro Portes and Rubén G. Rumbaut, *Immigrant America: A Portrait* (Berkeley: University of California Press, 1990).

3. Our research in Monterey Park began in 1986; it has focused on local issues as they affect, and are affected by, relations between established residents and immigrant newcomers within formal and informal political arenas. We have used a variety of methods and data sources appropriate to a community study: analysis of newspaper articles, pamphlets, and demographic and electoral data, interviews with community leaders, and most of all, ethno-

graphic observation of daily events. Our research team of two sociology professors and four graduate students has been multiethnic and multilingual. Since 1988 the research has been funded by the Changing Relations Project, sponsored by the Ford Foundation, and by the Institute of American Cultures and the Asian American Studies Center of the University of California, Los Angeles.

4. This approximated the actual ethnic breakdown of registered voters; as recent immigrants, a large proportion of the Asian population had yet to qualify for citizenship and, thus, for voting rights.

5. Of those who signed CHAMP's petition, 67 percent were residents (though not necessarily citizens and voters), and of these, 81 percent were Chinese, 13 percent Latinos, and 6 percent Anglos.

6. Elsewhere in the San Gabriel Valley, Asian American business owners won a federal court suit against a Pomona city ordinance requiring at least 50 percent English on their signs; the mandate violated the First Amendment, according to Judge Robert M. Takasugi (*see pp.* 284–87).

7. Berkley Hudson, "Heavily Asian Town's Mayor Holds Tight to Controversial Views," *Los Angeles Times*, July 16, 1989, sec. III, p. 4.

Chapter Five

How the English Only Initiative Passed in California[1]

José Zapata Calderón

The English Only movement has been thriving in the current climate of recession, unemployment, declining services, and rising immigration. In November 1987 California voters by a wide margin of 73% to 27% made their state the first in the nation to adopt a constitutional amendment declaring English its official language. Similar bills are being introduced in 31 states including New York, Colorado, North Carolina, Florida, Texas, Connecticut, Arizona, Alabama, New Hampshire, Washington, and Wisconsin. State legislators have bypassed the voting public and passed various versions of English Only in the six states of Georgia, Illinois, Indiana, Kentucky, Nebraska and Virginia (Perez, 1987).

How do we assess the social meaning and impact of the English Only movement? Will its commitment to the common sense and patriotic principle that all Americans should speak English hasten or impede the assimilation of new immigrants? Will the movement promote cooperation and unity or division and racism? What groups are behind the movement and what is the basis for their wide support in minority as well as majority communities? Has there been organized resistance to the English Only movement, and how effective has it been? Finally, what does the movement tell us about the theory and practice of racism in contemporary America?

The tentative answers to these complex questions come from a preliminary analysis of the ideology, tactics, and consequences of the movement. While emphasizing the national origins and scope of the movement, this study focuses largely on California where ethnic diversity has always been the demographic, but not always the political reality.

NATIONAL ORIGINS

The English Only campaign which is currently sweeping the country has its roots in both the anti-immigrant and reactionary ecologist movements. The campaign's program is advocated through a national organization called U.S. English that is led by former senator S. I. Hayakawa and a Michigan ophthalmologist, Dr. John Tanton. Before co-founding U.S. English with Hayakawa, Tanton started a Planned Parenthood Center in Petoskey, Michigan and joined the board of directors of Zero Population Growth (ZPG), the country's largest political organization devoted to population reduction (Trombley, 1986A).

He left ZPG in 1979 and founded the Federation for American Immigration Reform (FAIR), the country's largest lobbying group devoted to restricting immigration. He also sits on the board of directors for Population Environment Balance, an organization which promotes population reduction worldwide and a cutting of U.S. assistance to foreign countries which do not seek to arrest their population growth. Among its original founders was William C. Paddock, an author of books that predict catastrophe in the Third World because of population growth. All these groups join hands with the U.S. English campaign in blaming immigrants for the problems of "strained resources and services in the United States" (Harrison, 1986A: 20–21).

With its national headquarters centered in Washington D.C., the organization allows membership only to "all who agree that English is and must remain the only official language of the United States" and calls for the following program to combat what it calls a "movement to turn language minorities into permanent power blocs" (Wright, N. d.: b–9):

- Repeal of laws mandating multi-lingual ballots and voting materials,
- Restriction of government funding for bilingual education to short-term transitional programs only,
- Control of immigration so that it does not reinforce trends toward language segregation.

CALIFORNIA ORIGINS

In California, the English Only movement has utilized the growing population of Asians and Latinos to whip up nativist sentiment and fears of an "alien takeover." Their literature includes a large map showing the Southwest flooded by immigrants from South America and Asia. Although California has had a long background of diverse ethnic groups and cultures and the original 1841 California state constitution was written in both English and

Spanish, English Only advocates now seek to wipe any traces of this tradition.

To bolster their arguments, English Only backers have been using a pamphlet, *Nation Within a Nation*, written by R.E. Butler, an aide to U.S. Senator Steve Symms (R-Ida). This pamphlet utilizes various works written by Chicano authors in the sixties and seventies to justify its contention that there is a growing Latino separatist movement in the U. S. similar to the French separatist movement in Quebec. According to the pamphlet there are various Chicano organizations and activists throughout the Southwest who are working to establish a Spanish-speaking nation of Aztlán in the southwest United States and northern Mexico. Latino organizations, including the Mexican American Political Association (MAPA), the Mexican American Legal Defense and Education Fund (MALDEF), and the League of United Latin American Citizens (LULAC) are accused of wanting to control Latino communities by keeping the people there in a "language ghetto, a language barrio, where they're out of touch with this country" (Butler: 1985). What they fail to point out is that the Quebec secessionist movement is due to deeply rooted historical factors of which language is just one manifestation. There is neither a comparable secessionist movement in the U.S., nor one, e.g., that simply advocates Spanish only or Chinese only.

Why then, did Californians overwhelmingly support the English Only initiative last November? There appear to be many factors behind why the proposition fared as well as it did statewide.

For all its misleading claims and ambiguous language, Proposition 63 tapped a simplistic sentiment in the state's voters: everyone in the state should speak English. What this simplicity masked, however, were the origins of the initiative and the not-so-subtle anti-immigrant and divisive sentiment whipped up amongst a sector of the population. The proposition found support among angry taxpayers who blamed immigrants for cutting into the budget as a result of their alleged use of education, literacy, health and jobs programs. Dissatisfaction amongst the general population over the funding of bilingual ballots and misconceptions around the quality of bilingual education also added to this ferment. Further, proponents of the initiative led taxpayers to believe that immigrants did not want to adjust or learn English. What they did not point out is that Latinos, Asians and other new immigrants dominate the long waiting lists for over-enrolled adult English classes. In Los Angeles alone, the waiting list exceeds 40,000 (Woo, 1986).

The overall message was, in a sense, a backlash against the growing political power of the state's minorities, particularly the Latino and Asian population. Calls for linguistic and cultural diversity were interpreted as separatism or as un-American.

THE EFFECTS OF ENGLISH ONLY

The English Only initiative aims to keep non-English speaking people from contributing to and entering the mainstream of society. Its supporters plan to end numerous language assistance programs or services including election assistance for citizens not fluent in English, bilingual emergency operators, and multi-lingual public service information such as pamphlets informing non-English speaking parents how to enroll their children in public schools.

While English Only proponents have proposed that the initiative will unify the state and country under one common language, its actual effect has been to create scapegoating and division wherever it has been passed. In the Ventura county town of Fillmore, there have been numerous protests from Chicano parents about an English Only ordinance and a vow by the city mayor to see to it that "election information and other things" do not come out in other languages. In Monterey Park, the regular city council meetings have been a stage for all those who want to blame every ill in the society on Asian and Latino immigrants. In a city which is 80 per cent Asian and Latino, there is presently only one Chinese- American on the city council and no Latinos.

The backers of Proposition 63 have already begun work to try and ensure that English is the only language used in all California institutions. For example, Assemblyman Frank Hill (R-Whittier) has promised to ask the state legislature to require that driver's tests, welfare applications, state university financial aid forms, and other state services be made available only in English. If the legislature refuses to support his proposals, Hill has promised to utilize the English Only network to put it on the ballot and pass it over the heads of the legislature (Trombley, 1986B). Stanley Diamond, Chairman of the California English Campaign, is reviewing California laws and regulations to see which ones need to be put in compliance with the passage of the English Only initiative. J. William Orozco, southern California spokesman for the Campaign, is fighting the Alhambra school district to ensure that school notices will not be sent home in any language other than English. Monterey Park city councilman Barry Hatch, elected as a supporter of English Only, has used the passage of Proposition 63 to renew his efforts to make Monterey Park a "model" English Only city. His efforts are aimed at tearing down non-English business signs, halting the translation of the city newsletter, and cutting funding to bilingual education. In addition, the U. S. English Campaign has promised to defeat all efforts at funding bilingual education in the California legislature. They also plan to campaign against bilingual education candidates on the local level to guarantee implementation of the amendment in the cities throughout the state (Ingram, 1986).

The effects of English Only have reverberated all the way into the courtroom. An English Only order was imposed on Latino employees at Huntington Park Municipal Court by three judges who found the use of the Spanish language offensive. In a hearing before the Los Angeles County Civil Service Commission to decide the validity of the order, Service Employees International Union (SEIU) staff attorney Kent D. Wong asserted that the rule was specifically an attack on Latino workers who were the only group subject to possible discipline for violating the rule. "The English Only rule deprives the appellants of part of their heritage and culture," said Wong. "It is tantamount to telling them that they should put a mask over their face and cover up part of their heritage and part of their background. It is an insult to all of the Hispanic people who work there, and it is an insult to all L.A. county employees" (Epic, 1988:1).

In a similar case, the U.S. Equal Employment Opportunity Commission recently filed suit against the Salvation Army to overturn a long-standing policy requiring all its employees to speak English on the job (Murphy, 1987).

WHAT IS AT STAKE

In California, the obvious significance of the passage of Proposition 63 was: (1) the establishment of the legal foundation for challenging bilingual programs and services and, should those challenges turn out to be successful, the harmful effect on the development and well-being of millions of adults and children; (2) the related message that the political aspiration for equality and a share of power by Latinos and Asians would not be tolerated; and (3) the subsequent nightmare of costs to the state in litigating lawsuits and legislation.

Hidden in this debate, however, is the deteriorating condition of education, literacy, and the preparation for international business interaction (e.g., language competency).

English Only or English First in this context, shows its real character. Whether a symbolic statement or as a constitutional amendment with a private right of action (allowing lawsuits against the state legislature to enforce English Only), the movement for English is nothing more than a sophisticated, patriotic-sounding racist attack and xenophobic diversion from the crucial issues facing California and the rest of the country. The patriotic demagogy has appealed to many honest frustrated citizens. But such demagogy has only served to retard and restrict the full development of the talents and abilities of people of all ethnic backgrounds.

The ideological strength of the English Only movement has been its appeal to universal American values. Indeed, the patriotic appeal and racist effect of the movement have been the result of what Immanuel Wallerstein has astutely called the compatibility of the seemingly antagonistic ideologies of universalism and racism (Wallerstein, 1983). While capitalism proclaims the universal values and standards of mobility, it historically practices racism through the ethnicization of society in the racially-segregated job market (differently evaluated ethnic groups ending up in differently evaluated jobs) and in neighborhoods (differently evaluated ethnic groups residing in differently evaluated neighborhoods). Hence, under the existing conditions of class and racial domination, the universalist appeal to English as the common medium for communication and mobility functions both to mask and to promote racism and anti-immigrant hysteria.

RESISTING THE ENGLISH ONLY MOVEMENT

The English Only initiatives *can* be defeated. In the California vote, the electorate did vote against it in many precincts throughout Oakland and Berkeley while narrowly passing it by a 7% margin in San Francisco (Harrison, 1986B). It passed in the more conservative city of Los Angeles but with significant opposition from ethnic minorities. Heavily Latino districts (such as East Los Angeles) voted down the issue and, especially, in low-income areas closest to the immigrant experience. Overall, throughout the state, seven in ten Latino voters rejected the proposition (Southwest Voter Research Notes, 1986).

Several board members of U.S. English actually quit as a result of the pressure of public criticism of the California initiative. Opinion polls in the latter part of the campaign, and the vote itself, turned out better than expected given the initiative's initially widespread acceptance.

There are really two steps to defeating this movement. The first is exposing the true character of the initiative and its proponents. Second is mobilizing people around the real issues and desirable values.

Exposing this initiative can be achieved in a number of ways. The California experience may prove useful. When the initiative process to qualify English as the official language of the state began, no one really took any action. It wasn't until the process qualified that a coalition, eventually called Californians United, came together as a statewide network. Californians United used the slogan "This is America," stressing that Proposition 63 was un-American, divisive and dangerous. In particular it attempted to show how such calls for English as the official language of other cities has led to increased divisions amongst ethnic groups; how subsequent lawsuits would probably lead to the loss of bilingual services, including emergency services; why bilingual programs in schools are necessary; why the cost to the state because of lawsuits would be a nightmare. This exposure did make a difference with many voters and press editorials generally agreed.

Yet, despite extremely hard work and the endorsements of Governor Deukmejian, Mayor Bradley, the Attorney General, and many others, the coalition could not hide the fact that it was loosely organized and poorly funded. On the one hand, the exposure could not overcome the patriotic, common sense notion of English as the official language of the state. On the other, the English Only forces spent over $1.5 million on their campaign while the Californians United raised less than $100,000 for its media and organizing work. Beginning late, being poorly funded and loosely organized did not stop many members of Californians United from developing a good network of support but it did keep them from reaching enough of the public. Even with effective exposure, and with time and money, the momentum against English Only cannot be sustained unless the voting public can be rallied around a forward looking agenda. This, too, has yet to be accomplished. Identifying the crucial issues in California.is not difficult. One is the quality of education. The stakes are high as our country's technological progress is based in a significant part on the quality of our students. Yet the reality shows a 40% dropout rate in the Los Angeles city schools, the second largest school system in the U.S. That figure skyrockets to over 50% in minority neighborhoods. It is no accident that forty-eight other countries have higher literacy rates than the U.S. Jonathan Kozol, author of *Illiterate America* estimates that 60 million adults in the U.S. are illiterate.

Rather than frontally assaulting this national dilemma, energy has been diverted toward seeking someone to blame. So, in the California debate on Proposition 63, many taxpayers came to see the English Only issue as one between those who supported immigrants and more funding for language programs, and those who didn't. Tired of "paying out so much in taxes and seeing immigrants taking those resources," many voted to support Proposition 63.

Reagan's campaign for less government (at least in social services and education) has also had an effect on the state's view of all education. In California, whose economy is highly dependent on the quality of education, voters have been consistently willing to tolerate a lower allocation of funds per child than the national average.

The value that needs to be promoted is the appreciation of and respect for the diverse cultures and languages of immigrants and minorities, and the desire to bring them into the economic and political mainstream. The State of California, and many other states, have been enriched by the contributions of immigrants through their revitalizing industries, hard work, cultures, taxes and consumerism. In a state with many immigrants and minorities (25% Latino, 10% Asian, 10% Black), we can deal with them as a tremendous resource and ally in struggle, or as a huge liability or a special interest that needs to be disciplined to behave "properly."

What Californians United was not able to do in its short duration was to promote the need and respect for language rights, i.e., the right to have English programs available, the right to expanded and improved bilingual (transitional) programs, the promotion of foreign languages as part of preparing our students for participation in the global economy, and the right to participate in the electoral process through the use of bilingual ballots. This struggle of language rights is an excellent opportunity to promote larger structural changes in our county's institutions and priorities, for example, the restructuring of our educational system and shifting federal priorities toward education and away from the military (the federal government spends $300 million per year on the military). Such a discussion is necessary if we hope to prevent the dismal scenario for the future of our country's schools and related standard of living from becoming a reality.

The English Only movement fooled many people, but did not mark a turning point. The truth is that parents and the general public have failed to assert their political strength with regard to education and literacy. They have not developed a critical mass to demand changes from national and local political bodies. The national movements of Latinos and Asians have not rallied behind language rights although groups have tried to promote English Plus, a campaign promoting English and other languages.

Whether in a state, local, or national context it is clear that this campaign cannot be won unless a program of action is effectively promoted to minorities and the general population. Further, there is both the need and the opportunity to build alliances among different minority groups and organizations. This is also beneficial in building local bases of community power since one issue can be linked to others. A good example of this happening have been numerous ongoing efforts by Asian and Black community leaders in Los Angeles to dialogue around common issues pertinent to both communities. Out of this beginning, various Black politicians and leaders of the National Association for the Advancement of Colored People (NAACP), the Southern Christian Leadership Conference (SCLC), and the Urban League, joined Asian and Latino groups in opposing the initiative (New York Times, 1986).

In conclusion, the English Only movement is widespread, divisive, and racist in its origins and effects. It pits old residents against new immigrants, particularly, Asians and Latinos. Its declarations, written into law, give the legal justification for depriving new immigrants of the tools for empowerment and mobility while blaming them for all the complex problems brought by rapid economic and demographic changes in the U.S. and world economies. Activists interested in explaining and resisting this movement have a dual task: (1) exposing its fraudulent universality and racism; and (2) proposing a program of empowerment and solutions to structural problems within a framework of genuine ethnic and cultural diversity.

NOTE

1. Copyright Acknowledgement: This chapter was previously published in the following: *Estudios Chicanos and the Politics of Community: Selected Proceedings National Association for Chicano Studies.* Editors: Mary Romero and Cordelia Candelaria. Boulder, CO: 1988.

REFERENCES

Butler, R. E. 1985. *On Creating A Hispanic America: A Nation Within A Nation.* Washington, D.C.: Council For Inter-American Security.

Cox, Gail Diane. 1986. "Legal Community Gives Lip Service to 'English' Fight." *Los Angeles Daily Journal*, October 20, p.20.

EPIC Events. 1988. "Setback For English Only In California," (1):1, 6.

Harrison, Laird. 1986A. "U.S. English Links To Anti-Immigrant Groups." *Asian Week*: 7 (51):20–21.

———. 1986B. "Prop 63 Rejected 3–1 By S. F. Asian Neighborhoods." *Asian Week*: (13):3, 16.

Ingram, Carl. 1986. "Prop 63 Backers Aim at Bilingual Education." *Los Angeles Times*, November 24, pp. 3, 16.

Kozol, Jonathan. 1985. *Illiterate America.* Garden City, New York: Anchor Press/Doubleday.

Murphy, Kim. 1987. "Salvation Army Sued Over 'English-Only' Rule." *Los Angeles Times*, November 27, p. 1.

New York Times. 1986. "Debates Growing On Use Of English: Ethnic Groups To Fight Official Language Plan in California," July 21, pp. Al, A8.

Pérez, Felix. 1987. "Official English Battle Widens." *Hispanic Link Weekly Report*, 5(16):p. 2.

Southwest Voter Research Notes. 1986. California Latinos Nix English Only Proposal. Vol. 1, No. 3, (December):1.

Trombley, William. 1986A. "Prop 63 Roots Traced To Small Michigan City." *Los Angeles Times*, October 20, part l, p. 3.

———. 1986B. "Assemblyman Vows To Carry The Ball For English-Only Action." *Los Angeles Times*, November 24, pp. 31, 32.

Wallerstein, Immanuel. 1983. *Historical Capitalism.* London: Verso.

Woo, Elaine. 1986. "Immigrants: A Rush to the Classrooms." *Los Angeles Times*, September 24, part I, pp. 1, 28, 29.

Wright, Guy. 1984. "U.S. English," *San Francisco Sunday Examiner & Chronicle.* October 14, p. B–9.

Chapter Six

"Hispanic" and "Latino"

The Viability of Categories for Panethnic Unity [1]

José Zapata Calderón

The question has been raised whether there is a Hispanic or Latino ethnicity that supersedes individual group identities (see López and Espíritu, 1990; Giménez, 1989a; Hayes-Bautista and Chapa, 1988; Padilla, 1985a). Félix Padilla, in his *Latino Ethnic Consciousness*, departs from the primordial interpretation of ethnicity to propose the viability of a panethnic identity based not on a transplanted cultural heritage but on situational and collective action that transcends distinctive national and cultural identities. This chapter discusses the viability of a panethnic identity among Latino groups in relation to the terms that are used to identify them as collective formations.

THE DIVERSITY OF HISTORICAL EXPERIENCE

Panethnicity should emerge out of a common collective experience, but the groups that are said to reflect a Hispanic or Latino ethnicity differ sharply in historical experience, socioeconomic status, and identity.

The Chicano people became an oppressed minority in the United States not only through immigration but as a consequence of the Mexican-American war in 1848. Before that time they had been as heterogeneous as any other Latino group. The three primary areas of settlement—Texas, California, and New Mexico—had developed in similar isolation from the Mexican central government. Neither Spain nor Mexico had been able to consolidate these regions because of such factors as distance, the resistance of Native American tribes, and continuing turmoil in the central government, and as a result they had developed regional characteristics. In New Mexico, a connection between villages and urban centers was facilitated by a class structure that included a local authority and a network of relations that sustained it (Moore, 1970: 466). In Texas, the quick takeover by American settlers resulted in the destruction of any Mexican political leadership or elite (Montejano, 1987). Similarly, in California the Mexican elite was left out of the political process. Because the early settlements were organized around landholdings, they lacked the internal social organization and cohesion to fight off land encroachments. Consequently, when gold was discovered in 1849 the sparse Mexican population was inundated by waves of American settlers. Adding to the heterogeneity, because New Mexico had had more of a development from an indigenous population many people there considered themselves different from Mexicans who immigrated later. In California and Texas the back-and-forth movement and eventual settlement of Mexican immigrants has produced a strong cultural tradition carried over from Mexico.

As a result of this early historical development, the United States's annexation of the Southwest, and the penetration of Mexico by U.S. interests, the Chicano people have a diverse historical experience. They can be divided into three main types, to some degree overlapping: (1) the original inhabitants of the Southwest (today located primarily in northern New Mexico and Southern California), (2) the immigrants to the United States since 1910, and (3) the descendants of both these groups. First-, second-, and third-generation Chicanos of various levels of acculturation have on the whole retained an ethnic identity (Keefe and Padilla, 1987: 187).

Unlike the Chicano people, the Puerto Rican people were not indigenous to the United States. The United States took over the island in 1898, governed it as a colony for the next 50 years, and granted the population citizenship through the Jones Act in 1917. In 1952 (with the approval of Congress) it was given the status of a commonwealth, the closest thing to statehood. In the 1920s and 1930s, an economic depression resulted in monopoly control of the island's sugarcane plantations, reducing the number of small farmers and putting an end to the subsistence economy. Subsequently, as much as one-third of the population immigrated to the United States. Today there are 1,800,000 Puerto Ricans in the United States (one eighth of all Latinos), with the largest concentration in New York City (Moore and Pachón, 1985: 32).

Like Puerto Rico, Cuba was acquired by the United States as a result of the Spanish-American War in 1898. However, its immigration flows have been quite different from those of the other two groups, stemming primarily from political rather than economic causes. In the 1950s, many Cubans fled the oppression of the Bautista dictatorship, and approximately 600,000 left the country after Castro's revolution in 1959. This wave of Cuban immigrants contrasted with other Latino immigrants in that most of them were well educated, middle-class, entrepreneurial, and professional (Portes and

Bach, 1985: 200–220). The 124,000 Cuban immigrants who entered the United States in 1980 were much poorer and less well-educated than earlier waves, and many were placed in detention camps because of the U.S. government's fears that they might all be criminals and social deviants.

Flowing from these diverse historical experiences, other factors distinguish the various groups. Chicanos and Cubans more than Puerto Ricans have made the United States a permanent home. Chicanos have the highest proportion (53 percent) born in the United States and the highest level of bilingualism (60 percent). Cubans, because of their higher educational level, are adapting rapidly to American life and (in contrast to other Latino groups) already showing a lot of political power. Because Puerto Ricans have more freedom to go back to the island, fewer have permanent status in the United States. Thus, only 18 percent were born in the United States, and the majority of those interviewed in a recent study indicated that they intended to return eventually to the island to live (Vigil, 1987: 26–27). In addition, each group is culturally pluralistic. For example, Borjas and Tienda (1985) found so many differences in socioeconomic status, labor market characteristics, job mobility, and fertility rates among the various Latino groups that they were forced to conclude that it made little sense to "lump them under a single 'Hispanic' rubric for either analysis or policy treatment."

THE PANETHNIC VIABILITY OF LATINO AND HISPANIC

The categorizing of Chicano, Puerto Rican, Cuban, and other Latin American groups under the term Hispanic seems to have arisen from external forces, including the use of the term by the media, the U.S. Census Bureau and other government agencies, and politicians on the federal level, rather than from any cohesion of the groups themselves (Moore and Pachón, 1985: 11; Vigil, 1987: 2; Giménez, 1989b; Munoz, 1990: 10, 11). Where some semblance of panethnic unity is developing, the term Latino is preferred as a means of uniting Latino groups whose identity is socially constructed by U.S. foreign policy (Hayes-Bautista and Chapa, 1987).

The term Latino has been around for quite some time in activist circles. In the early and middle 1970s, when national coalitions involving Puerto Rican and Chicano movement groups developed, it was popularized to symbolize the commonalities in issues and collective action. At no point, however, did it come to imply a separate ethnic identity as has the term Hispanic. In the 1960s, Chicano groups fought hard to popularize the word Chicano as a replacement for Spanish-American, which implied the assimilation of the Chicano people into U.S. society, left out the Indian heritage, and implied that Chicano history had its origins in Europe. Whereas Spanish-American had been acceptable to the larger society, Chicano (or even Mexican-

American) was viewed as militant. For Chicano activists, the term became a badge of honor (as the term black was for African-Americans) and symbolized the reawakening and organization of a people that had lost its land. When the term Spanish-American fell into disuse, the U.S. Census Bureau and other government agencies, with the blessing of various Latino politicians, replaced it with the term Hispanic.

Although Latinos cannot be considered a homogeneous group with a distinct identity, there are commonalities that have the potential to unite the groups around collective action. The city of Chicago, where Puerto Ricans and Chicanos have a history of collective mobilization, is an example of some degree of Latino panethnicity. Community leaders here have popularized the term Latino to represent the collective concerns of the Spanish-speaking population in response to common structural conditions in the areas of education, politics, and economics (Padilla, 1985a). The two groups have a common language, an awareness of being different from other social groups in the United States, a low standard of living, and a common desire to eliminate the inequalities created for the Spanish-speaking by the larger society.

Even here, however, Latino ethnic identity is only "situationally specific." According to Padilla, Puerto Ricans and Chicanos would have had to come to grips with their own particular identities before accepting Latinismo. His research reveals variation in patterns of interaction and communication among the groups and heterogeneity in "the ideological formulations" of Latino political consciousness (Padilla, 1985b: 339).

In the city of Monterey Park, where I have been both an activist and a researcher, there have also been manifestations of panethnic unity among Latinos, but here too they are situationally specific. My interviews revealed both an acceptance of assimilation and the view that it is all right to be proud of one's heritage and to identify oneself as something other than American (Latino, Hispanic, Californio, Mexican-American), to oppose English-only proposals, to support bilingual education, to sympathize with new immigrants, to see America as a country built on diversity, and to work to promote that diversity in the development of the community (Calderón, 1991). While these opinion leaders reported that ethnicity did not play much of a role in their political lives, they evaluated it in the context of particular interests. A former Mexican-American city council member went so far as to relate from his experience that, although Latinos might organize along multiethnic lines in Monterey Park, ethnicity was used to serve particular political interests:

> The people that encouraged me to get involved were people that knew me and felt that there was an opportunity to exploit it [being a Hispanic]. . . . So I went into it with that in mind . . . being the second Hispanic to serve on the city

council kind of made me proud, and I was really aware of the fact that Hispanic, Mexican-American groups, do need role models (Calderón, 1990: 89).

This perception is consistent with the view of some academicians that ethnic groups are primarily political interest groups—united not just on the basis of culture but around common interests (Bentley, 1987). Erik Olin Wright (1979; 1982) proposes that these interests are related not simply to competition over resources but to manifestations of income and position in the production process.

The Latinos interviewed at the city council and administrative levels owned property and had a stake in the local economy, and they were unwilling to affiliate with a political identity that might jeopardize their positions. They saw themselves as part of a middle-class community and a middle-class culture, holding political positions that were fluid, ambivalent, and middle-of-the-road. Although they said that ethnicity had very little to do with their identity, they were still trying to hold onto some aspects of their heritage and culture. Those at this level who preferred to use the term Hispanic submitted that it was politically safer and more acceptable to the mainstream than others.

The identity and political positions of these Latinos represent what Wright (1982) calls contradictory class locations. Those interviewed or observed in city positions were primarily managers who had some control over the production process—semiautonomous employees or employers. For example, one had managed a store before he became a city manager and now ran a consulting business. Another was the principal of an elementary school, and a third was a developer. Because of their contradictory locations in the class structure, they were characterized by ambivalent perspectives of themselves and the issues around them.

Their loss of the Spanish language and their social mobility into an integrated middle-class community motivated them to see themselves as "Americans like everybody else." Consequently, they did not place much importance on ethnic identity or unity. At the same time, ethnicity did serve as a basis for political organizing around issues that they found threatening. Although they agreed that the Latino people lacked cohesiveness and political power, they were active around issues that took on a class character and involved economic and political interests that went beyond anyone particular ethnic group. Their emphasis on "issues," however, was situationally specific according to the alliances that emerged. Where Latinos were distinguished from other groups along lines of power or class, they responded panethnically.

While Hispanic was the most widely used term at the city council level; the term Latino was most prevalent at the neighborhood level, in organizations and coalitions comprised primarily of professional and working-class people. In the main, the organization that had been advancing the use of the term Latino was the West San Gabriel Valley League of United Latin American Citizens (LULAC). Centered in Monterey Park, it included people of Mexican, Central American, and Puerto Rican origin. The PTAs, neighborhood associations, and sports clubs in which LULAC was active also included some Cuban residents. The Coalition for Harmony in Monterey Park, which in 1987 defeated a city council resolution that would have made English the official language of the city, also popularized the term Latino. It went beyond being a catalyst for panethnic unity among Latino and Asian groups in the community by building a multiethnic alliance around the specific issue of language rights.

Another example of multi ethnic coalition building can be found in the nearby Alhambra School District, where in the spring of 1991 several racial incidents involving Latino, Asian-American, and Anglo students led Latino leaders and parents to develop the Coalition for Equality, composed of 35 individuals and organizations. Although there were initial differences, the coalition developed panethnic unity around the idea of restructuring the school system to meet the needs of a growing Latino and Asian-American population. This initial unity led to the formation of a multiethnic task force that included representatives from the Asian-American, Latino, and Anglo communities and eventually produced a series of proposals including a multicultural curriculum, school-based management, and parent involvement in all levels of the district's decision making.

CONCLUSION

Panethnic unity among Latino groups is becoming a reality and a necessity. The terms used to describe this panethnicity, however, have a lot to do with the class and ethnic forces that have an interest in their definition. The term Hispanic has apparently been imposed from outside rather than developing from the cohesion of the groups themselves. Chicanos, Puerto Ricans, and Cubans have such distinct historical experiences and cultural, socioeconomic, and political backgrounds that a distinct Hispanic identity is unlikely. The use of the word Hispanic is still unpopular in Chicano activist circles, where it is seen as an attempt by the government to assimilate and Eurocentrize Chicanos. In contrast, the term Latino does show the capacity for developing some panethnic unity. Although the Latino groups in the United States are somewhat diverse even internally, commonalities may sometimes be found around particular issues reflecting similar conditions of inequality.

Panethnic unity for collective action and the development of a historically distinct and separate ethnic identity are, however, two different things. In both the Chicago example and that of Monterey Park, a situationally specific panethnic unity among Latino groups developed over time as a collective response to structural conditions that threatened their particular class and ethnic interests. Whether Hispanic or Latino became dominant in the course of these struggles depended on the particular class and ethnic interests of the leadership. In Monterey Park, those who called themselves Hispanic had a stake in protecting their property and managerial positions and were unwilling to affiliate with a political identity that might jeopardize them. Those who used the term Latino tended to build panethnic unity around issues that threatened the interests of the entire Latino community and to form coalitions with other oppressed groups around structural issues they had in common.

NOTE

1. Copyright Acknowledgement: This chapter was previously published in the following: *Latin American Perspectives*, June 1992.

REFERENCES

Bentley, G. Carter. 1987. "Ethnicity and practice." *Comparative Studies in Society and History* 29 (January): 25.

Borjas, George J. and Marta Tienda. 1985. *Hispanics in the U.S. Economy*. Orlando: Academic Press.

Calderón, José. 1991. "Mexican American politics in a multi-ethnic community: the case of Monterey Park: 1985–1990," Ph.D. dissertation, University of California, Los Angeles, 1990.

Giménez, Martha E. 1989a. "Latino/Hispanic-who needs a name? The case against a standardized terminology." *International Journal of Health Services* 19: 557–571.

———. 1989b. "The political construction of the Hispanic," pp. 66–85 in Mary Romero and Cordelia Candelaria (eds.), *Estudios Chicanos and the Politics of Community*. Selected Proceedings, National Association for Chicano Studies.

Hayes-Bautista, David and Jorge Chapa. 1988. "Latino terminology: conceptual bases for standardized terminology." *American Journal of Public Health* 77: 61–68.

Keefe, Susan and Amado Padilla. 1987 *Chicano Ethnicity*. Albuquerque: University of New Mexico Press.

López, David and Yen Espíritu. 1990. "Panethnicity in the United States: a theoretical framework." *Ethnic and Racial Studies* 13: 198–224.

Montejano, David. 1987. *Anglos and Mexicans in the Making of Texas*, 1936–1986. Austin: University of Texas Press.

Moore, Joan. 1970. "Colonialism: the case of the Mexican American." Social Problems 17 (Spring): 463–472.

Moore, Joan and Harry Pachón. 1985 *Hispanics in the United States*. Englewood Cliffs: Prentice-Hall.

Múñoz, Carlos, Jr. 1990. *Youth, Identity, Power*. London: Verso.

Padilla, Félix M. 1985a *Latino Ethnic Consciousness: The Case of Mexican Americans and Puerto Ricans in Chicago*. Notre Dame: University of Notre Dame Press.

———. 1985b. "On the nature of Latino ethnicity," pp. 332–345 in Rodolfo de la Garza et al. (ed.), *The Mexican-American Experience: An Interdisciplinary Anthology*. Austin: University of Texas Press.

Portes, Alejandro and Robert L. Bach. 1985. *Latin Journey: Cuban and Mexican Immigrants in the United States*. Berkeley: University of California Press.

Vigil, Maurilio. 1987. *Hispanics in American Politics: The Search for Political Power*. Lanham: University Press of America.

Wright, Erik Olin. 1979. *Class Structure and Income Determination*. New York: Academic Press.

———. 1982. "Class boundaries and contradictory locations," pp. 112–129 in Anthony Giddens and David Held (eds.), *Classes, Power, and Conflict*. Berkeley: University of California Press.

Chapter Seven

Situational Identity of Suburban Mexican American Politicians in a Multi-Ethnic Community[1]

José Zapata Calderón

This chapter addresses the situational character of ethnic identification of middle class Mexican American politicians in Monterey Park, a multiethnic middle-class suburb undergoing rapid demographic changes.[2]

Specifically, Monterey Park is a microcosm of larger political and social transformations taking place in Los Angeles County, where racial minorities and new immigrants are becoming a majority, and where the dual issues of growth and increasing immigration have become important concerns of public debate.

In Monterey Park, as a result of this process, there is an imbalance being created in the power structure between the new majority of Latinos and Asians, who differ in economic and political power, and a dwindling Anglo minority who still control local political institutions.

The main material for my research has been taken from interviews with various Mexican American opinion leaders in the city council arena, including city politicians, elected public officials, and politically active businesspersons. The interviews were complemented with field notes written from my lived experience as a resident in the community, from participating in Latino organizations, and from working as a researcher in the "Changing Communities" project funded by the Ford Foundation in 1989.

Since opinion leaders do influence trends and public opinion, it is important to focus on their perceptions[3] and how they see themselves within a multiethnic community at a time when sharp demographic transformations are taking place around them. In this chapter, I begin to draw out the nature of Mexican American politics in the context of these changes by focusing on how a select group of suburban Mexican American leaders identify themselves politically in the city hall arena. An analysis of their perceptions can help in discerning what role class and ethnic factors play in the politics of "middle-class" Mexican Americans and in their relations with other ethnic groups in this multiethnic setting.

I will, first of all, give a brief overview of the demographics of Mexican Americans and Latinos in Monterey Park, and, secondly, an example from my work of the situational character that Mexican American opinion leaders exhibit in their identity and in their perceptions on the existence or nonexistence of a homogeneous Mexican American political community.

DEMOGRAPHICS

Mexican Americans in Monterey Park are part of a growing Latino majority in a region, the San Gabriel Valley, which has been targeted nationally by the Southwest Voter Registration Project as having the most potential in the southwest United States for voter registration and political empowerment campaigns.[4]

Until 1960, Monterey Park's population consisted of 85 percent Anglo, 3 percent Asian, and 12 percent Latino. In the 1970s, however, there were a number of external changes that deeply affected the city. Briefly, these included the federal government's recognition of mainland China and the exclusion of Taiwan from official diplomatic status; the emergence of the Pacific Rim as an interrelated economy; a dissatisfaction of incoming immigrant Asian families with the conditions in older and nearby Los Angeles ethnic neighborhoods; and a significant increase in the Latino population within the city. By the 1980 census, Monterey Park's population had radically changed to 40 percent Asian, 37 percent Latino, and 20 percent Anglo.

Spurred on by developers and realtors advertising and selling Monterey Park property in Hong Kong and Taiwan, the population continued its shift in 1990. In 1990, the Asian population became a majority with 56 percent while the Anglo population declined to 11.7 percent, and Latinos dropped to 31.3 percent.

As Latinos have been confronted with these rapid demographic changes, they have developed the commonality of having to work with other ethnic groups in the political arena to have some say in the decision-making process. At the same time, they have aligned themselves on varying sides of the political interests that dominate the city's power struggles.

PERSPECTIVES ON SITUATIONAL IDENTITY

The recent works of Felix Padilla have raised the issue of the situational character of Latino identity. His works stress that Latino ethnic consciousness is "situationally specific" according to the common conditions of inequality and the need for Latino groups to take action around similar concerns.[5] This perception goes along with the view of some academicians who define ethnic/racial identity as being in a constant process of being recreated,[6] and ethnic groups as being primarily political interest groups who organize themselves around common political interests.[7]

I argue that these interests are not only related to competition over resources, but also have a class foundation. The political positions of the Mexican American politicians interviewed for the purposes of this chapter take on a character of what sociologist Erik Olin Wright calls contradictory class locations.[8] These positions, often generalized under the term "middle class," are contradictory in that they sway between various class interests. As managerial professionals, they are considered part of the power structure in being able to supervise workers and in having significant say over the production process. On the other hand, they do not own the resources of production and they can be fired at any time by their employer.[9] When applied on a micro scale, all those interviewed or observed in city positions are primarily managerial professionals who have some control over the production process. For example, to name a few, a former city council member managed a store before he got into the profession of being a city manager. Today, he runs his own consultant business and employs a staff of individuals. One of the Mexican American former councilmembers is the principal of an elementary school where he supervises other employees in the school. A Mexican American developer, who has held various positions in city hall, also employs and manages others. A corporate public relations officer also has others working under him, has flexibility in his time, and has some control over how he carries out his work.

These individuals, affected by their contradictory locations in the class structure and the rapid demographic changes occurring around them, are being forced to rethink their ethnic identity in relation to newcomers and to the political power of Mexican Americans overall.

In this context, how these politicians identify themselves takes on a situational character incorporating both shared historical experiences and individual class interests.

SITUATIONAL CHARACTER OF IDENTITY

A former Mexican American city official who aligned himself more with growth interests exemplifies this situational character when he states his unclarity as to why he identifies himself as Hispanic:

> Hispanic origins. Hispanic? It's just a nice category. It doesn't mean anything to me. It is a way to classify yourself. I eat Mexican food but I don't speak the language. But, retain my culture—retained what culture? My parents consider themselves Californios. You know I belong to—am active in the California Historical Society, in the Southwest group and those kinds of things. Well, you know, I'm not too sure what else it would mean.

In identifying himself as a "Californio," this former city official referred to his class lineage as being rooted in the early 19th century California upper class of *hacendados* or landowners.

Although calling himself and his ancestors Californios, he used the term "Hispanic" repeatedly when talking about the contemporary Mexican American. At the same time, he admitted that he didn't identify to a large degree with the Mexican American culture, that his family didn't speak any Spanish, and that the broken Spanish he had once acquired was now lost because he was around "educated" people.

Another former city councilperson and businessman, now in his early sixties, related that people of his generation used to call themselves Mexican Americans but that he now primarily called himself Hispanic. Although calling himself Hispanic, he still strongly identifies with his Mexican roots:

> As a child my father left to go—he was an officer in the Mexican army and so he came here to get my mother and take her back. My mother was with her family and they didn't want her to go back. So he came and he left. And so as a result he left when my mother was pregnant with me. I never did know my father. So my father was from Mexico City. My mother was born in New Mexico. My grandfather was Eustos Zapata and he got involved in the revolutions and I guess he rode with Pancho Villa.

Another Mexican American elected leader in the community also prefers to call himself Hispanic and identifies the term with its relationship to other groups who are from Latin America:

> Hispanic is a good, easy common term. You know, it used to be Chicano or Mexican American. Now, I think there's more activity going down. There are other people who are similar to me but maybe don't have specific national origins. They don't come from Mexico but come here from Central America or Latin America.

SOCIAL CLASS AND ASSIMILATION

The responses of these Mexican Americans all manifest the common charac-
teristic of aligning themselves with powerful developer class interests, on the
one hand, and accepting their assimilation into a middle-class community, on
the other. Acknowledging that they have lost use of the Spanish language,
they are willing to identify themselves as Hispanic. However, they also exhibit an ambivalence in their beliefs that this term has any real meaning for
their political identity.

Instead of any unifying identity, they propose the absence of an ethnic
political community among Latinos in Monterey Park for various reasons,
including divisions within the group, apathy, and the effects of a middle-
class suburban culture.

Where Mexican Americans do identify with political activity, they agree,
and are more apt to identify with the established mainstream political parties
and civic groups. These leaders are no exception and take a "middle-of-the-
road" attitude as to which political party they align themselves with.

The former councilperson explains his reason for being a Republican as a
means of letting young people know that there were two parties in contention:

> And even being a Republican, isn't so much because I'm strong on Republi-
> cans. Sometimes in my life I thought that it was important that young people
> know that there are two parties. Because if we get strength politically, I don't
> think that we can be Mexican Americans and all Democrats. So I just thought
> that being a Republican-like I say once again, maybe that was a little naïve that
> being a Republican and being Mexican American might be something some of
> the young people may want.

The former city official explains he is a Republican but that he usually votes
either way:

> You know, I've been a registered Republican for years but I tend to vote either
> way. I'll probably be voting mostly Democratic this time. I guess you could
> say I really should have changed my registration. But I consider myself neither
> a Democrat or Republican.

Another Mexican American, a public relations officer for a corporation,
explains that although he is a Democrat, he does not want to be counted as
being firmly on one side and considers his politics to be "in the middle."

The former city official goes as far as to say that Latinos are both conservative and something other than Democrat:

> Middle-income Hispanics can be very conservative. I keep reading that they
> are involved as Democrats. I don't think they are Democrats. I think they are

just as prone to vote against stopping all phases of development as the Anglos would.

An ethnic political identity, according to these Mexican Americans, is held back by the class divisions that exist in the community. Those who are upper income or upper middle class are thought to associate more with issues that affect the larger community than with issues that could be called "Mexican American." For example, the local city official perceives ethnic issues as being primarily the possession of lower-income Latinos:

> As far as the Hispanics go, you've got really two different income levels here. You've got the old line old-timer, real middle class, or upper-middle income. They don't see any Hispanic issues. Ok, now you've got the lower-income Hispanics who don't vote. They are the ones that are minimum income—don't have adequate housing, etc.—and they see this general income situation as being an Hispanic issue. But the ones, the Hispanics that have it, they don't see it as an Hispanic issue.

A similar perspective is expressed by the Mexican American developer who believes that Latino unity is being held back by Latinos who have assimilated into the upper echelons of the middle class:

> There are a lot of Hispanics in Monterey Park that are "White Latinos." If they (the White Latinos) had a choice to vote for an Hispanic or a Jones, they would vote for Jones. These White Latinos consider themselves middle class or upper class. They average $40,000 a year. But all of them don't turn away. Some monied Latinos will give money to elections. Some will even help Latinos who are running. But the ones I am talking about are the ones who don't want to be called "Chicano." The ones who say "I'm an American citizen." The barrier to the unity of Latinos is the "White Latino."

Since Mexican American opinion leaders in the city council political arena propose that their identity is tied to the way they align themselves on issues, they also agree that the history of Mexican American political organizing in Monterey Park has been primarily through established civic groups and not through ethnic-based organizations. The corporate relations officer expresses this view:

> I've witnessed the Rotary Clubs, Soroptimist, and things like that. You know a lot of them are strictly, you know, Hispanic or are Jewish or something like that.

So does the former city council person:

> I don't know. I can't identify a place or time in my, say in my four years in office, where I can say there's a Mexican coffee klatsch or—other than your

church groups that may be just simply a Mexican American in the church in
the city where they are going to meet anyhow but there's—no organization. . . . But I don't recall being involved or invited in the city to any function
that had primarily Mexican American or Hispanic organization.

At the same time, he goes a bit deeper to explain that the lack of Mexican
American political organizing is related to the process of assimilation:

I still have a feeling though that Monterey Park is not only a middle-class city,
it's a middle-class status for Mexican Americans and it's a status that we've
not enjoyed for too many years. And I think a lot of people have the feeling
that I am here, I've got it made, and I've arrived. I've achieved. And have
become complacent with that. Why make waves to do anything else and go
any further than what I am? I am into the melting pot and I'm just as good as
anybody else or as much of an American as anybody else.

A former city councilperson agrees that the assimilation process may be
responsible for his primary involvement being on "nonethnic" civic and
agency advisory boards. This is also true for other Latinos, according to him,
who see no viable Latino organizations bringing Mexican Americans together. The participation that is beginning to take place in the political arena, he
claims, is occurring on city commissions. While he agrees that this is a good
step toward getting the Mexican American people to participate, he doesn't
see any organization or coalition that has the capacity to unite the Mexican
American people with other ethnic groups.

DISCUSSION

Overall, all the Mexican Americans interviewed in the city council political
arena are part of more established community civic groups and institutions
that are multiethnic. They don't affiliate with organizations or groups that are
strictly ethnically separate. They all have doubts as to whether distinct Lati-
no/Hispanic or Mexican American politics exists. Instead, they are pretty
much united that Mexican Americans and Latinos in general are moved more
by issues than by ethnicity. In this context, Mexican American political leaders in Monterey Park, particularly those who have held elected offices, have
the characteristics of a politically ambivalent middle class [10] and one that is
very much like what is called the Mexican American generation. This generation, according to Carlos Muñoz in his book *Youth, Identity, Power,* is a
generation whose political ideology leans toward assimilation while de-em-
phasizing Mexican roots. [11] It also follows along the lines of what other
Mexican American academicians have written about the characteristics of the
contemporary Chicano middle class. The historian Juan Gómez Quiñonez
proposes that, in the contemporary period, leaders in the Chicano community

"nearly always come from the middle class, and are increasingly homogenous in educational background, moderation in posture and style, and cautious about overemphasizing ethnicity."[12] In a study of political socialization among Chicano youth, Martin Sánchez Jankowski characterized the middle-class Chicano as wanting to become assimilated into the political system:

> There is a feeling among members of this group that politics can be an effective means of creating an economically secure future. . . . The political goals of middle-class Chicanos are to obtain as many advantages as possible without offending those who now hold power. These attitudes emerge from having been members of an ethnic group with a history of occupying the lower rungs of the socioeconomic ladder and from understanding that they have managed to become middle-class in spite of discriminatory practices by Anglo Americans.[13]

Monterey Park Mexican American leaders in the city council arena see themselves much along these lines: part of a middle-class community and a middleclass culture with political positions that are fluid, ambivalent, and middle-of-the-road. Although they say that ethnicity has very little to do with their identity, they still try to hold on to some aspects of the Mexican American heritage and culture. By calling themselves "Hispanic," they do identify themselves ethnically. However, the use of the term "Hispanic" is perceived as a politically safe term and as more acceptable in the mainstream than the term "Chicano."

However, when the interests of these Mexican American city officials are threatened, or when ethnicity can be used as a means of mobilization against them, then ethnicity comes to the political forefront.

For example, when former mayor Barry Hatch defined American identity in terms of supporting English as the official language, all the Mexican Americans on the city council arena opposed him. Similarly, on the issue of English Only and English on signs in the city, the former Mexican American city council official took a strong stand against it:

> Well, you know, the original outcry about the signs it was really just brought about by people suddenly seeing too many signs that they couldn't read and were mainly Chinese. Whether they were Chinese or whatever they were, it was kind of a slap at you because it was suddenly there. I did take a very strong stand on the English language thing and maybe politically stronger than I should have.

The Mexican American developer also took a stand against it as long as business signs could have some section in English:

Hatch is not satisfied. He wants "English Only" and no other language on those business signs. I support having a portion of signs being in English, but not all English. English Only is discriminatory.

The former city manager was also strongly opposed to English Only and supported bilingual education as long as it didn't lead to separatism:

I think it was a bunch of bullshit—I didn't agree with it. I was opposed to the whole idea. I think if bilingual education can help people out of a hole you've got to give them a chance. Now, I do agree that we are in a real danger if everyone keeps insisting on cutting themselves up into ethnic and language groups. I mean I'd rather have it cohesive. It makes it very difficult to develop a cohesive country.

The former city manager parroted a common sentiment among all those interviewed, that the Americanism of Hatch was really meant to exclude others:

Hatch is 1950s. I mean Joe McCarthy in the 1950s wrapped himself in the American flag and anyone he didn't like he branded. And I noticed that the way he talked about Americanism that he also makes it clear as he goes through.

CONCLUSIONS

The various conceptions of identity, in this context, are related to how the demographic changes are perceived and how individuals see that they are affected by them. Barry Hatch represents an extreme right-wing view in defining who is or is not a so-called "American." He advocates English Only, believes that immigrants are creating many of the ills in the society, and wants to preserve the purity of what he considers to be American. That purity is enveloped in an image of the United States as being predominately for Anglo, English-speaking people with a heritage dating back to European explorers. The Mexican Americans interviewed here, although middle-class and accepting of assimilation, responded with a situationally specific ethnic viewpoint as to their identity. This viewpoint accepts that it's all right to be proud of your heritage and to identify yourself as something other than American (Latino, Hispanic, California, Mexican American), to be against English only, to support bilingual education, to sympathize with new immigrants, to see the United States as a country built on diversity, and to work to promote that diversity in the development of the community. At the same time, there are ambivalent perceptions among these Mexican Americans arising out of a feeling of being displaced. With the new influx of Chinese immigrants into the city, Mexican Americans see the need to form coalitions.

However, they don't agree on what type of coalitions. Some see the need for coalescing with the new immigrants while others see them as a threat.

Although proposing that ethnicity does not play much of a role in their political lives, they do perceive of ethnicity in the context of particular interests. A former Mexican American councilmember goes so far as to relate from his experience that, although Latinos may organize along multiethnic lines in Monterey Park, ethnicity can sometimes be used to serve particular political interests:

> But at the time I was approached and I declared I was the only Hispanic on the ticket. And the people that encouraged me to get involved were people that knew me and felt that there was an opportunity to exploit it. I am not too sure it had that much bearing on anything. So I thought well why not. So I went into it with that in mind. . . . So, you know, being the second Hispanic to serve on the city council that kind of made me proud and I was really aware of the fact that Hispanic, Mexican American groups, do need role models.

Overall, what appears to be ambivalence of identity among these politicians is really, at its base, the situational use of identity to meet particular class goals.

On the one hand, as middle-class Mexican Americans who own property, they have a stake in the local economy and are not willing to affiliate with a political identity that may jeopardize their positions. Their loss of the Spanish language and social mobility into an integrated middle-class community motivates them to identify as "Americans like everybody else." Consequently, they argue that they do not place much importance on ethnic identity or unity. On the other hand, ethnicity comes forth as a basis for political organizing around issues that they find threatening.

Their emphasis on "issues," however, is situationally specific according to the alliances that emerge. Where Mexican Americans are distinguished along lines of power or class, in comparison to other groups, they respond ethnically.

At the same time, although they agree that the Mexican American people lack cohesiveness and political power, they are active around issues that take on a class character involving economic and political interests that go beyond anyone particular ethnic group.

NOTES

1. Copyright Acknowledgement: This chapter was previously published in the following: "Situational Identity of Suburban Mexican American Politicians in a Multi-Ethnic Community." *Chicanas and Chicanos in Contemporary Society,* edited by Roberto M. De Anda. Boston: Allyn & Bacon, 1966: 179–189.

2. Here, I use the terms which the participants used to identify themselves. I use the term Mexican American primarily and Chicano/Chicana secondarily in reference to a group of

people of Mexican descent who permanently reside in the United States. Mexican refers to recent immigrants from Mexico. Latino refers to all people of Latin American descent in the United States. Although all subjects interviewed in Monterey Park were of Mexican origin, they identified themselves as Hispanic, Mexican American, Californio, Mexican, and Latino. While Hispanic was the most widely used term at the city hall level, Latino was most prominently used at the neighborhood level. Although the majority of Latinos in Monterey Park are of Mexican descent, the participant observations also included Latinos from Puerto Rican, Cuban, and Central American backgrounds.

3. Mario T. Garcia, in *Mexican Americans* (New Haven: Yale University Press, 1989), proposes the study of Mexican American leadership is a basis for understanding the dynamics of change and politics within the larger Mexican American community. Another source: John Higham, "Current Trends in the Study of Ethnicity in the United States," *Journal of American Ethnic History* (Fall, 1982: 8–9) emphasizes the importance of studying ethnic leadership as a means of grasping the nature of ethnic groups in the United States.

4. Edmond Newton, "San Gabriel Valley Becomes the New Power Base of Latino Voters," *Los Angeles Times* (21 January 1990), Bl.

5. Felix M. Padilla, *Latino Ethnic Consciousness* (Notre Dame, IN: Notre Dame University Press, 1985). Also his "Latino Ethnicity in the City of Chicago," in Susan Olzak and Joanne Nagel (eds.), *Competitive Ethnic Relations* (Orlando, FL: Academic Press, 1986), 153–171.

6. George L. Hicks and Philip E. Leis, *Ethnic Encounters: Identities and Contexts* (North Scituate, MA: Duxbury Press, 1977). Also see Nina Glick Schiller, "Ethnic Groups Are Made, Not Born: The Haitian Immigrant and American Politics," in George L. Hicks and Philip E. Leis (eds.), *Ethnic Encounters: Identities and Contexts* (North Scituate, MA: Duxbury Press, 1977) 25–36.

7. G. Carter Bentley, "Ethnicity and Practice," *Comparative Studies in Society and History*, 29, 1 Jan. 1987) 25. Also, Joanne Nagel, "The Political Construction of Ethnicity," in Susan Olzak and Joanne Nagel (eds.), *Competitive Ethnic Relations*, 93–108.

8. Erik Olin Wright, *Classes* (New York: Verso, 1985).

9. Mario Barrera has also written about the segmented nature of the U.S. class structure and specifically about the Chicano professional-managerial class segment. He proposes that Chicanos remain a small percentage in the professional-managerial category and are still situated at the lower socioeconomic levels of that class segment. See *Race and Class in the Southwest* (Notre Dame, IN: Notre Dame University Press, 1979), 214–217.

10. Mark E. Kann in *Middle Class Radicalism in Santa Monica* (Philadelphia: Temple University Press, 1986) writes about the ambivalence of the middle-class as being rooted in their trying to "reconcile their professional ideals of autonomy, rationality, and public service with their material contribution to human dependence, social control, and even tyranny in the political economy."

11. Carlos Munoz, Jr., *Youth, Identity, Power* (New York: Verso, 1989), 19–46.

12. Juan Gómez-Quiñonez, *Chicano Politics: Reality and Promise: 1940–1990* (Albuquerque: University of New Mexico Press, 1990), 208.

13. Martin Sanchez Jankowski, *City Bound: Urban Life and Political Attitudes among Chicano Youth* (Albuquerque: University of New Mexico Press, 1986), 224.

Chapter Eight

Multi-Ethnic Coalition Building in a Diverse School District[1]

José Zapata Calderón

CONFLICT AND COALITION LITERATURE

Because of a tendency in the literature to view ethnic relations in terms of black and white, there is very little written on the question of political relations between Latinos and Asian-Pacific Americans. The early sociological literature on ethnicity focused primarily on interracial conflicts between blacks and whites (Blauner, 1969; Van den Berghe, 1967; Harris, 1964).

In recent years some important works have gone beyond the black/white dichotomy to look at both the heterogeneity of the Latino and Asian-Pacific populations as well as at the conflicts and commonalities between U. S. ethnic/racial groups (Omi and Winant, 1994; Takaki, 1993; Hardy-Fanta, 1993; Lamphere, 1993; Espiritu, 1992; Villareal and Hernandez, 1991; Nyden and Wiewel, 1991; Andersen and Collins, 1992; Davis, 1990; Garcia, 1988; Keefe, 1988; Santillan, 1988; Borjas, 1985; Moore, 1985; Padilla, 1985). Some literature has also been written on Black-Latino political conflict (Conciatore .and Rodriguez, 1995; Falcon, 1988) and on how Puerto Ricans compete with Blacks and other recent immigrants for scarce resources (Ginorio, 1987). Other literature has examined how the experiences of Mexican, Latin American, and Southeast Asian immigrants are quite distinct from that of European groups (Portes, 1979, 1985; Borjas, 1985; Kwong, 1987; Cheng and Bonacich, 1984).

In this realm, some works have been written on the politics of conflict between Latino immigrants and African Americans (Davis, 1994; Oliver and Johnson, 1984) and between African Americans and Korean immigrants (Cheng and Espiritu, 1989). The work by Oliver and Johnson is exemplary in exploring the economic structural reasons for inter-ethnic conflict Their study is placed in the tradition of early urban theorists who analyzed ethnic conflict as related to the conditions of urban growth and development However, they go one step further by emphasizing racial and economic factors that were not as prominent in the early American industrial city.

Oliver and Johnson stress that there is a great need for studying the impact of new immigrants and their interaction with the resident population and that there is also need for studies that highlight the ways in which cooperative relations are established (Oliver and Johnson, 1984).

A recent work, *Politics in Black and White: Race and Power in Los Angeles* by Raphael J. Sonenshein (1993), moves in this direction by looking at the role that leadership and ideology play in the development of biracial coalitions. Sonenshein proposes that the success of biracial coalitions depends primarily on an ideology or set of beliefs that are shared by groups who are commonly seeking political power. Although focused primarily on the incorporation of African Americans in the electoral arena, this work is a significant contribution to how biracial coalitions develop at both the mass and elite political levels. As a contribution to the practical aspects of this literature, I utilize the concepts of leadership and ideology in examining the development of multi-ethnic coalition-building in a diverse and changing Southern California school district.

THE SETTING

The Alhambra School District represents the larger demographic changes taking place throughout California. The district serves a diverse student population of 20,526 including 51.2 percent Asian, 39.0 percent Latino, 8.1 percent White, 0.7 percent Black, and 0.1 percent Native American (Alhambra School District, 1993).

It includes the city of Alhambra and almost all of the city of Monterey Park and now has the largest concentration of Chinese students anywhere in the United States.

The city of Monterey Park exemplifies the larger changes taking place within the school district. Up until 1960, Monterey Park's population consisted of 85 percent Anglo, 3 percent Asian, and 12 percent Latino. By the 1980 census, its population had radically changed to 40 percent Asian, 37 percent Latino, and 20 percent Anglo. In 1990, while the Anglo population dropped to 11.7 percent, the Asian population grew to 56 percent and Latinos dropped to 31.3 percent.

The city of Alhambra has had similar demographic changes. In 1982 the ethnic breakdown included 23 percent Asian, 37 percent Latino, and 39 percent Anglo. By 1991, Asians were the largest group with 36 percent, followed by Latinos with 32 percent and Anglos with 30 percent. The demographic changes in the two cities and in the school district overall have resulted in ethnic relations that are characterized by examples of both conflict and cooperation. [2]

Although city politics were historically dominated by growth and developer interests, a controlled growth movement emerged in the 1980s. This movement included some residents who were genuinely in favor of improving the quality of life in the region and others who had a tendency to blame all the "growth" problems on the new Chinese immigrants.

In 1986, alarmed by the growing number of Chinese residents and businesses in the city, an all-white city council endorsed a resolution making English the official language of the city. This resolution called for the U.S. Congress to immediately close the national borders, the use of English in all city literature, non-support to any city that supported sanctuary for new immigrants, and the use of city police in supporting the deportation of so-called "illegal." In November, 1987, a multi-ethnic coalition, the Coalition for Harmony in Monterey Park (CHAMP) was able to defeat the resolution and lead a trend at the city government level toward more cooperation between the different groups.

Alongside the tensions at the city government level, there were numerous racial incidents involving Latino, Asian, and Anglo students. In 1986, one fight led to the stabbing of a Chinese student at Mark Keppel High School in the Alhambra School District.

Although the school district established a series of cultural "harmony" retreat programs to sensitize student leaders to the diverse cultures in the area, the tensions between the various ethnic groups now shifted from the city government level to the high schools.

On March 9, 1991, a fight between Latino and Chinese students at San Gabriel High School occurred when students began taunting each other with racial slurs. The fight escalated to include at least ten Latino students and two Chinese students. Subsequently, a special panel of school district employees held expulsion hearings for five of the Latino students. This hearing decided not to expel the five Latino students, citing a lack of evidence and positive identification of those involved.

On March 29th, another fight took place, also racially motivated, between two Vietnamese American students and two Anglo students at San Gabriel High School. One of the Anglo students involved in the fight was the son of an Alhambra policeman who placed pressure on the District Attorney's office to file charges. Subsequently the Vietnamese students were charged with battery on school property.

Out of these two incidents, two separate coalitions developed. The Coalition for Equality, led by members of the West San Gabriel Valley League of United Latin American Citizens (LULAC), was primarily made up of Latino parents and educational professionals. The Asian Coalition, led by the Chinese American Parents and Teachers Association of Southern California, included 21 different Asian groups. This group was largely composed of Chinese professionals including teachers, teachers' aides, and bilingual social service workers. They questioned the District Attorney's office directly as to why the Vietnamese students were singled out when the Latinos involved in a similar incident were not charged. They requested an investigation into the issue and pressured the school district to acknowledge that there was a racial problem in the school.

While the intention of the Asian coalition, according to the President Marina Tse, was to have the charges dropped, the District Attorney's office responded by filing charges of battery on school property against the Latinos involved in the first incident.

School officials did not help the matter and denied there were racial tensions in their school. One school principal blamed the whole incident on "machismo" while another blamed it on the natural "hormones" of teenagers.

SEPARATE COALITIONS

At first, the two coalitions were not able to come together because of perceived class and cultural differences. Within the Latino coalition, there were some individuals who perceived the Chinese as being primarily an entrepreneurial elite with substantial funds and resources. These individuals, although primarily from the professional and managerial sector themselves, perceived that members of the Asian coalition were predominantly Chinese businessmen of a higher class than themselves.[3]

Similarly, the Asian coalition was having identical discussions about the Latino community. Some members of the Asian coalition proposed that the Latino community was better situated to wield political power since they had a good number of visible politicians and established organizations that could represent their interests. Although both coalitions were primarily made up of members from the professional sector, it was difficult for the two coalitions to come together because of how they perceived each other's power.

As a result of these perceived differences, the Asian Coalition and the Coalition for Equality met separately over the summer months. Although meeting separately, the coalitions diligently took up the cases of the Latino and Vietnamese students by involving the parents of the students charged, ensuring legal representation, attending all pre-trial hearings, speaking at school board meetings on their behalf, and communicating the coalitions' concerns with the District Attorney's office.

MULTI-ETHNIC LEADERSHIP IN COALITION-BUILDING

One of the primary components for the building of biracial coalitions is the existence of an "interracial leadership" that can develop trust and equal political status over time (Sonenshein, 1994).

Although the coalitions functioned separately over the summer, the leaders of LULAC and the Chinese American PTA began to meet informally to find ways to bring the two coalitions together. These meetings were essential; had they not taken place, the media and school officials could have further divided the groups.

Some local media printed articles that made it sound as though the Chinese American PTA had been responsible for the filing of charges against the Latinos. Further, at various school board meetings, some school board members took the heat off themselves by also pointing the finger at the Chinese American organization.

The leaders of the Asian Coalition and the Coalition for Equality came together every time a divisive issue came up. Further, these divisive issues were openly discussed at the general meetings of the two coalitions. Gradually, those members which were openly blaming other ethnic groups for the problems became a minority.

By the end of the summer, the two separate coalitions were able to overcome the divisions and tensions by focusing on the structural reasons for the problems. In December, 1991, at a meeting attended by 70 individuals from both coalitions, the Multi-Ethnic Task Force was formed which included representatives from the Asian, White, and Latino communities.

COMMON IDEOLOGY AND INTEREST

Sonenshein proposes that biracial coalitions are more likely to develop if the different groups are close in ideology and if leaders are able to help in ameliorating any conflicts of interest (Sonenshein, 1993).

In the Alhambra School District coalition-building effort, the coalition participants were primarily from professional occupations. Sociologist Erik Olin Wright has categorized these positions in the stratification structure as being in "contradictory locations" since they have a tendency to vacillate between class interests (Wright, 1985). Hence, as in the Canadian example described by Richard Thompson (1979), the ideological similarities or differences could not be discerned by merely examining the occupational statuses of the participants since they were all part of the professional category. Here, the use of ethnographic description and interpretation proves useful for drawing out how the intersection of class and ethnicity can unite and divide members of the same social stratum (Thompson, 1979).

Before the Asian Coalition and the Coalition for Equality merged into one coalition, they both had individual members that espoused a "narrow nationalist" ideology. This ideology promoted the practice of "doing only for one's own group" and blaming other racial/ethnic groups for "one's" gains or losses. It differed with the leadership's ideology in both coalitions which sought to overcome the divisive tactics of insensitive school administrators, the district attorney's office, and the media and instead to focus on the institutional and structural foundations of the conflict.

The leadership in both coalitions was able to neutralize the ideology of separatism by uniting the majority of members around ten different proposals aimed at changing the status quo in the school district. These proposals included: a review of disciplinary procedures, the application of conflict resolution programs, the implementation of multi-cultural curriculum, sensitivity training for all school personnel, and the involvement of parents, students and teachers in the decision-making process. The "separate" coalitions evolved into one coalition by agreeing that ethnic/racial tensions in the school district involved larger inequities that required multi-ethnic collaboration. These inequalities included the question as to why Latinos have had such a high expulsion and drop-out rate in the school district. A school board report of the academic years 1989–92, written by Assistant Superintendent Diane Saurenman, showed the Latinos comprised 56 percent of all student drop-outs. At a meeting with the Multi-Cultural Community Association in the Fall of 1993, school administrators informed the group that this pattern had been going on for 20 years and they did not know how to explain it.

In terms of the number of high school graduates completing a six-component group of requirements for admittance into college, the figures were even more dismal when Latinos were compared to other groups in the schools. In the years 1990–1992, Latinos ranked the lowest of all ethnic groups in completing the requirements at all three high schools. At Alhambra High School only 17 percent of Latinos completed the requirements as compared to 38 percent of Asians and 26 percent of others. At Mark Keppel only 3 percent of Latinos completed as compared to 28 percent of Asians and 8 percent of others; and at San Gabriel High the pattern was 4 percent for Latinos as compared to 29 percent for Asians and 12 percent for others.

What followed from these figures were the post-graduation aspirations by ethnicity. In the period 1989–1992, the average at all three high schools revealed that while 80 percent of Asian graduating seniors aspired to four-year colleges, only 11 percent of Latinos had such plans. Instead, at Alhambra High, 60 percent of Latinos opted for vocational/technical schools and 64 percent chose military service or the work force (Saurenman, 1993).

While school officials utilized expulsions, arrests, and the police as a means of dealing with the increased tensions on the campus, the Multi-Cultural Community Association rallied the various ethnic groups around abolishing a tracking system which grouped Latino students at the lower class levels based on ability. The Association utilized participant observation studies carried out by Pitzer College students to argue that most Latino students were tracked into the lower-level A, B, C, courses and not into the honors and advanced placement levels.[4] Simultaneously, the Association led coalition efforts around issues that affected all students. In a presentation to the school board on March 21, 1993, a parent with two children in Alhambra school district spoke for the Multi-Ethnic Task Force in pointing out that:

> School discipline procedures (i.e., suspension, expulsion, the calling in of city police, and the filing of criminal charges) rarely deal with why students are in conflict, but tend to focus on the actions (on the fighting) that it took to resolve the conflict. Consequently, the underlying basis for conflict remains unresolved. On the one hand, it is important to laud the academic accomplishments of Asian students in the schools. On the other, there is a need to get at the roots of why, overall, the Alhambra School District is failing to meet the educational needs of Latinos.

Continued pressure by the Multi-Ethnic Task Force on school administrators to focus on these issues led to the establishment of an official advisory group to the school board, the Alhambra School District Human Relations Advisory Committee. This 30-member committee has broad representation from the Multi-Ethnic Task Force, PTAs, teacher's unions, staff, administrators, and student representatives from the district's three high schools.

In May, 1993, this committee wrote and passed through the school board, a policy to deal with hate crimes. This policy requires all principals to develop a school-wide plan for "creating an environment which allows all persons to realize their full individual potential through understanding and appreciation of society's diversity of race, ethnic background, national origin, religious belief, sex, age, disability, or sexual orientation." As part of this policy, the school district also agreed to promote conflict resolution techniques and to provide a voice for students regarding these issues.

The passage of this policy, as well as continued incidents of racial conflict between Latino and Asian students, gave impetus to the Multi-Ethnic Task Force transforming itself into a membership organization. Calling itself the Multi-Cultural Community Association, the organization took the lead in obtaining funding for the institutionalization of conflict resolution classes as part of the curriculum.

CONCLUSION

Although the participants of coalition-building efforts in the Alhambra School District had the commonality of being professionals, they divided along ideological lines. In both the Asian Coalition and the Coalition for Equality, a "narrow nationalist" ideological interest that emphasized "doing only for your own group" kept the coalitions from merging into one. Only when a leadership emerged to combat the divisiveness of school and state institutions was the ideology of separatism able to be neutralized. Rather than focusing on the cultural and perceived class differences between the various ethnic groups, this leadership built an effective multi-ethnic coalition by uniting on a common ideology that focused organizational efforts on the structural foundations of conflict.

The success of coalitions between ethnic groups from varied cultural and historical backgrounds, as the Alhambra School District example has shown, depends on a type of leadership and ideology that can build short-term tactical alliances into long-term strategic goals for systemic and institutional change. This is crucial to whether the institution can be moved to make the types of changes needed to meet the demands of an increasingly diverse population.

Many schools are still structured in a traditional top-down hierarchy which was used at one time to meet the demands of an assembly line type of society. With advances in new information-oriented technologies and the trend toward a more interdependent world, there is a need to reform school districts in the direction of diversifying the curriculum and governance structure to involve parents, teachers, and students in the decision-making process. Whether such efforts succeed will go a long way toward establishing whether coalition-building between different ethnic/racial groups is a short or long-term development.

NOTES

1. Copyright Acknowledgement: This chapter was reproduced by permission of SAGE Publications, London, Los Angeles, New Delhi and Singapore, from *Critical Sociology*, 21, 1 (1995):101–111.

2. Recent literature on the Monterey Park and Alhambra region includes: Calderón (1988, 1990). Horton (1989, 1992), Horton and Calderón (1990), Saito (1993), Pardo, (1990), Fong (1993), and Yen Fen Tseng (1994).

3. A recent study by Associate Professor Paul Ong of the UCLA Asian American Studies Center shows the inaccuracy of these perceptions. Although the median income of Asian-Pacific Americans is higher than that of the White population, they have more people in poverty (14 percent compared to 9 percent of Whites). Although Asian American entrepreneurs comprised 2.6 percent of all firms in 1987, they accounted for only 1.7 percent of all receipts. Further, there are a disproportionate number of Asian Pacific Americans concentrated in low and mid-level positions with little hope of advancing into the managerial strata.

4. Pitzer College students, as part of a project funded by the Ohio Campus Project and a class titled "Community and Social Responsibility," expressed concern not only about the disproportionate number of Latino students grouped in lower-level classes but also about the teacher expectations that varied according to class level.

REFERENCES

Andersen, Margaret L. and Patricia Hill Collins. 1992. *Race, Class, and Gender*. Belmont, CA: Wadsworth Publishing Company.

Blauner, Robert. 1972. *Racial Oppression in America*. New York: Harper & Row.

Borjas, George J. and Marta Tienda. 1985. *Hispanics in the U.S. Economy*. Orlando: Academic Press.

Calderón, José. 1989. How The English Only Initiative Passed in California." Pp. 93–109 in *Estudios Chicanos and the Politics of Community*, edited by Mary Romero and Cordelia Candelaria. Oakland, CA: Cragmont Publications.

———. 1990. "Latinos and Ethnic Conflict in Suburbia: The Case of Monterey Park." *Latino Studies Journal* 1(2):23–32.

Cheng, Lucie and Edna Bonacich. 1984. *Labor Immigration Under Capitalism*. Berkeley: University of California Press.

Cheng, Lucie and Yen Espiritu. 1989. "Korean Businesses in Black and Hispanic Neighborhoods: A study of Inter-group Relations." *Sociological Perspectives* 32(4):521–534.

Conciatore, Jacqueline and Roberto Rodriguez. 1995. "Blacks and Hispanics: A Fragile Alliance." In *Race, Class, and Gender in the United States*, edited by Paula S. Rothenberg. New York: St. Martin's Press.

Davis, Mike. 1990. *City of Quartz*. New York: Verso.

———. 1994. "Compton Blues." *The Nation* 295(8):268–271.

Espiritu, Yen Le. 1992. *Asian American Panethnicity: Bridging Institutions and Identities*. Philadelphia: Temple University Press.

Falcon, Angelo. 1988. "Black and Latino Politics in New York City: Race and Ethnicity in a Changing Urban Context." Pp. 171–194 in *Latinos and the Political System*, edited by Chris F. Garcia. Notre Dame, IN: University of Notre Dame Press.

Fong, Timothy P. 1994. *The First Suburban Chinatown: The Remaking of Monterey Park, California*. Philadelphia: Temple University Press.

Garcia, F. Chris. 1988. *Latinos and the Political System*. Notre Dame, IN: University of Notre Dame Press.

Ginorio, Angela B. 1987. "Puerto Rican Ethnicity and Conflict." Pp. 182–206 in *Ethnicity and Conflict: International Perspectives*, edited by Jerry Boucher, Dan Landis, and Karen Arnold Clark. Newbury Park, CA: Sage Publications.

Hardy-Fanta, Carol. 1993. *Latina Politics, Latino Politics*. Philadelphia: Temple University Press.

Harris, Marvin. 1964. *Patterns of Race in Americas*. New York: Norton.

Horton, John. 1989. "The Politics of Ethnic Change: Grass-roots Responses to Economic and Demographic Restructuring in Monterey Park, California." *Urban Geography* 10(6):578–592.

———. 1992. "The Politics of Diversity." Pp. 215–245 in *Shaping Diversity*, edited by Louise Lamphere. Chicago: University of Chicago Press.

Horton, John and Calderón, José. 1990. "Language Struggles in a Changing California Community." Pp. 186–194 in *Language Loyalties*, edited by Jim Crawford. Chicago: University of Chicago Press.

Keefe, Susan E. and Amado M. Padillo. 1987. *Chicano Ethnicity*. Albuquerque: University of New Mexico Press.

Kwong, Peter. 1987. *The New Chinatown*. New York: Hill and Wang.

Lamphere, Louise. 1993. *Structuring Diversity*. Chicago: University of Chicago Press.

Moore, Joan and Harry Pachon. 1985. *Hispanics in the United States*. Englewood Cliffs, NJ: Prentice-Hall, Inc.

Nyden, Philip W. and Wim Wiewel. 1991. *Challenging Uneven Development*. New Brunswick, NJ: Rutgers University Press.

Oliver, Melvin and James H. Johnson, Jr. 1984. "Inter-Ethnic Conflict in an Urban Ghetto: The Case of Blacks and Latinos in Los Angeles." *Research in Social Movements, Conflict, and Change* 6:57–94.

Omi, Michael and Howard, Winant. 1994. *Racial Formation in the United States*: From the 1960's to the 1980's. New York: Routledge and Kegan Paul.

Padilla, Felix M. 1985. *Latino Ethnic Consciousness*. Notre Dame, IN: University of Notre Dame Press.

Pardo, Mary Santoli. 1990. "Identity and Resistance: Mexican American Women and Grassroots Activism in Two Los Angeles Communities." Ph.D. dissertation, University of California Los Angeles.

Portes, Alejandro. 1979. "Illegal Immigration and the International System: Lessons from Recent Legal Mexican Immigrants to the United States." *Social Problems* 26(4):425–438.

Portes, Alejandro and Robert L. Bach. 1985. *Latin Journey: Cuban and Mexican Immigrants in the United States*. Berkeley: University of California Press.

Saito, Leland. 1993. "Asian Americans and Latinos in San Gabriel Valley, California: Ethnic Political Cooperation and Redistricting 1990–92." *Amerasia Journal* 19(2):55–68.

Santillan, Richard. 1974. "Latino Politics in the Midwestern United States: 1915–1986." Pp. 99–118 in *Latinos and the Political System*, edited by F. Chris Garcia. Notre Dame, IN: University of Notre Dame Press.

Saurenman, Dianne. 1992. *Alhambra School Board Report According to Policy and Regulations 5113.2*. Alhambra, CA.

Sonenshein, Raphael J. 1993. *Politics in Black and White: Race and Power in Los Angeles*. Princeton, NJ: Princeton University Press.

Takaki, Ronald. 1993. *A Different Mirror: A History of Multicultural America*. Boston: Little Brown and Co.

Thompson, Richard H. 1979. "Ethnicity Versus Class: An Analysis of Conflict in a North American Chinese Community," *Ethnicity* 6:306–326.

Tseng, Yen-Fen. 1994. "The Chinese Ethnic Economy: San Gabriel Valley, Los Angeles County." *Journal of Urban Affairs* 16(2):169–189.

U.S. Bureau of the Census. 1980. *Statistical Abstract*. Washington, DC: U.S. Government Printing Office.

———. 1986. *Statistical Abstract*. Washington DC: U.S. Government Printing Office.

———. 1990. *Statistical Abstract*. Washington DC. U.S. Government Printing Office.

Van den Berghe, Pierre L. 1967. *Race and Racism: A Comparative Perspective*. New York: Wiley.

Villareal, Roberto E. and Norma G. Hernandez. 1991. *Latinos and Political Coalitions: Political Empowerment for the 1990's*. New York: Praeger.

Wright, Erik Olin. 1985. *Classes*. New York: Verso.

Chapter Nine

Doing Sociology

Connecting the Classroom Experience
with a Multi-Ethnic School District

José Zapata Calderón and Betty Farrell[1]

Practical and applied courses in the college curriculum are becoming more prevalent (Neapolitan 1992; Schultz 1992). Some recent articles in *Teaching Sociology* have discussed how a rigorous academic curriculum in the class-room can be combined with theory and experiential learning, or "doing sociology" in the community (Bricher 1993; Miller 1990; Porter and Schwartz 1993; Schmid 1992). In the same context, other articles have focused on how the sociological perspective can go beyond the classroom to create "transformative action" and social change (Flint 1993; Schmid 1993).

Although these articles begin to discuss the relationship between theory and praxis, they offer few concrete cases in which experiential learning has led to structural change in the institutions involved. In this paper we describe a class at Pitzer College, "The Roots of Social Conflict in Schools and Communities," which connected coursework with experiential learning. In the process, it served as a catalyst for structural change in three high schools in our region that were undergoing rapid demographic and social changes. At the same time, we address the tension in finding a balance between theory and praxis, which many instructors and students face in experiential courses.

THE ALHAMBRA SCHOOL DISTRICT

The field setting for this class, the Alhambra School District, is located five miles east of downtown Los Angeles in a San Gabriel Valley suburb. This district is a particularly interesting field site because it is a microcosm of many of the larger demographic changes taking place throughout California. Currently the district serves a diverse student population of 20,526, of whom 51 percent are Asian, 39 percent are Latino, and 9 percent are "other," including Anglo/white, African American, and Native American. The Alhambra School District, which includes the city of Alhambra, part of San Gabriel, and almost all of the city of Monterey Park, now has the largest concentration of Chinese students anywhere in the United States.

The city of Monterey Park illustrates the larger changes occurring in the school district. Until 1960, Monterey Park's population was 85 percent Anglo, 12 percent Latino, and 3 percent Asian. By the time of the 1980 census, the population had changed to 40 percent Asian, 37 percent Latino, and 20 percent Anglo (U.S. Bureau of the Census 1980).[2] The demographic trends of the 1970s continued through the 1980s: the Asian population grew to 56 percent by 1990, Latinos held relatively steady at 31 percent, and the Anglo population declined further to 12 percent of the city's 62,000 residents (U.S. Bureau of the Census 1990). The neighboring city of Alhambra (population 71,000) has seen similar demographic changes, although the proportions of the three ethnic groups—36 percent Asian, 32 percent Latino, and 30 percent Anglo—were roughly equal by 1991.

As a result of these striking demographic changes in the two cities and in the school district, ethnic relations are characterized by both conflict and cooperation.[3] Alongside tensions at the city government level over urban development issues and the status of English as the "official" language, numerous racial incidents have involved Latino, Asian, and Anglo students in the schools. In 1986 one fight led to the stabbing of a Chinese youth at Mark Keppel High School in Monterey Park. In 1991 several fights broke out at San Gabriel High School between Latino and Chinese students and between Vietnamese and Anglo students. Differences in disciplinary actions following these incidents led to an escalation of tensions between Latino and Asian parents and to the formation of several ethnically based community coalitions.

In December 1991 a broader coalition—the Multi-Ethnic Task Force (later renamed the Multicultural Community Association)—was formed, uniting members around 10 different proposals to effect structural changes in the school district. These proposals included a review of disciplinary procedures, the application of conflict resolution programs, the implementation of a multicultural curriculum, sensitivity training for all school employees, and the involvement of parents, students, and teachers in the decision-making process. The first author, a resident of Monterey Park and a parent of children in this school district, was elected a chair of this new coalition, and thus provided an important link to crucial gatekeepers in the community and school system.

"THE ROOTS OF SOCIAL CONFLICT IN SCHOOLS AND COMMUNITIES: GOALS AND RESULTS OF THE COURSE"

In this context, the course "The Roots of Social Conflict in Schools and Communities" was developed. In January 1993 Pitzer College received a competitive course development grant from the Ohio Campus Compact. This grant supported the development of courses that addressed the connections between service, participation in the political process, and public policy development. Over two semesters, we involved 40 students in participant-observation research in the three high schools of the Alhambra School District.[4]

We had several goals in designing this course. At the college level, it helped to implement a new educational objective promoting an understanding of "the ethical implications of knowledge and social action"—that is, enhancing a sense of social responsibility for students, especially in relation to work in surrounding communities. At the departmental level, it was part of a pilot program for a new sociology requirement that would allow majors to engage in the craft of "doing sociology." At the undergraduate course level, the class was designed to link an internship in the public schools with the academic study of communities and school systems that have been affected significantly by the demographic changes and subsequent interethnic conflicts in the Los Angeles metropolitan region.

In the first semester, 20 Pitzer College students, in teams of three or four, were admitted as observers in several classes in each school.[5] The selected classes represented all grade and ability-group levels. All of the students kept extensive field notes of their observations; these notes served as the basis of research papers that they prepared at the end of the semester. Following the standard guidelines of ethnographic research, the students were expected to record all observable data rather than focusing on predetermined questions or research areas.[6] Given the open-ended nature of their observation assignment and their placement sites, they tended to concentrate on the microcosm of classroom interaction. Through their initial observations, they were able to identify several patterns.

First, a number of observers from the college wrote that the classroom structure and the teachers' interaction styles made a difference in students' perceptions about school and in their achievement levels. Because Asian students tended to be tracked in the upper-level classes and Latino students in the lower-level classes in these high schools, differences in teachers' behavior, use of language, style of teaching, and expectations about students' abilities had the potential to reinforce group divisions and to perpetuate different achievement outcomes.

A second pattern observed by our students was the racial/ethnic segregation that shaped interaction inside and outside the classroom. Several observers noted, for example, that the voluntary seating arrangement in many classrooms tended to replicate the intraethnic friendship networks that appeared in the cafeteria and the schoolyard. One unintended consequence was that any collaborative work in the classroom tended to reinforce these networks because students who sat next to each other were often assigned to work together. Thus one significant opportunity to bring together different combinations of students for a common task was lost.

Finally, our students observed that the limited resources for the English as a Second Language (ESL) courses and the resulting "burn-out" among teachers lowered the morale in these courses. Because the recent wave of immigration to the San Gabriel Valley has contributed so substantially to the rapid demographic transition of this school district, ESL courses offer many first-generation students an especially important introduction to American society in general, and specifically to the culture of American high schools. Therefore these classes seemed to our student observers to offer an important but often missed opportunity to include significant multicultural education with the instruction in basic language skills.

Because educational reform was a topic of great concern to the newly formed Multicultural Community Association, and because the first author was co-chairing that group, all of these student observations were used to develop policy recommendations for the Alhambra School District. Coalition members, for example, began to question school district officials about the systematic grouping of Latino students at lower ability levels; they also began to address the effectiveness of disciplinary programs in the schools and to argue for the development of a more multiculturally sensitive curriculum. These concerns became part of a districtwide "goals action program," which was passed recently by the school board.

During the summer following the first phase of this project, the instructors met once again with Alhambra School District administrators and agreed that the second phase would focus on developing and implementing multicultural lesson plans. As a result, during the following fall semester, another 20 students were assigned to high school classes in psychology, world history, English, journalism, mathematics, art, and ESL with the goal of developing and teaching their own lesson plans. Encouraged by school district administrators, principals, and teachers to move from observers to active participants, sophomore- and junior-level college students worked closely with teachers, asking questions and exploring strategies to shift seating patterns, encourage cooperative learning, and open the curriculum to more multicultural approaches.

As they developed specific lesson plans, the students focused on introducing multicultural teaching strategies into the classroom. All the lesson plans actively involved the high school students through group discussions and writing exercises. In a lesson plan for a world history class, for example, students wrote down their initial reaction to images depicting people of different ethnicities as a means of starting a discussion on stereotyping. In an English class, students responded to "Dear Abby/Ann Landers" letters on issues of prejudice and discrimination. Members of another class compared themselves to characters on the TV show *Beverly Hills 90210*. A student teacher from the college even devised a multicultural lesson for a mathematics class by surveying the students on social issues relevant to their lives and then using the survey results to engage them in a lesson on circle graphs. The lesson ended with a discussion of the use and misuse of statistics.

At the college, the students participated in a weekly seminar organized around varied readings about the region, including educational stratification, demographic changes, and the Latino and Asian immigrant experiences. One book, *Always Running*, chronicled the experiences of writer Luis Rodriguez, who grew up in San Gabriel, attended Mark Keppel High School (one of our observation sites), and belonged to a local gang. The readings provoked lively discussions as the students related the materials to their own lives. The opportunity to draw connections between families, communities, and schools from their personal experiences, their fieldwork, and the course readings made this sociology seminar particularly engaging.

The Alhambra Schools Project culminated in a day-long conference at which our students shared their experiences as observers and teachers with an audience of high school teachers, school district administrators, and the press. Although some teachers and administrators initially had expressed reservations about the project, they now complimented the students on their energy and creativity.

Significant results continue to emerge. Teachers have reported that some of the high school students have formed new friendships in and out of class. The lesson plans still inspire new approaches among some of the teachers who participated, and they are being distributed to educators throughout the school district. Also, a number of our students have decided to make teaching their career choice. New opportunities for this type of experiential learning have opened up as other school districts contact us about developing a similar program in their schools. Finally, new types of coalitions—such as one formed recently between Pitzer College, the Alhambra School District, and the Southern California Edison Company, a corporation willing to support a multicultural education and conflict resolution program—have begun to change some of the institutional relationships in our region.

CONNECTING THEORY TO EXPERIENCE

One challenge—central to the sociological enterprise, but highlighted especially in this course—was to complement students' understanding of *culture* a crucial variable of social interaction with the equally crucial but much less

visible variable of *social structure*. In their high school classroom observations, for example, our undergraduates could readily identify the cultural
barriers of language and custom that had led to specific instances of interethnic conflict in the schools and to considerable general misunderstanding in
the wider community. They were able to develop and teach lesson plans that
effectively challenged racial/ethnic stereotypes and to engage high school
students at all levels in a dialogue about the meanings and consequences of
such cultural stereotyping. Yet when they were faced with dramatic data
from these schools showing great divergences between Asian and Latino
students' achievement levels and college preparatory tracks, our students
were overwhelmed and dismayed by the implications of the same cultural
explanations that they had earlier adopted rather uncritically to account for
group differences.[7]

In logs recording their responses to readings on the high educational
achievement levels of recent Southeast Asian immigrants, the college students puzzled over the striking differences in the ethnic group patterns they
had observed in their high schools. Thinking culturally, in this case, made
our students uncomfortable because they anticipated that discussions about
culturally based differences would only reinforce patterns of inequality. They
were concerned that if cultural values were the source of these differential
achievement levels, acknowledging and describing this phenomenon would
only reify it as a justification for continued inequality. Wishing to celebrate
diverse cultural values as the basis for group empowerment, they were dismayed that these same values might have harmful consequences for the
social structure.

In our weekly seminar discussions, which focused on the history of racial/
ethnic stratification in the United States and on the nature of structural discrimination, students began to question some of their own cultural assump-
tions in favor of more social structural and institutional analyses of group
difference. Key sociological texts played an important role in raising these
theoretical issues at various points throughout the semester.[8] Yet only by
observing classroom interaction and by working directly with high school
teachers and students did our students begin to discover the social consequences of concrete structural arrangements such as those in seating patterns,
study group organizations, and the institutionalized tracking process through
which students are channeled in the educational system. These insights were
tentative, however, in the course of one semester they only began to challenge the primacy of the cultural explanations for behaviors that enjoy so
much legitimacy today.

The challenge of making students understand the complex interplay between cultural values and social structure conditions is at the heart of experiential education. We believe that this understanding should become a central
goal in teaching such courses. In this case, our students began to recognize

that attributing ethnic inequality to cultural differences can lead to the tendency to blame the victim and can reinforce segregation and stereotyping. This discovery was rooted in their fieldwork experience, but it acquired greater depth and breadth when complemented by key supporting texts from the sociological literature. Through readings and experience that forced them to reconsider their initial single-causal explanations for differential group patterns in school achievement (e.g., "bad teachers," "an irrelevant curriculum," "cultural differences"), these undergraduates could begin to develop more complex structural and institutional explanations for the ways ethnic inequality can be perpetuated and maintained through the public school system—an institution in American society that has long been credited with offering meritocratic opportunities for social mobility.

A critique of an exclusively cultural analysis of group differences developed quite spontaneously in this class from the juxtaposition of readings with field experience. We now recognize many more opportunities to build the kind of creative tension between theoretical concepts and practical observation that this example illustrates by assigning more specifically contrasting perspectives in the readings and by organizing more in-class debates in future classes. Although there are many good reasons to use the seminar to process the fieldwork experience, we expect that students will benefit more in the long run by engaging in more critical dialogues involving theoretical ideas based on sociological readings and insights acquired in the field.

SOME DILEMMAS OF EXPERIENTIAL TEACHING

Although this course was highly successful from both the students' and the teachers' perspectives, we encountered some problems that may be generalizable to other experiential teaching situations. These problems are familiar to other qualitative researchers; they may be categorized generally as issues of establishing access and of developing continuity.

ESTABLISHING ACCESS

Many immediate advantages accompanied the kind of direct access to a community coalition and to a school district allowed by the first author's position as chair of the Multicultural Community Association. The opportunity to introduce students into a community setting where serious educational issues are being debated and reform measures are proposed is invaluable. The first author's leadership position in the coalition provided leverage with the school district administrators, who otherwise might have been less willing to admit college students as observers during a period of heightened tensions in their schools. Yet because the students gained access to a field site through an activist coalition's political clout, it was also harder to separate the project of the college course from the coalition's agenda of educational reform. Administrators, who initially saw the project in terms of its potential to evaluate their programs, were quite reluctant to admit "untrained" undergraduate observers to their schools. In this case, some of their concerns were alleviated by the involvement of two faculty members in this course, only one of whom was identified with the community coalition, and by extensive discussions about the techniques and goals of participant observation research. By promising the school district administrators that our students would not give interviews to the press during their participant observation research, we also helped to moderate the concern that this project would become politicized. Thus, although we had more initial opportunities to gain access to this field site than many other college teachers, our channels of access were not always perceived as unbiased and interest-free.

DEVELOPING CONTINUITY

A project of this kind requires much groundwork, not only with the school district administrators, who were the initial gatekeepers, but also with the participating high school teachers. In the first stages of the project we gave insufficient attention to the hierarchical structure of the urban public high school, and particularly to the frustration felt by many teachers when confronted with top-down decision making by their administrators. Several of the teachers initially chosen by their principals to participate in this project were less than enthusiastic about receiving our students in their classrooms. They saw few immediate benefits to working with college students, and they feared that field notes could be appropriated too readily for administrative review. In the face of such perceptions and potential opposition by important gatekeepers, the participant observation experience is seriously compromised.

In the future, we resolve to work more directly from the beginning with all teachers involved in this project. Although students benefit by learning to negotiate with a highly bureaucratic organization or to cope with the mistrust and anxiety of gatekeepers at all levels, we now recognize that we must play a more visible role as mediators between our students and the high school teachers. In many cases, these are teachers who feel besieged by the new demographic pressures, the political demands, and the economic constraints in their district.

Developing and maintaining a viable working relationship between our college and this public school district has also led us to consider our longer-term commitments more carefully now than at the beginning of the project. Recently we have faced the issue of how and what to give back to the high school students, teachers, and administrators who have worked with our students over the past year. We would like to challenge the perception that this project has primarily benefited the college students. Consequently we have begun to develop several ancillary projects that build on our relationship with the school district, including campus visits to introduce more "at-risk" students to a college environment and a one-on-one tutoring/mentoring program, located on our campus, for high school students. Supported by additional grant money, which was awarded because of the success of the initial course, we are establishing a resource center for conflict resolution studies on our college campus; this will allow us to gather materials and sponsor workshops on conflict resolution strategies and multicultural curricular development for local high school teachers. Our longer-term goal, with the support of our college administration, is to design college faculty internships with the local public school district, which will complement and enhance the program of students' experiential learning.

CONCLUSION

Our experience in coteaching this course has been highly positive. The collaborative effort enriched our teaching experience; we also learned much about the culture and social structure of the American public school system from our students' field notes and discussions, as well as from our own negotiations with school administrators at all stages of the project. Occasionally we found ourselves caught in a mediating position between our student participant observers, who wanted to investigate the sources of ethnic conflict; the Alhambra School District administrators, who were concerned about possible negative publicity associated with "problems" discovered in their schools; and members of the community-based Multicultural Community Association, who were concerned with implementing policy for social change. As instructors, we sensed some competing forces in this project: concern with preserving an open and flexible learning environment for our students, on the one hand, and the constraints created by politically charged school and community issues, on the other.

A key lesson that we learned from this teaching experience is that it is often more demanding but also more rewarding to practice the craft of sociology both inside and outside the classroom, alongside our students and in local communities. In many ways this innovative teaching experience has brought us—as well as our students—back to the heart of the sociological enterprise, with its roots in praxis as well as in theory.

NOTES

1. Copyright Acknowledgement: This chapter was previously published in the following: *Teaching Sociology*, (with Betty Farrell). January, 1996, Vol. 24: 46–53.

2. Several external changes that deeply affected the city and the region in the 1970s help to account for this dramatic demographic shift. Briefly stated, these include the federal government recognition of mainland China and the exclusion of Taiwan from official diplomatic stats; the emergence of the Pacific Rim as an interrelated economy, along with more lenient U. S. immigration policies for this region; incoming immigrant Asian families' dissatisfaction with conditions in older ethnic neighborhoods in nearby Los Angeles; and the movement of middle-class Latino families from East Los Angeles to the San Gabriel Valley suburbs.

3. Some of the recent literature on the Monterey Park and Alhambra region includes: Calderón (1989, 1990), Fong (1994), Horton (1989, 1992, 1995), Horton and Calderón (1990), Pardo (1990), Saito (1993), and Tseng (1994).

4. Pitzer College, with a student population of 730, is a four-year liberal arts college in the process of expanding its efforts to include multicultural understanding and community outreach in its curriculum. As part of its educational objectives, the College is emphasizing the need for students to appreciate other cultures through direct involvement in institutions that advance the development of a multicultural world. These objectives have already produced results: Numerous professors and students have taken up the challenge of involving themselves in communities that are microcosms of the larger demographic changes occurring in California.

5. Because we learned about the grant funding at the beginning of the spring semester, we had no time to develop a separate class to focus on the project. Consequently, 20 students volunteered from four different classes that we were teaching. With very little time for pretraining, we met with students every two weeks and gave them introductory material from Lofland and Lofland's (1995) *Analyzing Social Settings: A Guide to Qualitative Observation and Analysis*. We reached an agreement with Alhambra School District administrators that our students would observe classrooms in the three high schools in the district. In return, we promised a final report outlining the students' findings.

6. It was crucial to explain to the district administrators, who generally had experience only with surveys and quantitative evaluation research, that qualitative researchers strive to develop concepts, insights, and understanding from patterns that emerge in their field notes. We stressed that the strength of this methodology is its flexibility and responsiveness to situations; ideally it allows the researcher to understand how social realities arise and operate, and how the various expectations and perceptions that people bring to particular settings shape individuals' behavior and organizations' response.

7. A School Board report for the academic year 1990–1991, written by Assistant Superintendent of Pupil Services Diane Saurenman (1992), showed that Latinos have the highest dropout rate of any ethnic group in the three high schools. In the four years from 1989 to 1992, Latinos accounted for 50 to 55 percent of the dropouts, as compared with 32 to 46 percent for the Asian students at Alhambra High School. In those four years, Latinos made up 57 to 65 percent of the dropouts at San Gabriel High School, as compared with 24 to 36 percent for Asians. In 1990–1992, Latinos at all three high schools also ranked lowest of all ethnic groups in completing college preparatory requirements. At Alhambra High School, only 17 percent of Latino students completed these requirements, as compared with 38 percent of Asian students and 26 percent of all others; at Mark Keppel High School only 3 percent of Latinos completed them, as compared with 29 percent of Asians and 12 percent of all others. These figures were also related to postgraduation aspirations by ethnicity. Between 1989 and 1992, surveys found that 80 percent of Asian graduating seniors at all three Alhambra District high schools aspired to attend four-year colleges; only 11 percent of Latinos had such plans. Instead, the great majority of Latinos at Alhambra High School indicated that they would opt to attend vocational/technical schools, enlist in the military, or enter the labor force following high school graduation.

8. As readings in this course, we also used Jonathon Kozol's (1991) *Savage Inequalities*, Mike Rose's (1989) *Lives on the Boundary*, Jeannie Oakes's (1985) *Keeping Track*, and Michael W. Apple's *Official Knowledge*. Each of these readings underscored the structural foun-

dations of inequality in the educational system. Other books that could be used for this purpose are: Ronald Takaki's (1993) *A Different Mirror*, Stephen Steinberg's (1981) *The Ethnic Myth*, and Michael Omi and Howard Winant's (1994) *Racial Formation in the United States.*

REFERENCES

Apple, Michael. 1993. *Official Knowledge: Democratic Education in a Conservative Age.* New York: Routledge.

Bricher, Marie R. 1992. "Teaching Introductory Sociology: Using Aspects of the Classroom as Sociological Events." *Teaching Sociology* 20:270–75.

Calderón, José. 1989. "How the English Only Initiative Passed in California." Pp. 93–109 in *Estudios Chicanos and the Politics of Community*, edited by Mary Romero and Cordelia Candelaria. Oakland: Cragmont Publications.

———. 1990. "Latinos and Ethnic Conflict in Suburbia: The Case of Monterey Park." *Latino Studies Journal* 1(2):23–32.

Flint, William. 1993. "Ideological Contradiction and the Problem of Closure in the Sociology Capstone Course." *Teaching Sociology* 21:254–57.

Fong, Timothy P. 1994. *The First Suburban Chinatown: The Remaking of Monterey Park, California.* Philadelphia: Temple University Press.

Horton, John. 1989. "The Politics of Ethnic Change: Grass-Roots Responses to Economic and Demographic Restructuring in Monterey Park, California." Urban Geography 10:578–92.

———. 1992. "The Politics of Diversity." Pp. 215–45 in *Shaping Diversity*, edited by Louise Lamphere. Chicago: University of Chicago Press.

Horton, John and José Calderón. 1990. "Language Struggles in a Changing California Community." Pp. 186–94 in *Language Loyalties*, edited by Jim Crawford. Chicago: University of Chicago Press.

Horton, John, with José Calderón, Mary Pardo, Leland Saito, Linda Shaw, and Yen-Fen Tseng. 1995. *The Politics of Diversity: Immigration, Resistance, and Change in Monterey Park, California.* Philadelphia: Temple University Press.

Kozol, Jonathan. 1991. *Savage Inequalities.* New York: Crown. Lofland, John and Lyn H. Lofland. 1995. *Analyzing Social Settings: A Guide to Qualitative Observation and Analysis.* Belmont, CA: Wadsworth.

Miller, Wesley. 1990. "Internships, the Liberal Arts, and Participant Observation." *Teaching Sociology* 18:78–82.

Neapolitan, Jerry. 1992. "Thee Internship Experience and Clarification of Career Choice." *Teaching Sociology* 20:222–31.

Oakes, Jeannie. 1985. *Keeping Track: How Schools Structure Inequality.* New Haven: Yale University Press.

Omi, Michael and Howard Winant. 1994. *Racial Formation in the United States.* New York: Routledge.

Pardo, Mary Santoli. 1990. "Identity and Resistance: Mexican American Women and Grass-roots Activism in Two Los Angeles Communities." Doctoral dissertation. University of California, Los Angeles.

Porter, Judith R. and Lisa B. Schwartz. 1993. "Experiential Service-Based Learning: An Integrated HIV/AIDS Education Model for College Campuses." *Teaching Sociology* 21:409–15.

Rose, Mike. 1989. *Lives on the Boundary.* New York: Penguin.

Saito, Leland. 1993. "Asian Americans and Latinos in San Gabriel Valley, California: Ethnic Political Cooperation and Redistricting. 1990–92." *Amerasia Journal* 19(2):55–68.

Saurenman, Dianne. 1992. *Alhambra School Board Report According to Policy and Regulations 5113.2*, Alhambra, CA: Alhambra School District.

Schmid, Thomas J. 1992. "Classroom-Based Ethnography: A Research Pedagogy." *Teaching Sociology* 20:28–35.

———. 1993. "Bringing Sociology to Life: The Other Capstone Mandate." *Teaching Sociology* 21:219–22.

Schultz, Martin. 1992. Internships in Sociology: Liability Issues and Risk Management Measures." *Teaching Sociology* 20:183–91.

Steinberg, Stephen. 1981. *The Ethnic Myth: Race, Class, and Ethnicity in America*. Boston: Beacon.

Takaki, Ronald. 1993. *A Different Mirror: A History of Multicultural America*. Boston: Little, Brown.

Tseng, Yen-Fen. 1994. "The Chinese Ethnic Economy: San Gabriel Valley, Los Angeles County." *Journal of Urban Affairs* 16:169–89.

U.S. Bureau of the: Census. 1980. *Statistical Abstract*. Washington, DC: U.S. Government Printing Office.

———. 1990. *Statistical Abstract*. Washington, DC: U.S. Government Printing Office.

Chapter Ten

Partnership in Teaching and Learning

*Combining Critical Pedagogy
with Civic Engagement and Diversity*[1]

José Zapata Calderón

Estoy comenzando en Español para traer enfrente una tema especial: la importancia de desarollar unidad entre nuestros colegios y la comunidad. Yo comienzo muchas de mis presentaciones en Español para demostrar el poder del lenguaje y para enseñar como algunas de nuestras comunidades han sido excluidas. Si no entiende el lenguaje de mi comunidad, como puede entender todo de lo que soy y lo que a sufrido mi comunidad? Al mismo tiempo, hay la necesidad de entender el lenguaje de ustedes y de sus comunidades para entender sus historias y quien son ustedes. Si no podemos hallar el puente para quitar lo que nos silencia y la ignorancia, no podemos unirnos en desarrollar un futuro mejor.

I will stop here, before some of you stop reading and turn the page. I have actually had some students walk out of my classes when I have used Spanish to demonstrate the power of language and to show how the simple denial of language and culture can be used as a form of oppression. My message, nevertheless, goes beyond language to the issue of translation. In order to translate each other's worlds, we must first understand each other. The connections between the classroom and community-based learning are all about translation. In looking for ways to help my students understand communities outside of themselves and to become engaged interpreters, I have been transforming the pedagogy in my classroom, extending the boundaries of the classroom, and rethinking the methods and purposes of undergraduate research. In this process, the academic world and its relation to its neighboring communities have become more central to the academic life of the students.

Students in my classes have been transformed as learners through community-based participatory research and through the social responsibility ethos promoted at Pitzer College. In one of my classes on social movements, for example, students spend the first half of the semester learning about Cesar Chavez, the history of farm workers dating back to the early 1900s, and contemporary efforts to build unions. During their spring break, the students travel to the headquarters of the United Farm Workers to carry out service projects, to work alongside the historic figures they have read about in their books, and to listen to stories spoken in the workers' own language. Throughout the semester, students gather field notes and write final research papers based on these experiences. Some of these students have used their research as foundations for community grant proposals, as presentations at undergraduate conferences and national associations, and as thesis papers for honors.

In using hands-on research to find creative solutions to compelling problems, these kinds of experiences help students develop as participant translators. By making connections between the academy and the community, my students and I have been involved in translating silence into critical consciousness.

THE POMONA DAY LABOR CENTER

In 1997, the city of Pomona passed an ordinance to impose a $1,000 fine and six months in jail on day laborers for seeking employment on street corners. Because of their experiences, my students understood that the academy and the community of Pomona were not bifurcated but interrelated, that the worlds of the day laborers and their worlds as students were not separate but part of one whole. Subsequently, the students and day laborers packed city hall to protest the ordinance, carried out research on how other cities had dealt with the issue, and applied for and received $50,000 to start the Pomona Day Labor Center, a nonprofit organization funded through city and private funds. The students and I have been partnering with this community-based organization ever since.

Presently, the students are continuing with their research and implementing various projects to empower the day laborers. In addition to holding language and computer classes every morning, the students have been instrumental in ensuring worker representation on the organization's board (Calderón, Foster, and Rodriguez 2005). In response to the city council's decision to minimally fund the Center in the future, we have utilized surveys, questionnaires, and focus groups to establish the amount of resources that the workers have and to explore how they can be maximized. Our collaborative research with the workers has resulted in grants from area foundations that have sponsored the development of health referrals, immigration rights pro-grams, language acquisition, computer training, and job-preparation pro-grams (Calderón and Cadena 2007). The establishment of weekly leadership training meetings has also resulted in worker/employer conflict-resolution sessions and pickets (led by day laborers) to retrieve wages from employers who have refused to pay.

Overall, the Center represents the new kind of hybrid organizational/ educational/civic space that is emerging around the edges of some of our college campuses today. It promises to be a transformative borderland where new forms of translation can occur that integrate the academic world with civic purpose, learning with action, theory with practice, and reciprocal re-search with collective social change.

NOT JUST SERVICE LEARNING

The formation of the Pomona Day Labor Center is not an isolated example at Pitzer College; it reflects the ethos of many programs that have emerged and taken off in the last few years. This ethos is rooted in the advancement of intercultural and interdisciplinary understanding as well as in the ideal of democracy translated as social responsibility. It is rooted in the idea that, through campus-community partnering, our students and faculty can engage in acts of collaboration that go beyond just charity or one-way service pro-jects. Keith Morton (1995) characterizes this as going beyond the charity model, with the provider in control of services, to a model of social change that builds partnerships of equality between all the participants, that gets at the root causes of problems, and that focuses directly or indirectly on politi-cal empowerment.

Further, this ethos is rooted in the concept of "community-based partner-ing," according to which research and action are carried out not merely for the benefit of academia but for the benefit of the community-based organiza-tion and its members in both the short and the long term. It joins the idea of service learning with the long-term goal of reciprocity. That is, service learn-ing is part of a larger program meant eventually to empower the participants, to develop their leadership, and to develop the foundations that will allow them to function as active participants in the larger world of policymaking.

THE CENTER FOR
CALIFORNIA CULTURAL AND SOCIAL ISSUES

This kind of community-based partnering is a cornerstone of the Center for California Cultural and Social Issues (now renamed the Center for Commu-nity Engagement). Created in 1999, CCCSI supports research and education initiatives that contribute to the understanding of critical community issues and enhance the resources of community organizations. As part of its mission to be a genuine partner in communities rather than to dispense so-called "expert" solutions to predefined needs, the Center supports numerous innovative community-based projects by offering research awards and technical training to faculty and students at Pitzer College. In addition, the Center has developed a small number of core partnerships with community-based organizations that last no fewer than four years.

The CCCSI also is linked to an external studies program that is based on participatory learning and on understanding different cultural perspectives. It is involved in cooperative projects with local community-based organizations in Nepal, China, Venezuela, Turkey, Italy, and Zimbabwe. Some of the students from this program return to use their newfound language skills through external-internal programs. The community-based Spanish program, for example, develops partnerships between students and their Spanish-speaking host families and the Pitzer in Ontario program (based in Ontario, California). Students immerse themselves in a multiethnic community that is undergoing dramatic demographic transformations. Through classes, fieldwork, internships, field trips, and participatory action research, students learn firsthand the processes of everyday life in suburban communities like Ontario and the effects of globalization and technological development on them. Through partnerships with local community-based organizations, students learn the principles of asset-based development and gain an awareness of sustainable development practices.

AN EQUAL RELATIONSHIP

In bringing students and faculty together with community-based organizations, all of these partnerships use the strengths of diversity, critical pedagogy, participatory action research, and service learning to work on common issues and to create social change. These collaborative efforts are examples of community-based models that require faculty and students to immerse themselves alongside community participants to collectively develop theories and strategies and to achieve common outcomes.

An essential component of this style of learning and research is its commitment to promoting an equal relationship between the interests of the academics and the community participants. Traditionally, academics have had a tendency to "parachute" into a community or workplace for their own research interests without developing the kind of long-term relationship and collaboration that it takes to create concrete change. In working to move beyond traditional research models, participating students and faculty collaborate in what Kenneth Reardon (1998) has described as "intentionally promoting social learning processes that can develop the organizational, analytical, and communication skills of local leaders and their community-based organizations." We have found that it is essential for faculty members to make a long-term commitment to the sites and communities where they have placed their students. Although students can only commit for a semester or until graduation, faculty participants are in a better position to sustain campus-community partnerships.

As these long-term partnerships are developed, students and faculty become a political force in their communities. They no longer are placed in the role of travelers passing by. Instead, they see themselves as participants with a stake in the decisions being made.

CONCLUSION

This type of civic engagement takes into consideration the meaning of community—which, as a whole, is made up of many competing interests. Those who are corporate growers, developers, and polluters call themselves part of the "community," although their profitmaking interests often place them in conflict with "quality of life" initiatives. The "communities" to which I refer are very diverse geographical, political, and spiritual places. They have different power relations, backgrounds, ideologies, and levels of stratification. These communities are facing inequality or are trying to improve their quality of life. Hence, the research and learning described above focuses on the sources of inequalities and on what can be done about them. While the dominant understanding of inequality tends to blame the "individual" for his or her "inadequacies," other theories and explanations focus on the historical and systemic foundations of inequality. The practices I have described in this chapter stand with the latter. They challenge students and faculty to find common grounds of collaboration with community institutions, unions, organizations, and neighborhood leaders to invoke social consciousness and long-term structural change.

NOTE

1. Copyright Acknowledgement: Reprinted with permission from "Partnership in Teaching and Learning: Combining Critical Pedagogy with Civic Engagement and Diversity," *Diversity & Democracy,* vol. 11, no. 2. Copyright 2008 by the Association of American Colleges and Universities.

REFERENCES

Calderón, J. and G. Cadena. 2007. Linking critical democratic pedagogy, multiculturalism, and service learning to a project-based approach. *Race, Poverty, and Social Justice.* Calderón (Ed.). Herndon , VA: Stylus Publishing, 63–80.

Calderón, J., S. Foster, and S. Rodriguez. 2004. Organizing immigrant workers: Action research and strategies in the Pomona Day Labor Center. *Latino Los Angeles: Transformations, Communities, and Activism.* Enrique C. Ochoa and Gilda Laura Ochoa (ed.), Arizona State University Press.

Morton, K. 1995. The irony of service: Charity, project, and social change in service learning. *Michigan Journal of Community Service Learning* 2, 19–32.

Reardon, K. M. 1998. Participatory action research as service learning. *New Directions for Teaching and Learning* 73, 57–64.

Chapter Eleven

A Multicultural and Critical Perspective on Teaching through Community

A Dialogue with José Calderón of Pitzer College[1]

Sandra Enos

José Zapata Calderón is an associate professor in sociology and Chicano studies at Pitzer College, in Claremont, California. After graduating from the University of Colorado, he returned to northern Colorado as a community organizer for 14 years. At Aims Community College and the University of Northern
Colorado, he taught courses that connected students with research in the Mexican-American barrios in Weld County. As an advocate ethnographer, Calderón
has published numerous articles and studies based on his community experiences and observations. The type of research and teaching methods described
below have served as a catalyst for other endeavors.

In 1991, after being hired as an assistant professor at Pitzer College,
Calderón led the development of a multiethnic coalition, the Multi-Cultural
Community Association, to find solutions to ethnic tensions between Latino
and Asian students in the Alhambra School District. As a parent in the district,
he was also elected as the chair of the Alhambra School District Human
Relations Advisory Committee. A grant that he wrote to Campus Compact in
1994 resulted in a course, Community and Social Responsibility, cotaught
with sociology professor Betty Farrell.[2] This class allowed Pitzer students to
carry out participant observation and multicultural study plans in the Alhambra
School District high schools. The project resulted in the development of multicultural and conflict resolution classes in the school district, the initiation of a
conflict resolution program at Pitzer College, and continued funding by the
Edison Company and other foundations.

For the last three years, Calderón has taken a class of (on average) 30
students to study and work with the United Farm Workers union in La Paz,

California. In return for the union's hospitality and shared knowledge, the students contribute their skills and abilities to various segments of the farm-worker community. On the last day of their stay, students present skits depicting what they have learned from the experience. This class was honored as the Curriculum-Based Alternative Spring Break of 1995 by the BreakAway Foundation. In the spring of 1996, together with film/video professor Alex Juhasz, Calderón taught a class, Film and Diversity, in which students created videos focused on issues of diversity, as part of a Ford Foundation-funded "ism" project. Most recently, Calderón has taught a class called Restructuring Community that focuses on the practical consequences of urban growth, the emergence of "growth machines," and alternatives to uneven development and inequality. The class provides students with service-learning experiences through local city governments as well as community organizations.

Enos: *Can you tell me about how you came to integrate service-learning into your classes?*
CALDERÓN: It came out of resolving a problem that I really had trying to connect the world of community activism with academia. I went to graduate school with the idea that academia would provide more flexibility to survive, on the one hand, but also to continue this tradition that I had, which was to use knowledge to create social change, or to develop policies based on building a better quality of life. After I graduated from the University of Colorado in the early 1970s, I was involved in community organizing for about 14 years before coming back and working on a Ph.D. I think the only reason I survived in the sociology Ph.D. program at the University of California-Los Angeles (UCLA) was because I found a means to apply what I was learning in the classroom to my concrete lived experience. Otherwise, I would have never stayed there. I was able to apply it to community service and activism, particularly in the city I was living in when I was working on the Ph.D., and to involve my entire family in particular sites we had been organizing in.

When I graduated from UCLA and was hired as a professor at Pitzer, I sought to continue this practice in all my classes. As a result, one of the most successful classes and a catalyst for more service-learning here at Pitzer was when I applied for funds from Campus Compact.

Betty Farrell and I developed and cotaught a class where we placed students in the Alhambra School District to do participant observations, on one hand, and give service, on the other hand. They worked with teachers and carried out mentoring and tutoring. In some cases, our students even helped to teach classes.

In the second semester, students helped teachers to develop multicultural lesson plans. Out of this, we were able to hook up with a coalition of parents, the Multi-Cultural Community Association, that I was part of. We were able to work together in advancing some structural changes in the schools. Through our efforts, a multicultural education curriculum was more institutionalized, a conflict resolution class was established, and alternatives to a traditional tracking system were implemented. These experiences helped solve my dilemma of how to connect the classroom with social change, and it gave me motivation to go even deeper into service-learning. Discovering Campus Compact and the connections to other people who were carrying out service-learning in other parts of the country motivated me and other professors on the Pitzer campus to integrate community service into our classes.

My lived experience as a farmworker also became an asset to this process. I grew up working in the fields alongside my grandparents, who were farmworkers all their lives. When I began teaching at Pitzer College, I wanted to develop a class that could let students feel what I felt when I went out to work with Cesar Chavez and the United Farm Workers (UFW) after I graduated. That experience had changed my life in terms of wanting to come back and organize in my own community back in Colorado. So in order to bring a flavor of that experience to my students, I developed a class called Rural and Urban Ethnic Movements, where students go work and live with the farmworkers. In preparation for their going, I utilize a number of books and a lot of literature that has been written about the farmworkers. The ties that I developed in the early 1970s have provided me with the contacts to allow for the kinds of relations that have developed between students at Pitzer and the United Farm Workers. In return for the union's hospitality and shared knowledge, the students work in various departments of the union. When they return to Pitzer, they organize a memorial celebration and support the union's boycott efforts throughout the year.

That pretty much relates to how I came to integrate community service. It came out of a passion, of trying to figure out how I could connect this passion for community activism and social change with the classroom and do it in such a way that I could survive in academia.

There seems to be a common profile of faculty who are drawn to the practice of service-learning.

A lot of the faculty whom I have met who are involved in service-learning have had some type of community organizing and service background. Because of their past experiences, they struggle to make education a non-alienating, relevant experience. Usually, these individuals care immensely about the state of the world and its inhabitants, and they are using their energies to make it a better place to live. I put myself in this group. Although we have stumbled over many hurdles, we tend to be optimists. We are constantly looking for new angles to teach, learn, and organize. There are never enough hours in the day to do all of this—but somehow service-learning creates the balance and the link.

I have students work with autobiographies in my class, and I clearly see this distinction. Many minority students do come from lower socioeconomic backgrounds, from immigrant families. Their fathers and mothers may be janitors now, may no longer be just farmworkers, but have that background. Consequently, they have particular issues that emerge on the campus that sometimes, unless there are other individuals on campus like myself who are sensitive to them, they hold in, and it can result in their dropping out. Those issues involve the lack of funds and feeling alienated, particularly if there isn't a whole lot of material about the history and identity of their particular community. Those histories need to be represented, and I think that is what diversity and multiculturalism are all about. It's not just something that minority students or women or gay and lesbian students need to know about, but something that the majority population needs to know about so that they can all be aware and work together on common issues. That's where the real issues emerge—the issue of affirmative action, the issue of making sure that history books are representative of the contributions of all groups.

My view is that in order to understand our commonalities, it is important to recognize our historical differences and why those differences exist. Then I think real unities develop, not just unities developed on superficial, feel-good levels, but unity based on an understanding of each other and where we do have commonalities.

Do you think that community service provides a platform where students can experience the sort of things that you are talking about? Students are in the world but may not be seeing the world. Do your students need the link to the community and to the academy to see what it is you are trying to teach?

A lot of students come right out of high school and are full of theories and ideas that they were taught in high school or by their parents. I find many students who come out of communities where they were not exposed to people of color or to issues having to do with race, gender, class, or gay and lesbian issues. In the Rural and Urban Ethnic Movements class, we get students from all different stratification levels. The students who are the most affected are not necessarily the minority students, because I think they know something about the social situation. The students who have been somewhat isolated and have not been exposed to the conditions of farmworkers and how farmworkers have emerged to organize themselves are the ones who begin to question why there has been this massive movement, why there have been all these books written about it, and why they have not been taught about it. The direct experience with the UFW affects them on a longterm basis, because it doesn't just follow how they have been taught in the past out of a book or a teacher feeding them abstract information.

The impact is long term; that is why it is hard to evaluate the effect of service-learning after one semester. Usually, students say that they had a positive experience and that they learned a lot. But the long-term impact is what we don't get right away. For example, I had this very conservative student who used to question the legitimacy of unions. He went on the service-learning alternative break. I recently got a letter from him in which he wrote that the class and experience had changed his entire life. He wrote that he decided to go into social welfare and empower people. Before, his outlook was to go into corporate America and make lots of money. His is not an isolated incident. If we started asking people involved in service-learning all across the country, I think we would find that this transformation occurs among many students. They end up working with the homeless, in unions, in nonprofits, in agencies, and in the community. Their values are now to use their lives, their knowledge, and their values to build a better community. That is what I have found. Again, some of the students who are most affected are not just students from minority backgrounds but those other students.

Have you made any changes in your courses since you began with servicelearning?

Many times over. I definitely learn new lessons every time I teach, and I use these lessons to continuously restructure my courses. One of the things that I have learned is to integrate more student-centered learning. Over and over, I have read Ira Shor's *Empowering Education* alongside *Pedagogy of the Oppressed* by Paulo Freire. These books have helped to take me away from traditional methods of lecturing and to understand the meaning of student-centered learning and that learning is a two-way process between students and teachers in the classroom. This method allows me to use problem-solving and critical-thinking techniques to draw out students. It allows for a continual process of reenergizing students, and I get energized as well. It certainly energizes me a lot more that students are energized when they return from their community site and are able to reflect upon it in relationship to class concepts. In my Social Stratification class, for example, I ensure that the students learn about some of the classical theories that emerged from Marx, Durkheim, and Weber. However, these theories become more concrete when we are able to talk about them in their relation to local communities or to the students' service experience. This really makes for more dynamic learning.

Service-learning has also led me to change the requirements for my classes. I primarily give essay examinations, and ask students to write reflection papers and research papers based on ethnographic methodologies. I especially promote that students learn about what participatory action research and advocate research are all about. I bring in books such as William Foote Whyte's *Participatory Action Research*, Michael Burawoy's *Ethnography Unbound*, Jim Thomas's *Critical Ethnography*, and Orlando FalsBorda's *Breaking the Monopoly With Participatory Action Research*. These books all demonstrate that it is good for students to be involved, to do research, to put themselves into the place of others, and to represent the voice and views of the oppressed. In terms of the books and articles I use for the class, I try to pick out materials that directly relate to lived experience and the type of community service that students carry out. I particularly like biographies and autobiographies. I now make it a practice at the beginning of each semester to allow students to review the syllabus—this has come out of my experience with Invisible College [an association of service-learning educators] and Campus Compact—to propose changes, and address any holes in the content. This practice allows us to make a contract with each other. I also periodically throughout the semester discuss with the students how the class is going and consider any changes that they might have. Many of these changes and modifications in my classes have come as a result of my deep involvement with service-learning and with individuals throughout the country who have shared their lessons with me.

Do you think Pitzer is an unusual school in terms of its location, its student body, its ability to accommodate the sort of work you do? Your president supports your work, I know. I can imagine that other institutions are more conservative in their orientation to service. While students on many campuses might be encouraged to serve soup in a soup kitchen, there may be fewer schools that have students out in the community doing critical analysis of the public schools and proposing reform and policy change.

Right. We have an administration and a faculty that are very supportive of service-learning. One of the foundations of our college, since its founding in 1963, is to integrate interdisciplinary intercultural perspectives as part of the liberal arts curriculum. Way back then, Pitzer had already begun to adopt three educational objectives. These were the interdisciplinary perspective, the intercultural perspective, and what was called a concern with the ethical implications or social consequences of the relationship between knowledge and action.

Pitzer is also unique in placing responsibility for educational quality with its faculty and its students. Rather than, for example, having academic departments, we have field groups. Academic departments, the faculty felt, lead to academic entrenchment and cut out the interdisciplinary character; they also create turf wars. Instead, Pitzer faculty organize themselves into what are called field groups that have no budgets and really have no department chairs. Field groups access curriculum with a concentration, and they make tenure recommendations. Faculty have membership in multiple field groups, not just one, so the system itself allows for continual development of inter-disciplinary courses and [initiatives] where faculty from many disciplines can find common ground. So there are a lot of faculty here from different disciplines that I coteach service-learning courses with who are strong colleagues. For example, last year I cotaught a course with professor Alex Juhasz called Film and Diversity. This course combined our strengths in video, and race and ethnic relations.

Another thing that has allowed Pitzer to advance is the Ford Foundation Diversity Initiative. Six years ago, the college began the process of introducing diversity into the curriculum. Over a two-year period, eight seminars were held involving two-thirds of the faculty. The purpose was for faculty to figure out how they would redesign their courses to be more inclusive of the role historically underrepresented groups played in the development of the United States.

Within this context, a broad array of courses with increased outreach to the community have flourished. So today, although there are some individuals who believe that service-learning lowers academic standards in higher education, on the whole here we have full support. Through our development of service-learning models, we are able to provide evidence that it is helping to enrich higher education. With those who are skeptical, we have shared studies that have come out of Campus Compact and other sources. We have shared articles written about how service-learning has advanced collaboration with local communities. We have been a catalyst for creating examples of how service-learning is academically rigorous. Our class with the Alhambra School District, for example, was a class that was academically rigorous for the students by making concrete connections between books, theories, and lived experience. The faculty support here has led to the institutionalization of a "social responsibility" objective that requires the students to take at least one class during their term here involving community service, community-based fieldwork, or an internship. This has been made a prerequisite for graduation. The Faculty Council also recently decided to give lab credit for courses that have a service-learning component. These initiatives have advanced the development of a career and community services center, which is able to help faculty with some of the logistics in developing classes that have a service-learning component. Our work in the Alhambra School District also led to the development of a conflict resolution center, which was initially funded by a grant. The campus is now looking into long-term funding, because the project is serving so many schools in the region.

Overall, Pitzer's history of innovative education together with recent service-learning initiatives have led to strong support by the faculty and administration.

Have you found that your own research and path of investigation have changed any by virtue of what the students have been involved in?

I think that it has been sort of a dual learning experience. For example, as the students began to work in the Alhambra School District, their observations resulted in a number of concrete findings that served as a foundation for a lot of changes in the school. As they shared those experiences, it influenced me to further expand the research that I was carrying out We began to collaborate on the research. Some students used their data to write their thesis papers. The class that Betty Farrell and I cotaught culminated in an article that appeared in *Teaching Sociology*. It also helped to fulfill our needs for doing research—which is necessary for promotion. I think a lot of young faculty are hesitant to go into service-learning because they are told that it will not help them in obtaining tenure. My own tenure recommendation included a substantial segment on the contributions I had made through service-learning. I would say that it is now being seriously considered in the evaluation of other faculty, as well. This didn't come overnight, it involved the creation of service-learning models and other faculty members' seeing the significance and importance of its being part of the tenure process. During my term at Pitzer, I've learned how to balance my teaching and service-learning with my research.

As service-learning becomes popular and faddish, and faculty talk about placements for students and work in the community, they worry that students aren't prepared and that maybe they don't belong in the community. On the other hand, do you think the potential benefits of students' being in the community supersede the need for a perfectly created placement in the community by a faculty member?

I lean toward the viewpoint that there are no guarantees in service-learning. It is positive in itself that some professors are attempting to try it out. I think that is where those of us who are involved in service-learning play a role. Those of us who have had a lot of experience in service-learning need to be catalysts on our campuses and share our experiences with others who are just beginning to get excited about it.

At Pitzer, we have institutionalized yearly meetings where we talk about our plans for how we are going to advance the service-learning curriculum on campus, what needs still are unmet. Every Friday, we have also institutionalized the meeting of a learning circle that brings faculty and students together to discuss service-learning projects and take up concrete issues on campus.

What are some of the lessons we share? One of the things we've learned is that service-learning means making a commitment to a particular site for a long period of time. The difference between students and faculty is that students usually take a course for one semester or carry out service-learning until they graduate and then they are gone. But that's not true with faculty. We're around for a longer period of time. I think too many communities have been burned by service-learning practitioners who parachute in to involve students over one semester or to gather research for a project, and then very little is given back to the community. What we have learned is that when those individuals go back to the community, they are not very well respected or accepted. Sometimes, they burn the field for other, sincere faculty who want to work there.

So, to me, it is better from the very beginning if service-learning is treated as a collaborative effort between the campus and the community and the institutions involved. That's why service-learning, if it is done well, takes so much time. I think faculty has to know that. The key to a successful service-learning class or a research project lies in the initial planning. For sure, it has to be carried out with the voice of the participants at the selected site. Throughout the term of the project, there has to be communication among all those involved. And when the term ends, it is important that faculty and the students summarize the results together. You can't guarantee that students aren't going to say or do things that might be insensitive or unconscious, but those are the risks we have to take. In the case of the Rural and Urban Ethnic Movements class, for example, not only do we have the class time to prepare students through readings, videos, and discussions, but we are also bringing speakers from the farmworkers themselves to talk about the issues. We also hold evening meetings where members of the UFW come and talk to the students about what they can expect when they go there. At the same time, we help the site by letting them know who the individuals are who are coming and what skills, abilities, and questions they are bringing with them. If we as faculty have developed a strong relationship with the site, and they know that we are going to be there for the long term, they will respect us. If mistakes are made, they will let us know, because it is that kind of relationship.

You have taught sociology for a while. Do you think service-learning is a particularly good tool to teach sociology as you understand the field?

I have always thought of sociology in terms of praxis and in terms of how the Brazilian educator Paulo Freire defined our capacity as human beings to create culture. I was an activist before I became a sociologist. How can we live in society, study social relations, teach about social problems, without actively promoting practical solutions? This involves seeing the world as a local community being connected to much larger worlds.

I have long grappled with the question of how to relate my academic world to a better society. Wherever I go to speak, I raise the question as to the role of higher education in helping to advance human development. What should be the role of higher education in promoting participation in the issues that are really facing us right now: a clean environment, quality of life, adequate child care, a quality education? My view is that higher education should meet these challenges head on. We have resources that can be utilized, not to "help" communities but to collaboratively utilize the energies and resources—research, teaching—to work with and alongside communities because we are part of those communities. The role of higher education should be to help develop campus-community partnerships that can present alternatives to some social, political, economic, and environmental inequalities.

We should be asking ourselves some questions: How can I use the position that I have in teaching, learning, and research without losing my humanity? How do I ensure the values of caring for others, values that may have come from experiences in activism, in the community, and in trying to build a better world? This is to me what sociology should be all about. We do have the capacity to be active participants in the process of social change. We can connect the tools of knowledge to finding solutions to the economic and social realities of our communities. Of course, we have to focus because we can only do so much. But to me, that's what sociology should be all about, not just carrying out research that gathers dust in some library.

It also occurs to me that we can look at higher education as an institution in the larger society that has basically been a somewhat neutral actor in some settings. High on the hill—doing the job of educating students—it is able to maintain a detached outlook on matters that are of important interest to the communities that surround it. How do you, as an active member of the community and as an engaged researcher, function in an institution that may have a smaller purpose than the one you think the organization or institution should be about?

It can be very frustrating sometimes unless there's some perspective to it. There are conservative professors who definitely teach their class with a bias. They say it is not biased. However, the theories that they use in the classroom have a bias to them. We also have a bias, and I don't hold back from relating to students my positions. The one thing that we can provide in this place that pretends to be neutral is that we can give students something that they may not have gotten elsewhere. To develop critical thinking in my classes I present literature so we can examine both sides of an issue. That allows for a lot of dialogue. Then if service-learning is tied to it, it becomes an even larger dialogue and more concrete.

At the same time, I think we can have a perspective and utilize that perspective to understand that faculty teach in a lot of different ways and that a thousand ideas can flow. This type of teaching can give room to be able to create critical thinking to help students to question and think to create change. This type of teaching gets away from the banking method of instruction, where the flow of knowledge is channeled primarily from the teacher to the student. I find my place within the institution by, on the one hand, being clear about the positions I hold on certain issues, while at the same time allowing students to critically think about their positions and where these positions fit into the larger picture.

I know that you've done a bit of traveling to campuses that are doing service-learning. What is your analysis of the variety of practices that are assumed under the service-learning rubric?

There are sharp differences in how various practitioners and institutions implement service-learning. There are those who primarily focus on the "service" aspect. Although the service-learning experience may have course materials and class discussions, its main goal is to place students in a particular institution or organization to provide a service. Still, this type of service-learning does benefit the community, and it affects students and faculty, as well. In some cases, this may be the first introduction to getting involved and giving service.

Another type of service-learning, which I am interested in, is based on a mutual process of empowerment, in which students, together with the community, are involved in a collaborative effort to find solutions to particular issues or problems. This type of service-learning requires the faculty and students to immerse themselves alongside community participants to do reflection and to collectively develop theories and strategies related to the problems that they are facing.

As service-learning is becoming more popular, there are new questions that are emerging in its application in institutions of higher education. In some institutions, the issues of liability, management, and governance have come to the fore. In others, the issues of control and power relations are becoming a reality. In one college I know, a professor got students involved in researching and protesting land development policies in an African-American community. It turned out that some of the developers were also on the college's board of trustees. This created tremendous conflict between the interests of the college, the land interests, and those interested in protecting the quality of life in their community.

For me, these are positive developments. As we begin to explore new types of service-learning, it makes for very exciting research and for finding new ways to deal with these issues. It is natural that once service-leaning is embraced by faculty and students, it will move to other levels that can include policy making and social change. When it moves to this level, there are no guarantees as to the involvement and support of the institution. There are no guarantees as to whom the students will confront, including those in powerful positions related to the institution. I don't see this as negative, but it certainly moves beyond the "safe" models that many institutions are comfortable with—the internship, service, and volunteer models. I personally support all these different models, because they serve different purposes and constituencies at different times and under different circumstances. At the same time, they can build upon each other.

It has been interesting speaking both with you and with Frank Furstenberg from the University of Pennsylvania, because you have both been involved as sociologists in work with public schools. You have significantly different entry points to the school setting and significantly different ways of determining the problem to be addressed.

As I have mentioned before, my entry point comes from my activist background. Coming from this background, I really laud students who get involved with community leaders and other participants in finding solutions to practical problems in their communities. I try to show through example that there is a need to get involved. There are many students coming out of high school these days who have a history of community involvement. The higher education experience can put a damper on that quality. Some of these students have a tendency to turn away from the academy and drop out.

I think service-learning can make a real difference for these students. I know that it makes a difference for faculty who have come out of an activist history and are trying to find a means to exist in academia without being coopted and without losing the values that give social meaning to their research or teaching.

My research and activism correspond with aspects of the participatory action research approach, particularly in the explicit connections made between social research and action. However, in my situation, in the city of Monterey Park, I became an activist before I became a social researcher. Consequently, I had to resolve the issue that my data were collected in the dual roles of researcher and advocate. I began to call this type of research "advocate research": a type of research where one could be involved in the process while simultaneously seeking to describe the world of the participants through their eyes. Of course, as ethnographers we have to seek to represent all sides. However, our involvement can give us an "in" that allows us to more fully understand the participants and to summarize the lessons learned.

What kind of impact do you think all this activity on the part of higher education is having on communities?

Certainly, the communities that I have been working with have been empowered to see campuses as having tremendous resources that the community can take advantage of. The labor unions, for example, are actively seeking to develop stronger ties among labor, campuses, and community activists. I am heartened by the efforts being made by labor organizers as well as faculty to become part of the communities that they live in—collaborating with neighborhood groups to advance local organizing efforts and political campaigns.

As the research efforts on our campuses are being used to create and change policies, the divide between campus and community is being diminished. Our communities don't see the campus as an island, and, more important, we don't see ourselves as an island. We see ourselves as an appendage of a larger community.

As students and faculty get involved in local political issues, they also begin to see that they can be a political force in the community. They no longer see themselves as travelers passing by, but as individuals with a stake in the decisions being made. Service-learning certainly helps to bring all these aspects together. Pitzer College, as an example, is developing a reputation locally and regionally as a place where there is a culture of service-learning. We get calls all the time from schools that want to utilize our resources in conflict resolution, early outreach, and curriculum transformation. As we get known for that sort of work, the strengths and advantages of service-learning get known.

This sounds like a wonderful example and somewhat unique in its bilateral and multilevel organizational involvement.

Yes, students and faculty are involved at all levels. It is based on where professors find their passion. Many service-learning practitioners come out of a background of activism. They realize that they have lost their idealism along the way. They find that they are so caught up in academia that they have lost ties with the community. The reason why some professors shy away from service-learning is that they don't have ties to the communities around them.

We are being innovative at all levels. Some professors have involved students in local unions. They have learned to use email and the Internet to communicate with union organizers and community members in other cities and in other nations. Some students are part of a partnership between the nearby city of Ontario and Pitzer that includes students' living with families in the targeted area, intensive writing courses with a focus on urban issues, and seminars led by a variety of scholars, agency directors, and community workers. These various curriculum initiatives have been complemented with institutional grants from the Irvine and Mellon Foundations. With these funds, faculty-development grants are providing opportunities for professors to develop classes in their fields that integrate experiential learning or to participate in internships themselves.

Do you find there are unique kinds of teaching and learning opportunities that are afforded by service-learning that cannot be achieved in any other way?

Yes. Through service-learning, students were "doing" diversity and multiculturalism without realizing it. In various classes that I have been involved with, students were drawn from different backgrounds in terms of race class, gender, and sexual orientation. What I found is that the students, in the process of working together in service-learning projects, have developed a sense of collectivity. In the case of the UFW experience, students work together in teams doing data entry, public action mailings, archival research, etc. In return for the union's hospitality and shared knowledge, the students present a reflection of what they have learned through the medium of theater. The beauty of this project is that it brings together students from diverse backgrounds to work together and to think critically and creatively. When they come back to campus, these ties are not lost but enriched. These are results that we cannot replicate in the classroom. These are results that reenergize me as a professor and remind me about the concrete meaning of collaborative learning.

Are you able to weave in sociological knowledge? What concepts and theories are students pointed to?

This is one thing that we are very careful of doing. In my Social Stratification class, I ensure that students learn about classical and contemporary stratification theories. However, I take it one step further and have students figure out how to apply these theories to multicultural novels and class presentations. In this class, for example, a group of students from varied ethnic backgrounds read the book *I Know Why the Caged Bird Sings*, by Maya Angelou, and applied its content to various stratification theories. In the process, they found connections to their own lived experience and shared their collective interpretation through the creation of a wall-size mural. As they worked on the project, I observed how students from varying ethnic, class, and gender backgrounds could come together to produce a masterpiece.

In a couple of classes that I cotaught with sociology professor Betty Farrell, Social Responsibility and Community, and Roots of Social Conflict in Schools and Communities, students participated in a weekly seminar organized around varied readings about the region, including educational stratification, demographic changes, and the nature of the Latino and Asian Pacific people's experiences.

In the Rural and Urban Ethnic Movements course, students learn about social movement theories and the difference between use values and exchange values as applied to the concepts of place, growth, gentrification, and community development. By virtue of their experience in the community, they are able to critically evaluate these theories.

In the courses that focused on local school districts [Alhambra and Garvey], most of the students wrote in their evaluations of the class that it was most difficult because of the requirements extensive reading, fieldwork, traveling to the site, working independently with the students, taking field notes, coding, and writing up the final results. As mentioned before, we ensured that the books that they were reading were concretely related to the site that they were involved in. This was also ensured through the Rural and Urban Ethnic Movements class. There are now a lot of books on the history, origins, and strategies of the farmworker movement. In the class, we spend a lot of time looking at all the different sociological theories that relate to this particular social movement. When we go out into the field, students see the theories in practice and how different strategies are being applied. As a result, their reflection papers are not based just on emotion or personal reflection but are about how the theories can be applied to what they have learned and observed.

For faculty, helping students to link experience to theories is a real challenge. I know that I am always trying to move students beyond their own experience so that they become awakened to the importance of reading and critically examining texts and meaning. In some cases, in a course such as The Family, for instance, the students want to base all their learning on lived experience, and often challenge our research because they are aware of a personal exception to the rule. Helping students to see the world in new ways via experience and theory is designed not to rid them of old ways of thinking but simply to help them understand where their own perspectives come from.

One of the lessons that I have learned about student-centered education is that if it is applied well, it leads to a more interactive classroom, where the roles of the faculty member are made more equal to those of the student. This is a good thing. However, I have also found (particularly in introductory courses) that many students have not been exposed to particular theories or different ways of looking at issues. Some students in this situation often become comfortable with sharing their experience but slight the importance of doing the readings. As professors, we can shirk our responsibilities if the class becomes primarily focused on lived experience. The students need to learn to be dialectical and critical of the various sides and implications of classical and contemporary issues and theories in the literature. They need to ask challenging questions: Why do people have different positions on issues? Why are individuals and groups stratified at different levels? How did I, as an individual, get stratified in the position that I am in today? Students should be able to explain the historical, economic, political, and social foundations of how individuals and groups have become stratified at different levels and how inequality in positioning is explained in ways by contending theories and theoreticians.

Overall, I think that this type of learning by "doing" sociology will stay much longer with them than if it were knowledge being taught merely out of a book. I am learning, more and more, how to develop combinations of lived experience, theory, and praxis in the classroom.

Do you find that students who come from backgrounds that are similar to the communities and people being served are having experiences that are different from students from more-privileged backgrounds?

Both are affected in deep ways. From reading reflection papers, I find that the more-privileged students respond in awe at having experiences with communities such as the farmworkers' communities in La Paz and Delano. They are struck time and time again by the realities that these communities have to face on a daily basis and how they are able to survive through resistance and organization. The service-learning experience often influences these students to change their career goals. Now, they begin to think about how they can use their lives after graduation.

However, I have found that the students who come from those communities are not surprised, but instead spend most of their time searching for answers. They are more affected by the strategies and efforts that the community advocacy organizations are carrying out to change things. These students become more interested in returning to their communities and using their education to join the efforts of others. Many minority or underrepresented students (including women and gay and lesbian students) fall in this category. They are sensitive to the issues on campus, issues that have a lot to do with their survival. These issues involve the lack of funds, role models, financial aid, and a relevant learning environment. Often, if the institution lacks a multicultural curriculum and faculty who can understand where the students are coming from, such students will drop out. All students and faculty need to realize that the inclusion of the underrepresented in the curriculum is something that serves not only the underrepresented but everyone, regardless of background. This country was built on the backs of diverse people. Unfortunately, some benefited and some didn't. That story needs to be told so that students from all backgrounds can sincerely and genuinely work together on common issues. The service-learning experience impacts both types of students, but the impacts are quite different.

As I look at the field of service-learning, it occurs to me that we have not established a useful framework that helps people to really understand what we mean by "community work." There are a variety of competing meanings here, and I think we assume understanding and agreement where none exists.

I think that we need a deep dialogue on this issue. The community, as a whole, is made up of many competing interests. Those who are corporate growers, developers, polluters—interests that may place profits over quality of life—are all part of what we call "community" When we talk about community, we are talking about a geographical, political, or spiritual place that is very diverse. This place has different levels of stratification, power relations, backgrounds, and ideologies. When you and I talk about community, we have a common sense that we are talking about communities of people who are facing inequality or who are trying to improve their living environment.

Ultimately, what communities we serve can have institutional implications, and this can result in conflict with the traditional power and decision-making interests. We need to debate some hard questions. What are the ethics of service-learning? Do we treat all communities the same? What communities are we talking about when we say that service-learning is all about "collaborating with the community"? This is an important question—because service-learning can be used to oppress and domesticate communities, to do all the things that we say that we are not about.

As we teach and develop critical thinking, some may take it to mean that it is only about "criticizing" and being oppositional. People today are asking for positive solutions, not just to hear what you are against. In this context, it is important to present and learn about all sides of issues that are affecting our communities. Our students need to learn the intricacies of research methodology and its strength in producing various options, answers, and outcomes. This sort of openness and exchange should be a hallmark of our service-learning classrooms. We have to teach our classes in such a way as to allow divergent perspectives to flow from the literature and from the students themselves.

It is my perspective that in the larger society students are not provided with many different ways to look at the world. The dominant understanding of inequality has a tendency to blame the "individual" for his or her "inadequacies." There are other theories and explanations that focus on the historical and systemic foundations of inequality. Students should learn to weigh the strength of the evidence for these explanations. What is liberating—as both Ira Shor and Paulo Freire would agree—is that first attempt at dialogue and critical analysis. From this can emerge consciousness that moves to the level of practice—empowering practice. If we as educators, who have direct contact with the students, are not the catalysts for this type of learning and community work, the students will most likely not get it from anywhere else.

NOTES

1. Copyright Acknowledgement: This chapter was previously published in the following: *Cultivating the Sociological Imagination: Concepts and Models for Service-Learning in Sociology*, edited by James Ostrow, Gary Hesser, and Sandra Enos. Washington, D. C.: American Association of Higher Education American Sociological Association, 1999.

2. Campus Compact, a national organization with offices in more than 20 states, works with member campuses and higher education in general to advance the practice of service-learning and community service on college campuses.

Chapter Twelve

Organizing Immigrant Workers

*Action Research and Strategies
in the Pomona Day Labor Center*[1]

José Zapata Calderón, Suzanne F. Foster,
and Silvia L. Rodriguez

After a local ordinance was passed in the city of Pomona, California, to get day laborers off street corners, a city policeman confronted a day laborer about his inability to read an antisolicitation ordinance in English. Asking a student to interpret for him, the policeman shook his finger as he scolded the day laborer.

> He is in violation of the law. If he is going to sit here now and say "I don't, understand, I don't speak English," he has to make a decision. That decision is, you can either learn to speak English to function in society, because that's what the signs are, they are in English, or find himself in violation of the law. It's that simple . . . learn English or go to jail. (Beetley-Hagler 2000)

The action of this policeman, captured on videotape by then-Pitzer College student Andy Beetley-Hagler, is not an isolated case. It is how city officials and law enforcement agencies have responded in many urban and suburban communities where Latino day laborers, known as *jornaleros*, congregate on street corners to seek jobs. Groups of men can be found gathering on urban street corners, hardware store parking lots, and truck rental facilities looking for work. These are men who do not have permanent jobs but are driven to work by circumstances on a day-to-day basis. According to a study conducted by Abel Valenzuela (1999), director of UCLA's Center for the Study of Urban Poverty, "Day laborers are overwhelmingly Latino, predominately from Mexico."

Changes in immigration laws and regional economic restructuring are credited for the thousands of Latino immigrants from Mexico, Guatemala, El Salvador, and other Central American countries entering the United States and accepting jobs in the low-wage and low-skill services sector (Soja and Scott 1996). The passage of the Hart-Cellar Act in 1965 increased the total number of immigrants admitted to the United States and inadvertently gave opportunities to approximately five million immigrants in the service sector (Waldinger and Bozorgmehr 1996). As described by Myrna Cherkoss Dona-hoe in this volume, the deindustrialization of Los Angeles led to a loss of jobs in the manufacturing sector, a restructuring process of growth in "high-skill, high-tech" employment, and the rise of a service sector based on low-wage workers and an informal economy (Pastor 2000; Valle and Torres 2000; Soja and Scott 1996; Waldinger and Bozorgmehr 1996). As Los Angeles deindustrialized with the loss of steel, automobile, and tire manufacturing between 1965 and 1992, new jobs were generated in the informal and service sectors that paid low wages, were nonunionized, and offered few protections and benefits. These transformations have contributed to a growth in both the Latino population and the low-wage manual labor pool that is used to advance economic growth (Soja 1996; Milkman 2000; Milkman and Wong 2000).

Some of these Latino immigrants have become part of the informal economy as day laborers or workers who are hired on a temporary basis in both the service and commercial sectors. The informal economy is characterized by low wages, usually paid by an employer in cash, and working conditions that are unregulated (Sassen 1994, 2001; Pardo 1998). In the Southern California region, it is estimated that there are twenty thousand day laborers looking for work on a daily basis (Añorve, Osborn, and Salas 2000). Of this number, 78 percent are Mexican, 20 percent Central American, 1 percent U.S.-born, and 1 percent born elsewhere (Valenzuela 1999).

With an increase of day labor sites and corners, thirty cities in the Los Angeles region have adopted some type of municipal ordinance against the solicitation of work in public spaces (Toma and Esbenshade 2000, 57). Some of these ordinances have been in response to complaints by local residents and businesses. Others have been as a result of an anti-immigrant sentiment that has been propagated by right-wing organizations and politicians who have blamed immigrants for everything from the loss of jobs and social services to the cyclical downturns in the U.S. economy (Waldinger and Bo-zorgmehr 1996, 445–55; Acuña 1996, 158–64). Pomona's Ordinance 3814, approved in June 1996, fines workers up to one thousand dollars and/or places them in jail for up to six months if they solicit employment on any street, public area, or parking lot. The city of Ontario, California, passed a similar ordinance prohibiting the solicitation of employment on public streets and at unauthorized commercial and industrial parking areas (Clark 2001, A1).

Unions affiliated with the American Federation of Labor-Congress of Industrial Organizations (AFL-CIO) have responded to these attacks by organizing immigrant workers and supporting legislation to give complete amnesty to undocumented workers. However, they held back on organizing day laborers. Hence, other grassroots groups, organizations, and individuals have recognized the need to fill that void (LópezGarza 2000, 162–63; Toma and Esbenshade 2000; Acuña 1996, 197–98; Hondagneu-Sotelo 2001, 221–29; Valenzuela 1999; Jones-Correa 1998).

This chapter focuses on a collaborative effort in the city of Pomona, where college students, a faculty member, community advocates, and day laborers joined together to establish an official site from which day laborers could negotiate employment. This case study is part of a larger story taking place throughout the Los Angeles metropolitan area and the United States, where workers are creating partnerships and coalitions to build power and defend their rights.

Our findings show that day laborers are difficult to organize. Unlike other low-wage workers such as janitors and gardeners who are more established in specific locations with specific employers, day laborers are highly mobile and dependent on different employers on a daily basis. These difficulties have manifested themselves in the use of various strategies to organize day laborers. One strategy depends on a top-down (business-union-type) model that excludes the voices of the workers and simultaneously uses anti-solicitation city government ordinances and law enforcement agencies to force day laborers off the streets. Another strategy, the participatory model, focuses on improving the long-term conditions of day laborers by advancing services aimed at improving their quality of life and involving them in the policy making and leadership building. This chapter, inasmuch as it is about building collaborative relations, is also about the different strategies that are being used to organize day laborers.

THE POMONA DAY LABOR CENTER

The Pomona Day Labor Center is situated in the city of Pomona, which is located thirty miles east of Los Angles. Similar to the demographic changes taking place in Los Angeles, Pomona's overall population has grown from 131,723 in 1990 to 149,473 in 2000, a 13.5 percent change. The population changes between 1990 and 2000 have resulted in the proportion of Latinos in the city's population growing from 54 percent (77,776) to 65 percent (96,370); Asian/Pacific Islanders remaining at about 7 percent (from 9,846 to 10,765); African Americans decreasing from 14 percent (19,013) to 10 percent (14,398); and Whites decreasing from 26 percent (36,687) to 17 percent (25,348) (U.S. Census Bureau 1990, 2000).

Since opening its doors on January 5, 1998, the center has been located in a business center west of downtown and east of the Corona Freeway. A Contractor's Warehouse is located on the south side of the business center. Employers gather materials at the Contractor's Warehouse and then proceed to hire workers who congregate in the parking lot. *La esquina*, as the corner in front of the center where some workers wait for employers is called, has an eighteen-year history of serving as a gathering place for day laborers.

On entering the center, a long bar-shaped table awaits the employer or employee. From this table a staff member greets employers and registers day laborers for employment on a first-come and first-serve basis. A roster is used to keep records about who works on any given day, the hours worked, the salary received, and the employer's information, such as license plate numbers. The day laborers who do not go on a work assignment for the day are given priority on the roster the following day.

Behind the table are some filing cabinets and office supplies, which are next to a used computer that sits on a desk. A plain wall, constructed by the day laborers, separates the front desk from a long room. The walls, painted a plain green by the student interns and day laborers, display various posters, including one with a United Farm Workers' Union flag. On any given day, one can see workers watching television at one corner of the room as others work diligently at a table of computers. At the other corner, half a dozen workers are observed sitting around a folding table playing cards. This room is also the site for various Pitzer College student-led efforts, which include language training, health care referral, and immigration rights services.

CAMPUS/COMMUNITY PARTNERSHIP

A partnership between Pitzer College and the day laborers in Pomona developed out of a common interest in community building. Pitzer College, a coeducational liberal arts college located in Claremont with an enrollment of approximately 850 men and women, has had a history of encouraging social responsibility through student participation in community service learning projects.

The authors of this article reflected this ethos by carrying out research and participating in various organizing efforts alongside the day laborers in Pomona. As part of a course in the spring of 1997 called "Restructuring Communities," Professor José Z. Calderón had college students interning in various local movements so that they could work with community activists. One of the student groups began to work with Fabian Nuñez, a community activist and Pitzer student (who is now the speaker of the California State Assembly). Meanwhile, Pomona city officials were debating ways to implement the municipal ordinance approved in 1996 to remove day laborers from public streets. Professor Calderón and his students joined Nunez, day laborers, and other Pomona community organizers in packing city hall to protest the ordinance. When city officials defended their actions by claiming that all day laborers were undocumented, Pitzer students presented evidence proving that permanent residents also made up a portion of those who solicited work on the street corners. Using Valenzuela's aforementioned 1999 study on day laborers, the students showed the council that a portion of day laborers had resided in the United States for ten years or more.

In addition, Pitzer students explored other alternatives to the punishment and incarceration proposed by city officials. Pitzer students visited day labor centers organized by the Coalition for Humane Immigrant Rights of Los Angeles (CHIRLA), which receive more than one hundred thousand dollars each from the city of Los Angeles. They gathered crucial information on the success of well-established day labor centers, which led to a funding proposal for a similar center in Pomona. The funding information in particular has been extremely useful in the struggle to receive more financial support from the city of Pomona and from private foundations for the Pomona Day Labor Center.

Ultimately, the Pomona City Council supported the establishment of a day labor center near the most popular day laborer corner. Although calling it "unlawful" to solicit work in public spaces, Ordinance 3814 proclaimed that a "designated day labor center" was the only "lawful" place to solicit work in the city. Subsequently, a coalition of community organizers and students formed a nonprofit organization, the Pomona Economic Opportunity Center (PEOC), which received fifty thousand dollars in seed money from the city of Pomona's Community Development Block Grant (CDBG) program to establish a day labor center (Tresaugue 1997). The city also appointed a board of directors that included city commission members, some independent consultants, and community representatives. Resulting from the college's involvement, the city council also appointed Professor Calderón and various students to the board.

An on-site director was hired to oversee the daily operations of the center. A lawyer on the board who had organized a day labor center in Glendale, California, suggested that the PEOC hire directors from outside the center. Unfortunately, due to high overhead costs and a lack of consistent financial resources, the PEOC was unable to pay the director a substantial wage or offer adequate benefits. This placed most of the pressure on the site director, because he worked 7 days a week and 365 days a year. Without adequate funds to hire a staff that could take care of the operational needs of the center, the burden of administering the nonprofit organization fell on the shoulders of the board of directors.

Embedded in the allocation of the seed money was the city's expectation that the center would be able to become self-sufficient. As a way to achieve self-sufficiency, the original organizers of the center encouraged the workers to pay dues of thirty dollars per month. Although the dues collections were sporadic, with many workers not paying at all, the dues eventually dropped to twenty dollars and then to ten dollars. The initial seed money and workers' dues, although helping to sustain the center's operation for two years, was not enough to cover the total costs. With the help of Pitzer College's Center for California Cultural and Social Issues (CCCSI), Professor Calderón urged more of his students to use their research at the center to write funding proposals to the city and various private foundations. Although the grants were relatively small and not enough to hire a full-time executive director, they were instrumental in keeping the center in operation.

PROMOTING SOCIAL CHANGE THROUGH PARTICIPATORY RESEARCH

The summer of 1999 served as a critical turning point in the development of the center. Under the direction of José Calderón, Pitzer students Suzanna Foster and Silvia Rodriguez (along with fellow student Jill McGougan) served as participants and researchers at the Pomona Day Labor Center from June 1999 until April 2000. They talked to the day laborers and listened closely to their experiences, including their transition from the corner to the center and their life stories. The methodology of participant observation was used in order to collect information about the center and to build a successful organization. The three students taught English as a Second Language (ESL) classes, trained new student interns working at the center, helped to advance the development of a health project, and wrote proposals to foundations for funding. Suzanne Foster, co-vice president of the center's board of directors in 2000, wrote a senior thesis entitled "Empowerment Services and Social Change at the Pomona Day Labor Center." Jill McGougan, who has served on the center's board of directors since 2000, also wrote a senior thesis entitled "The Internal and External Factors Impacting a Day Labor Center."

In contrast to traditional research methods, our research team focused its inquiries on those issues that primarily benefited the day laborer community. Rather than setting ourselves apart from the community that we were researching, we sought to participate alongside the day laborers in finding solutions to the problems that they were facing (Nyden et al. 1999). We applied aspects of the action research method, where both the researchers and community participants collaborate to produce knowledge with the express purpose of taking action to promote social change and analysis (Greenwood and Levin 1998). The kind of change that this methodology refers to is one that is pragmatic and involves the community participants in the decision-making process so that they can negotiate having more control over their lives. Our research team participated in all aspects of the day labor center's activities. We informed the workers about our research and shared our findings as a means of advancing collaboration around grant proposals, policy changes, and board decisions. Because of the highly mobile character of day laborers based on their fluctuating opportunities for work, we were not able to involve them directly in the research methodology on a daily basis. Nevertheless, we shared our research process, findings, and written work with them.

In seeking to apply a methodology that could involve the workers in the research process, the research team began with the premise that trust had to be an essential component of a just relationship with the day laborer community and that this could only be accomplished through equal participation and compassion. Raúl Gomez, an ex-day laborer who visited the center in June 1999, expressed to Foster the importance of having mutual respect as a foundation for the success of any project at the center. He commented that "the workers are very sensitive to being talked down to or to being made to feel stupid," and that without respect on the part of all the participants, the researchers "shouldn't volunteer, nor should anyone else."

The research team took this advice into serious consideration as it met with CHIRLA, the Institute of Popular Education of Southern California (IDEPSCA), and the Community Learning Network (CLN) in order to assess their methods of organizing day laborers and use of popular education. Based on our meetings with these groups, our research team determined that the so-called top-down model of organizing is an ineffective way to organize day laborers and that a more effective model is one that emphasizes "worker participation, confrontation, pressure from arenas other than the worksite itself, and strategic planning" (Sherman and Voss 2000, 84).

TOP-DOWN ORGANIZING MODEL

The top-down model of organizing day laborers can be compared to the traditional models of unionism that rely primarily on dues in exchange for a staff that handles the problems of the members (Sherman and Voss 2000). This type of organizing places the primary power in the hands of the staff and treats the worker as a secondary participant.

This business-unionism model best characterized the practice of two consultants working on day laborer issues for a national hardware supply company. The consultants (whose names have been changed) began their participation with the Pomona Day Labor Center when the nonprofit board of directors was in its developmental stages. Alice Smith, one of the consultants, described herself as a student from the University of California, Los Angeles (UCLA) carrying out research on day laborers. The other consultant, Winston Nelson, introduced himself as a lawyer who volunteered his services to help establish day labor centers in the region. Both of the consultants immediately moved into leadership positions at the center by claiming that they had created models for establishing day labor centers in other Los Angeles area cities like Glendale and El Monte.

When the center first opened, Smith and Nelson implemented a membership structure in Pomona that they had used in other cities. This structure defined members as those who used the services of the center and paid the thirty dollar dues. Smith and Nelson originally imposed the dues component as a means of persuading the workers to follow the center's rules and to develop a basis for self-sufficiency. They negatively labeled those day laborers who chose not to become members of the center as *piratas* (pirates), a name that workers at the center continue to use to this day. Further, they persuaded some of the first directors of the center to portray the piratas publicly as being drug and alcohol users. The directors were also trained by Smith and Nelson to enforce the ordinance and use the police to force the piratas to register as members of the center. This tactic involved getting members of the center to distribute flyers at the parking lot entrance that spoke negatively about the piratas, advising employers of the city's ordinance, and calling on employers to hire day laborers only from the city-sanctioned center. Smith used cameras and two-way radios to pinpoint the so-called piratas. The center's director was instructed to call the police to report fights and disturbances, even when such activities were not happening. Later, the police officers realized that the calls were placed solely to instill fear and to force the workers to become members of the center and to generate revenue. Two police officers were present at a board of directors' meeting on August 18, 1999. They announced that they would no longer respond to what they called "fraudulent calls." Even after the police department took this position, Smith and Nelson insisted that the phone calls were necessary to implement the ordinance and to stop the growing concentration of day laborers on the corner.

The strategies used under the direction of Smith and Nelson divided the day laborers, created conflict between those who were considered members of the center and those who were not, and increased animosity between the day laborers and the center's board of directors. Subsequently, the board of directors began to question Smith and Nelson on criticisms raised by the day laborers about the workers' lack of representation in the center's decision-making processes. For example, pursuant to the recommendations of Smith and Nelson, the board of directors agreed to charge the day laborers thirty dollars per month in dues. According to Smith and Nelson, these were the wishes of the day laborers themselves. Later, through meetings between members of the board and the day laborers, the board learned that the workers had never voted or reached a consensus on paying this amount. According to the workers, the idea of paying dues and the amount were imposed on them by Smith and Nelson.

The board also questioned Smith concerning the reason that worker representatives no longer attended the board meetings, as prescribed by the bylaws of the organization. She reported that the worker representatives had problems with their board membership and "had decided to resign." Smith did not explain the reasons for the workers' resignations nor did she attempt to recruit more day laborers to the board. Instead, Smith committed herself to being present at all the meetings and serving as a liaison between the board and the day laborers. Meanwhile, Nelson proposed a change in the organization's bylaws to have a five-member board instead of the original eleven to thirteen members, five of which were designated as day laborers. Although Nelson's proposed bylaw change was never voted on, the day laborers stopped coming to the meetings and Smith took the liaison position.

By January 1999, Nelson and Smith had moved into the positions of president and treasurer of the board of directors. Since the other board members did not have the time to devote to these positions, no one objected to their appointments. Their role as liaisons, however, resulted in a lack of communication between the board of directors and the day laborers. Further, the day laborers began to raise questions about the center's expenditures and, in particular, how their dues were being used.

THE NEEDS OF THE WORKERS

Although recent studies of new immigrants have found a high rate of labor force participation and a low usage of public assistance, this does not mean that they do not have needs related to quality-of-life issues (Pastor 2000). Largely because of their undocumented status, day laborers turn to places such as day labor centers to help provide employment and education opportunities.

The research team soon learned of the day laborers' criticism of Smith for her failure to implement the English classes she had promised for at least a year. From the day laborers' perspectives, English was essential for gaining employment, negotiating a decent wage, and contesting mistreatment. Manuel Gonzalez, one of the day laborers at the center, emphasized this point at a general membership meeting. He said that the day laborers had all agreed to come to the center in the beginning because it promised job training, English classes, and other benefits, but the workers never received these services. He was angry because the workers had been promised these programs and services but had received only an organized system of work distribution, shelter, and a bathroom. As reported in Foster's July 1999 field notes, the workers didn't even have any drinking water.

Smith and Nelson's strategy centered more on meeting employers' needs for workers who worked hard and did not question anything or complain. This exemplifies the situation that some studies describe where employers prefer immigrant workers as a "controllable labor force" that works hard and keeps quiet about working conditions for fear of deportation (Ong and Valenzuela 1996).

The desire of the day laborers to improve their quality of life required a move beyond the marketplace strategies of supply and demand. It demanded that the workers be treated as "subjects," not as "objects," in the process (Freire 1993). This was a difficult transition to implement, particularly when the workers were caught in the immediacy of survival. Author Henry Giroux proposes that the "notions of critical thinking, culture and power disappear under the imperatives of the labor process and the need of capital accumulation" (1983). The necessity of trading labor for wages becomes the primary focus of many people's realities, although critical thinking, culture, and power are perhaps equally significant. The labor process does not freely allow access to education and critical thinking because of its strong demands on people. Although gaining employment is an essential piece of the puzzle, attaining empowering education and services significantly aids a strategy for organizing workers.

The urgent requests of the members of the center for certain services demonstrated that, although employment was a priority, it certainly was not the only valued goal. For example, several men wrote *"superar"* (to advance, or succeed) when asked what they most wanted on their membership application for the center. Although an equal number, if not more, answered "work" to this question, it could not be denied that these men had additional goals and dreams that deserved to be addressed. One man, Miguel Venustiano, answered the same question on July 5, 1999, in this way: "Quiero triunfar, para sacar adelante a mi familia, y asi devolverles la felicidad y la paz que ellos me ofrecen" (I want to triumph, to move my family forward, and by doing this return to them the happiness and peace that they have given me).

The experience of a seventy-five-year-old immigrant worker at the center exemplifies this issue. Originally a farmer in Mexico, Pepe Sánchez is considered a grandfather by the day laborers and placed in honor at the top of the roster list for jobs daily. Realizing that Sánchez was getting too old to work, the site director looked into the possibility of obtaining some type of social services for him. As with other immigrant workers, the case has become entangled in the bureaucratic process of proving permanent resident status. The day may well come when Sánchez is physically unable to work but has no one to look out for him. This elderly day laborer's case brought forward the need to move beyond employment services to also provide immigration rights, education, and health care services at the center. The center now emphasizes community building along with employment and encourages everyone to look out for each other.

The men at the center have a wide range of skills and educational levels. Some have not completed a sixth-grade level of education, whereas others have earned their university degree in their country of origin. Some have completed or almost completed high school in the United States. Others have received training all of their lives, in different areas like manufacturing, construction, or agriculture. Although there is no lack of skills at the center, there is a lack of knowledge regarding local resources and services that would allow the workers to improve and build on what they already know or even earn a more advanced degree. Some workers, like Tomas Rios and Antonio Guerrero, do not feel that they can attain their goals in a system that is not in their language, or in a country that is not officially their own. Attaining these skills or knowledge can improve their socioeconomic status, improve their outlook on life, and help them find permanent employment. This knowledge and provision of services are essential to their empowerment as human beings and as working immigrants.

Smith and Nelson pitted the need for employment against the need for other types of services. Calderón's field notes from June 22, 1999, reflects a meeting between our research team and Smith in which she claimed that the most effective strategy for running a day labor center was to implement what she called a "union" model. This model, according to Smith, allows the workers to restrict the supply of their labor and to force the employers to pay a living wage above the minimum. Smith suggested that the union model was currently used at the center. She added that this strategy had resulted in the day laborers agreeing collectively on a minimum hourly wage of $7.00 to charge employers. She stated that other day labor centers (particularly those directed by the organization CHIRLA) implemented the "social service agency model that do[es] not have a collective minimum wage" and "will accept paying the workers only $5.00 an hour, and even below." Smith went on to explain that the service model practiced by CHIRLA resulted in the day laborers using the centers primarily for the free services and not to reach financial stability. "The day laborers protest against freebies," said Smith during our meeting. Our research of CHIRLA day labor centers revealed that they do have an established collective minimum wage of $8.00 an hour and, as described later in this chapter, that they provide access to an array of services.

One Pitzer student researcher, Heather Miller, found that some day laborers shied away from available services, but not for the reasons stated by Smith. As the Pomona Day Labor Center began to sponsor health screenings and eye exams, it was noted that some day laborers hesitated because of their immigration status and because of their need to make work the primary focus of their lives. Others openly mentioned a lack of trust in established institutions (Miller 2001).

THE PARTICIPATORY MODEL
FOR DAY LABORER ORGANIZING

Jeremy Brecher and Tim Costello, in *Building Bridges*, propose that successful organizing strategies among workers, in addition to ensuring their full democratic participation, involve the advancement of coalitions between worker and community organizations "that go beyond the traditional limits of collective bargaining" (1990, 196).

CHIRLA and IDEPSCA are carrying out all aspects of this participatory model when organizing day laborers. In mid-1999, the research team met with two CHIRLA representatives, Day Laborer Project coordinator Pablo Alvarado and Worker's Rights Project coordinator Victor Narro. They introduced their projects and their methods to involve day laborers in all facets of the organizing effort. Alvarado explained that in 1989, CHIRLA assisted the city of Los Angeles in opening the first day laborer site in the nation, located in Harbor City. CHIRLA organizers assisted in the creation of the site, but did not get directly involved in the operation of the center. Rather, the Harbor City site was considered a pilot project and was first operated by the city of Los Angeles. In 1990, the city opened another site in North Hollywood. Between 1989 and 1996, both centers were operated by the Los Angeles Community Development Department. The department viewed the day laborers' presence primarily as a health and safety issue, and therefore did not allow the workers to organize or to initiate marketing campaigns about the center.

CHIRLA soon began to move beyond informal organizing at street corners to organizing around the issues that affected day laborers throughout Los Angeles. During this time, CHIRLA's efforts were concentrated at one corner in the Ladera Heights community, where there was a local movement to criminalize day laborers. Here, CHIRLA organized a multiracial coalition to defend the rights of day laborers and to protest against a citywide initiative targeting day laborers. In 1994, the Los Angeles County supervisors passed a local ordinance, similar to the one later passed in the city of Pomona, against labor solicitation on public and private property in unincorporated areas. Rather than calling for any specific penalty, the supervisors left it up to property owners to implement the ordinance. In response, CHIRLA developed a "free speech zone" where collaboration occurred among the police, local residents, Home Depot, community organizations, and the day laborers. The Los Angeles County Human Relations Commission facilitated collaborative meetings where a number of conflict resolution sessions were held between the residents and day laborers. These sessions resulted in policies that benefited the status of day laborers in other areas throughout the county. In addition to ensuring respect for free speech areas for day laborers, it advanced the implementation of similar "human relations models" in places such as Woodland Hills, the area centered in Maria A. Gutierrez de Soldatenko's discussion of Justice for Janitors in this volume. Here, government officials sought to stop the concentration of day laborers on corners by employing police on horseback. CHIRLA proposed the alternative of organizing day labor centers as community-based organizations that included the voices of day laborers. According to the CHIRLA representatives, the city of Los Angeles began receiving a great deal of criticism for not finding solutions to day laborers gathering on corners, an issue that some city officials categorized as *el patito feo* (the ugly duckling), or a problem that no one wanted. In 1996, the city of Los Angeles sought to address this issue by releasing requests for proposals (RFPs) and inviting community organizations interested in administering the various day laborer centers to submit bids. In the first round of RFPs, CHIRLA and IDEPSCA were the only agencies that applied. City officials opened up another round of RFPs with the intention of getting more applications, with no result. In the absence of other interested organizations, CHIRLA and IDEPSCA were given a contract to operate the various sites and to implement various conflict mediation programs. According to Calderón's field notes from July 6, 1999, CHIRLA and IDEPSCA were then receiving up to $112 thousand from Community Development Block Grant funds annually for each of four different centers.

Moving beyond the health and safety models developed by the city of Los Angeles, CHIRLA introduced three participatory components for organizing day laborer centers:

1. Ensure the basic civil, labor, and human rights of day laborers by involving them in advocacy efforts on issues that directly affect them.
2. Develop employment opportunities through outreach and marketing strategies organized by day laborers.
3. Advance a practice of civic engagement by involving day laborers in their communities (initiating volunteer community cleanups, remodeling old housing, organizing soccer leagues, and so forth).

In contradistinction to the perspective of Alice Smith, the CHIRLA representatives rejected the idea of a day laborer organization being narrowly configured along the lines of a service agency model. Mayron Payes, a CHIRLA organizer, explained that CHIRLA uses "different approaches" to ensure the "full participation" of the day laborers. CHIRLA provides services such as assistance with wage claim cases both to encourage participation in the center and to defend workers' rights. He added that these services do not make workers more dependent, but improve the conditions of their lives so they can fully participate in all aspects of civil society. Since the majority of the day laborers are Latino, CHIRLA has sought to tap the cultural aspects of this particular community. Payes gave various examples of this approach, including the organization of a soccer team, *teatro* (theater) group, and a musical group. In addition, a group of workers was collaborating at that time to produce a newsletter for day laborers. Other day laborers join in a yearly day labor conference where organizing strategies are discussed. For Payes, these "nontraditional" approaches to organizing allow "day laborers to participate, to grow as persons and as a community, and to reduce their alienation." In terms of empowerment, the CHIRLA representatives also spoke about another group of day laborers organizing themselves into a union, El Sindicato de Jornaleros. The workers have also organized themselves and lobbied their state representatives to pass a bill supporting the right of undocumented workers to obtain driver's licenses or state-sanctioned identification cards. In this way, CHIRLA representatives claim, day laborers move beyond the individual needs of getting a job and securing good wages to organizing around the policies that affect their everyday lives.

CHIRLA supported this process of empowerment by holding a day laborer leadership school. The leadership school provided a forum for discussion and education on how institutions function in the United States, how the global economy affects day laborers, and how they can become participants in the decision-making process. The success of the leadership school could be seen at the day labor centers and corners, where the workers take the lead in implementing their own rules, devising their own processes of distributing work each morning, holding general decision-making assemblies, and participating in monthly advisory board meetings.

CHIRLA's strategy of organizing has been implemented in the approximately 150 corners throughout Los Angeles where day laborers gather. Since it is impossible to acquire funding for so many day labor centers, Pablo Alvarado states that CHIRLA has found an alternative by building collaborative relationships among residents, city officials, and day laborers at these various sites:

> With a little organizing and conflict mediation, we have been able to turn tense situations at some of these corners into places where the workers have negotiated their responsibilities to these communities by developing agreed-upon rules of conduct and designated employment pickup sites.

CHIRLA and IDEPSCA utilize a participatory model based on popular education in the delivery of their services and in their organizing principles. Similar to various workers' rights centers organized in Los Angeles, the work of CHIRLA and IDEPSCA goes beyond social services. Their organizing principles empower the workers. The workers understand the world around them. In addition, they receive leadership training to create changes in their conditions (Bonacich 2000, 146). According to the CHIRLA representatives, this holistic approach serves the needs of the day laborers and advances the goal of creating "self-sustaining communities."

POMONA'S DAY LABOR CENTER:
BUILDING THE PARTICIPATORY MODEL

An effort to duplicate the participatory model at the Pomona Day Labor Center faced a serious challenge. The research team discovered that Smith and Nelson had been writing fraudulent progress reports to the city of Pomona claiming to be implementing various services at the center, including ESL classes; translation and mediation services between workers and employers; referring workers to appropriate agencies for services; and conducting tax workshops (City of Pomona 1999). This same report revealed some important figures that the day laborers had no knowledge about:

> A help to the Pomona program are the materials and expenses donated by [a national hardware supply company] of $9,280.40 in the last year, and the two consultants paid by the [company] to facilitate the program, a lawyer [Nelson] and a day laborer organizer [Smith] who organized [a nearby city's] program as well as others ($55,532.50 in the last year, actual billed hours). (City of Pomona 1999)

Smith and Nelson were asked by the center's board of directors to account for these funds. As noted in Calderón's field notes from November 17, 1999, a board member requested an itemized budget reflecting how the consultant fees were spent, the conditions under which the funds were granted, and the actual use of the funds in relation to the center. Nelson's response to the request was that the consultant fees were not anyone's business but his own, and that he didn't ask where anyone else's "personal paychecks came from."

Under fire from the day laborers and the board, both Smith and Nelson resigned their positions as treasurer and president, respectively. Their resignations gave way to a more democratic process in which workers were involved in decision making at the center, the development of partnerships was strongly emphasized, and the particular services that the workers had been asking for were finally implemented.

A partnership developed that, like the participatory model, sought to use a holistic approach with a combination of employment opportunities, leadership training, various services, projects, meetings, and organizing efforts to sustain the center. Through a collaborative effort with the Community Learning Network (CLN), an organization based at Claremont Graduate University, several Pitzer students (including the coauthors) began to develop an ESL curriculum for the center. CLN's organizers advised the Pitzer students on implementing a participatory action model of education and organization that focused on the community's assets rather than its deficiencies (Kretzmann and McKnight 1993). The model CLN used seeks to overcome the practices of many community initiatives, which, rather than advancing a "positive capacity-building venture," serve only to perpetuate "feelings of dependency" (Kingsley, McNeely, and Gibson 1997). CLN sought to advance this communitybuilding process by assessing the needs of the community, connecting to its skills and resources, and working on common issues.

The CLN organizers and the Pitzer students used focus groups as the primary vehicle to gather information on the needs and assets at the center. The focus groups identified the needs for work, ESL classes, and information on immigrants' rights. The focus groups also determined that the men had a vast amount of personal knowledge about their experience as immigrants, crossing physical and political borders, and trading their labor for wages. The ESL classes, then, were taught in such a way that acknowledged the workers' experiences and areas of expertise. Further, the curriculum helped to draw out the workers' opinions on issues at the center and other needed resources.

This participatory model of communication and education was implemented with the intention of empowering the workers to examine critically the issues in their realities, to connect them with other issues in a process of problematizing their similarities, and to reflect upon their common themes for social change (Freire 1993, 89). Through the process of dialogue, the students and teachers together created a curriculum that focused on experiences and themes that were important to them, including employment, tools, and health (Bentley 2001).

A health project emerged after a student found out that a worker was very ill and did not have access to health care. After the student took this individual to a doctor, many other workers asked for similar help. A partnership was soon created between the center and the Western University of Health Sciences in Pomona and regular health screenings and health referrals were implemented. More than thirty medical interns and doctors from Western University's Pomona Community Health Action Team (PCHAT) performed physical exams at the center. Eighty workers attended the health fair and more than fifty workers received physicals—some for the first time in many years.

Presently, Pitzer students continue to expand the health project to include eye and dental care. One man, in his sixties, had experienced difficulty with his vision for ten years. When the students took him to get an eye exam and bought him glasses through the program, he related that a whole new world had opened up to him. Now he could see things around him that he had never seen before.

An immigration rights project was also launched at the center. An immigration rights lawyer held a workshop on recent changes in immigration laws. Some student interns were involved on various legal cases, including one where an employer refused to pay three workers a total of three thousand dollars owed to them. Through the simple process of training and educating the workers on how to prepare and file a small claims suit, the full amount was eventually retrieved.

TRANSFORMING LOS ANGELES
THROUGH COALITION BUILDING

With the transformation of the Los Angeles region to a postindustrial urban economy there has been an expansion of high-wage professionals, on one end, and low-wage unorganized manual laborers, on the other. These developments have led to an increase of day laborers in the informal economy, which has resulted in various efforts aimed at organizing them.

Some initiatives, led by conservative anti-immigrant groups, have sought to abolish various services and programs, such as bilingual education and adult literacy programs, that can help build the economic and political capacity of immigrant workers (Ono and Sloop 2002; Crawford 1992; Calderón 1989). There are others who promote municipal ordinances either to criminalize day laborers or to promote their exploitation as a cheap labor force. What these groups have in common is a top-down strategy that aims at dividing immigrant workers from the working class and excluding them from the growing political voice and clout of a growing Latino and "minority majority" population.

The story of the implementation of participatory strategies through collaborative partnerships described in this chapter shows that there is no contradiction between the use of education as a service and an organizational form that is inclusive of the day laborers' voices and leadership. Through the use of nontraditional methods that allow for critical dialogue and the involvement of the participants, the goals of an empowering education can be achieved. Ira Shor, a pacesetter in the field of critical education, defines the goals of an empowering education as relating "personal growth to public life, by developing strong skills, academic knowledge, habits of inquiry, and critical curiosity about society, power, inequality, and change" (1992, 15). The collaboration between Pitzer College and the Pomona Day Labor Center, although confronting many obstacles, has advanced the development of a participatory action model between the day laborer and campus communities, a culture of bottomup decision making by all the partners involved, and a connection between the needed services of day laborers and an organizational form to advocate for their rights.

NOTE

1. Copyright Acknowledgement: This chapter was previously published in the following: *Latino Los Angeles*, Edited by Enrique C. Ochoa and Gilda L. Ochoa © 2005. The Arizona Board of Regents. Reprinted by permission of the University of Arizona Press.

REFERENCES

Acuña, Rodolfo. 1996. *Anything but Mexican.* New York: Verso.

Añorve, Raúl, Torie Osborn, and Angélica Salas. 2000. "Jornaleros Deserve Dignity." *Los Angeles Times*, Aug. 27.

Beetley-Hagler, Andy, dir. 2000. *La Lucha de Trabajar en Pomona.* Pitzer College.

Bentley, Sarah. 2001. "English-as-a-Second-Language (ESL) Curriculum Development and Implementation at the Pomona Day Labor Center." Senior thesis, Pitzer College, Claremont, Calif.

Bonacich, Edna. 2000. "Intense Challenges, Tentative Possibilities: Organizing Immigrant Workers in Los Angeles." In Organizing Immigrants: *The Challenge for Unions in Contemporary California*, edited by Ruth Milkman. Ithaca, N.Y.: Cornell University Press.

Brecher, Jeremy, and Tim Costello. 1990. "American Labor: The Promise of Decline." In *Building Bridges: The Emerging Grassroots Coalition of Labor and Community*, edited by Jeremy Brecher and Tim Costello, New York: Monthly Review Press.

Calderón, José. 1989. "How the English Only Initiative Passed in California." In *Estudios Chicanos and the Politics of Community*, edited by Mary Romero and Cordelia Candelaria. Oakland, Calif.: Cragmont.

City of Pomona. 1999. "Pomona Day Labor Center Quarterly Report." Sept.

Clark, Deborah. 2000. "Day Laborers Fate Debated." *Ontario, Calif., Daily Bulletin*, Sept. 18, A1.

Crawford, James. 1992. *Language Loyalties.* Chicago: University of Chicago Press.

Foster, Suzanne. 2000. "Empowerment Services and Social Change at the Pomona Day Labor Center." Senior thesis, Pitzer College, Claremont, Calif.

Freire, Paulo. 1993. *Pedagogy of the Oppressed.* Rev. ed. New York: Continuum.

Giroux, Henry. 1983. *Theory and Resistance in Education: A Pedagogy for the Opposition.* New York: Bergin and Garvey.

———. 1992. *Border Crossings: Cultural Workers and the Politics of Education.* New York: Routledge.

Greenwood, Davydd J., and Morten Levin. 1998. *Introduction to Action Research: Social Research for Social Change.* Thousand Oaks, Calif.: Sage.

Hondagneu-Sotelo, Pierrette. 2001. *Doméstica: Immigrant Workers Cleaning and Caring in the Shadows of Affluence.* Berkeley: University of California Press.

Jones-Correa, Michael. 1998. *Between Two Nations: The Political Predicament of Latinos in New York City.* Ithaca, N.Y.: Cornell University Press.

Kingsley, Thomas G., Joseph B. McNeely, and James O. Gibson. 1997. *Community Building Coming of Age.* Washington, D.C.: The Urban Institute.

Kretzmann, John P., and John L. McKnight. 1993. *Building Communities from the Inside Out: A Path Toward Finding and Mobilizing a Community's Assets.* Evanston, Il.: Acta.

López-Garza, Marta. 2000. "A Study of the Informal Economy and Latina/o Immigrants in Greater Los Angeles." In *Asian and Latino Immigrants in a Restructuring Economy: The Metamorphosis of Southern California*, edited by Marta López-Garza and David R. Diaz. Stanford, Calif.: Stanford University Press.

McGougan, Jill. 2000. "The Internal and External Factors Impacting a Day Labor Center as Part of a Social Movement." Senior thesis, Pitzer College, Claremont, Calif.

Milkman, Ruth. 2000. Introduction to *Organizing Immigrants: The Challenge for Unions in Contemporary California*, edited by Ruth Milkman. Ithaca, N.Y.: Cornell University Press.

Milkman, Ruth, and Kent Wong. 2000. "Organizing the Wicked City: The 1992 Southern California Drywall Strike." In *Organizing Immigrants: The Challenge for Unions in Contemporary California*, edited by Ruth Milkman. Ithaca, N.Y.: Cornell University Press.

Miller, Heather. 2001. "Culture and Gender-Based Internal Barriers to Health Care among Latino Day Laborers." Senior thesis, Pitzer College, Claremont, Calif.

Nyden, Philip, Anne Figert, Mark Shibley, and Darryl Burrows. 1999. *Building Community: Social Science in Action*. Thousand Oaks, Calif.: Pine Forge Press.

Ong, Paul, and Abel Valenzuela Jr. 1996. "The Labor Market: Immigrant Effects and Racial Disparities." In *Ethnic Los Angeles*, edited by Roger Waldinger and Mehdi Bozorgmehr. New York: Russell Sage Foundation.

Ono, Kent A., and John M. Sloop. 2002. *Shifting Borders*. Philadelphia: Temple University Press.

Pardo, Mary. 1998. *Mexican American Women Activists: Identity and Resistance in Two Los Angeles Communities*. Philadelphia: Temple University Press.

Pastor, Manuel, Jr. 2000. "Economics and Ethnicity: Poverty, Race, and Immigration in L.A. County." In *Asian and Latino Immigrants in a Restructuring Economy: The Metamorphosis of Southern California*, edited by Marta López-Garza and David R. Diaz. Stanford, Calif.: Stanford University Press.

Sassen, Saskia. 1994. "The Informal Economy: Between New Developments and Old Regulations." *Yale Law Journal* 103, no. 8 (June): 2289–304.

———. 2001. *The Global City: New York, London, Tokyo*. Princeton, N.J.: Princeton University Press.

Sherman; Rachel, and Kim Voss. 2000. "Organize or Die: Labor's New Tactics and Immigrant Workers." In *Organizing Immigrants: The Challenge for Unions in Contemporary California*, edited by Ruth Milkman. Ithaca, N.Y.: Cornell University Press.

Shor, Ira. 1992. *Empowering Education: Critical Teaching for Social Change*. Chicago: University of Chicago.

Soja, Edward W. 1996. "Los Angeles, 1965–1992: From Crisis-Generated Restructuring to Restructuring-Generated Restructuring." In *The City: Los Angeles and Urban Theory at the End of the Twentieth Century*, edited by Allen J. Scott and Edward W. Soja. Berkeley: University of California Press.

Soja, Edward W., and Allen J. Scott. 1996. "Introduction to Los Angeles: City and Region." In *The City: Los Angeles and Urban Theory at the End of the Twentieth Century*, edited by Allen J. Scott and Edward W. Soja. Berkeley: University of California Press, 1996.

Toma, Robin, and Jill Esbenshade. 2000. *Day Laborer Hiring Sites: Constructive Approaches to Community Conflict*. Los Angeles: Los Angeles County Human Relations Commission.

Tresaugue, Matthew. 1997. "Pomona OKs Labor Center." *Los Angeles Times*, July 31, A1, A6.

U.S. Bureau of the Census. 1990. *Statistical Abstract*. Washington, D.C.

———. 2000. Statistical Abstract. Washington, D.C.

Valenzuela, Abel. 1999. "Day Laborers in Southern California: Preliminary Findings from the Labor Survey." Working Papers Series, Center for the Study of Urban Poverty, UCLA.

Valle, Victor M., and Rodolfo D. Torres. 2000. *Latino Metropolis*. Minneapolis: University of Minnesota Press.

Waldinger, Roger, and Mehdi Bozorgmehr. 1996. "The Making of a Multicultural Metropolis." In *Ethnic Los Angeles*, edited by Roger Waldinger and Mehdi Bozorgmehr. New York: Russell Sage Foundation.

Chapter Thirteen

Immigration Raids in the Inland Empire

A Historical Pattern and Its Responses

José Zapata Calderón

On June 4th and 5th of 2004, a Mobile Patrol Group from the U. S. Border Patrol station in Temecula, California carried out a series of immigration sweeps in Southern California cities that resulted in the arrests of 420 Latino immigrants. In addition to creating a climate of fear and hysteria in immigrant communities, it also affected citizens and residents who, for the simple reasons of having brown skin, were stopped by the border patrol and questioned about their citizenship status.

Similarly, in January, 2007, in the Inland Empire region and in other parts of California, a series of immigration raids, named Operation Return to Sender by ICE (Immigration Customs and Enforcement) officials, resulted in the arrests of over 760 immigrants. As part of this deportation project, the raids resulted in more than 13,000 arrests nationwide (ICE, 2007). Calling them "sweeps" rather than raids, Immigration and Customs Enforcement officials claimed that their enforcement was only aimed at targeted fugitives who had overstayed their visas or who had ignored deportation orders. Yet, numerous eyewitness and news media accounts reported that this was not fully the case. The San Francisco Chronicle newspaper, in a January 23rd article reported that ICE agents, in addition to the so-called 119 immigrant criminals that they targeted in Contra Costa County, "also picked up 94 other undocumented immigrants they encountered in the process (Hendricks, 2007: B-8)." In an article by the Associated Press on January 23rd, where reporters rode along for the first day of the "sweeps" in Orange County, they reported that the agents "fanned out to houses in Anaheim and Santa Ana" and that the criminal fugitive that they arrested was merely a 29-year-old undocumented immigrant "wanted for a driving under the influence conviction (Flaccus, 2007)." At a second stop where the agents were looking for a "convicted rapist" (that had moved out weeks before) they, "instead, arrested six men who could not provide legal papers (Flaccus, 2007)." Timothy Aiken, deputy director of ICE in San Francisco, commented "We want to go after the worst of the worst; we go after people who have ignored a judge's order—but we can't be blind to someone who doesn't have lawful status in the U. S. We wouldn't be doing our job if we ignored these people (Hendricks, 2007: B-8)." By their own words, immigration officials admitted that their actions were random, creating a climate of fear and tension in immigrant communities. In the city of Pomona, there were various eyewitness accounts where immigration agents used the pretext of going after so-called "convicted fugitives" to stop and detain people randomly. For example, the husband of Pomona resident Maria Morales, a mother of two children, was picked up off the street as he walked to his job. In an incident near the Pomona Day Labor Center, ICE agents claim that they went to the area in search of a "criminal." Eyewitnesses, instead, saw them chase after immigrant workers who were looking for jobs in that area. Similar reports emerged from residents at a local apartment complex in Pomona where, under the pretext of looking for a "fugitive" began to knock on doors and arrest individuals randomly. These types of actions are confirmed as occurring in other parts of California by Jerry Okendo, President of the Northern California League of United Latin American Citizens chapter. He is quoted in the San Francisco Chronicle as criticizing ICE agents for carrying out "sweeps" in the cities of Concord and Richmond without "properly identifying themselves" and carrying out arrests without search warrants. According to Okedo, ICE agents "were sweeping through apartment complexes and picking up anyone who could not provide proof they were living in the United States legally (Hendricks, 2007: B-8)." Richmond City Councilman John Marquez complained that ICE agents "were identifying themselves as police" helping to break up the good relations that he said had been established between the police department and the Latino Community.

HISTORICAL PATTERN OF IMMIGRATION RAIDS

The character of these recent raids follow a historical pattern by the U. S. government to round up immigrants when the country is experiencing an economic downturn or when there are social conditions and cutbacks that need a scapegoat. When the economy went downward during the depression of the 1930s, for example, the U. S. Government gave consular offices the charge of deporting anyone who might add to the "public charge" numbers

(Bernard: 1998:67). During this period, at least half a million people of Mexican origin were put on trains and deported (Acuna: 2000: 220–225; Gonzales, 1999:146–149). In the early years of the depression, any Mexican-origin person who applied for welfare, unemployment, or any type of social service was forced to leave the country under the U.S. government category of "voluntary repatriation." Approximately half of those deported were U.S. citizens, a clear violation of both their civil and human rights.

Raising concerns over national security issues as a result of World War II, the U. S. government instituted the Smith Act in 1941 to deny visas and deport anyone who "might endanger the public safety (Bernard, 1998:67)." A similar bill, the Internal Security Act, was passed in 1950 to deport anyone suspected of being a member of the Communist Party or any of its affiliated organizations (Bernard: 1998:69).

When the U. S. entered World War II, and there was a need to fill labor shortages in agriculture, the federal government established the Bracero Program (Acuna, 2000: 285–289; Takaki: 1993: 391–392). The program was extended after the war as Public Law 78 and was justified as a means of meeting labor shortages caused by the Korean War. The program ended in 1964 with 5 million Mexicans used in the peak years between 1954 and 1962. With the establishment of a regulated labor pool, the United States Immigration and Naturalization Service began a massive drive known as "Operation Wetback" to deport undocumented immigrants to Mexico. Again, similar to the round-ups of immigrants during the depression, Operation Wetback grossly violated the civil rights of Mexican immigrants including those who were legally in the U. S. as citizens and permanent residents (Calavita, 1998). Hundreds of Mexican-origin people were arrested and harassed. They were threatened and forced to produce "proof" of their citizenship. Only a few of the thousands of those deported had formal hearings. When the project ended, more than a million persons had been deported to Mexico (Barrera, 1979: 116–30).

CONTEMPORARY CONDITIONS FOR RAIDS

In this contemporary period, on an international level, there is a movement of immigrants from poorer countries to more developed ones (Sutcliffe, 1993: 84–107). The response in the U. S. and in European countries has been twofold: on the one hand, the companies (and even some government officials) see the need for immigrants to fill employment voids (particularly when these countries are faced with an aging population). On the other hand, these countries do not want to acknowledge them as human beings with basic human rights.

There are "open borders" for multi-national corporations when it comes to investment, trade, and moving jobs (Sutcliffe, 1998). However, when it comes to the free migration of immigrants, the meaning of democracy does not exist. That is why there is a backlash to this meaning of democracy in Latin America where a growth in international investment has meant increasing unemployment and the forced removal of the peasantry from their rural lands to the urban cities (Gonzalez, 2001).

Up until September 11, 2001, there was a movement toward some form of legalization for the estimated 12 million undocumented immigrants in the U. S. However, after September 11th, the issue of immigration became a national security issue. The most significant measure was the passage of the USA Patriot Act which allowed wide latitude for law enforcement agencies to conduct searches, to use electronic surveillance, and to detain persons suspected of being terrorists. The act expanded the definition of "terrorists" for the purposes of removing any immigrants certified by the U. S. Attorney General as having engaged in terrorist activities (Hom, 24–26).

THE RAIDS AND NATIONAL SECURITY

It was in this climate that California experienced the recall of Governor Gray Davis in November, 2003 and where his opponents raised the specter of immigration as an issue of national security. One candidate Tom McLintock went as far as to promise that he would use the full strength of the National Guard to patrol the border. The eventual Governor Arnold Schwarzenegger, who had supported Proposition 187 (a ballot initiative to deny social services, health care, and public education to undocumented immigrants) and had been listed on the Board of an organization, U. S. English, that advocates the exclusive use of English in public institutions, used the issue of national security as a reason for turning down a bill that would have given immigrants the right to obtain a driver's license.

In accordance with this perspective, U. S. Border Patrol officials have argued that the immigration raids are connected to the "war on terrorism." When Tomas Jimenez of the Border Patrol, was asked by a Channel 54 reporter on the reasons for raids that were carried out in 2004, he responded that "the mission of the Border Patrol, the primary objective at this time, is to prevent the entering of terrorists and terrorist arms to the United States" (Noticiero, 2004).

In a meeting with various representatives of Latino organizations in the Inland Valley, Border Patrol officials agreed with Jimenez's assertions and proposed that the raids were about "intelligence gathering."

At the same time, the Border Patrol officials proposed that these raids were "routine" and not part of any change in national strategy. They proposed that the actions were only part of a local plan initiated by the officials in the Temecula office. The contradiction is that, when asked if they had the power to stop the raids, their response was that they needed to confer with the Deputy Director in the region and with "higher-ups" in Washington. Those "higher-ups," such as Department of Homeland Security Under Secretary Asa Hutchison, only backed off and tried to place the blame elsewhere when they were pressured by Congressional members of the Latino Caucus and massive demonstrations throughout California.

It is no coincidence that the 2004 raids took place a few months before the national elections. For, in addition to the long history of scapegoating immigrants during an economic downturn, this country has had a history of politicians attacking immigrants to get elected or re-elected. The most prominent example is that of California Governor Pete Wilson who, in 1994, in order to take the blame away from his administration for an ailing economy, created an image that immigrants were taking away jobs, ruining the schools, and overtaxing social services. He personally took the reins of Proposition 187 and used its momentum to get re-elected (Hayes-Bautista, 2004).

Similarly, before the election, President George Bush presented an immigration proposal that boiled down to nothing more than a contemporary revised "Bracero" program. On the other, President Bush had to simultaneously prove to the conservative wing of the Republican Party of his toughness on immigration.

Pressured to stop the raids in Southern California, the lower level officials consistently replied that they were in no position to stop the raids and that they had to confer "with Washington" higher-ups for any change in strategies.

Meanwhile, fifty Republican Congressmen, under the leadership of Colorado Congressman Tom Tancredo, signed a joint letter on June 26, 2004 praising the actions of the Border Patrol and urging Hutchison to continue the raids. In their letter, the lawmakers proposed that "this kind of interior enforcement is desperately needed across the country" . . . and that "the success of the unit operating from the Temecula station is ample evidence of the need for this activity nationwide" (Tancredo, 6/26/04).

As a follow-up to these actions, the conservative wing of the Republican Party ran openly one-issue anti-immigrant candidates against the Latino representatives, such as Congressman Joe Baca and Assemblywoman Gloria Negrete-McCloud, who openly opposed the raids. In California's sixty-first Assembly district, for example, a retired police officer Alan Wapner challenged incumbent Assemblywomen Negrete-McCloud through open support from California Governor Schwarzenegger and through the use of leaflets and press conferences that called for securing "our borders through beefed-up border patrols" and improving the "tracking of illegal aliens by linking governmental databases, births, deaths, and immigration status (Wapner for Assembly, 2004)."

ORGANIZED RESPONSE TO RAIDS

An important lesson in the aftermath of the immigration raids in 2004 and 2007 in the region—was the response by Mexican and Latino organizations.

Within a week of immigration raids in 2004, various organizations including Estamos Unidos, Hermandad Mexicana de Ontario, the Latina and Latino Roundtable, The Labor Council for Latin American Advancement (LCLAA) and the Riverside-based National Alliance for Human Rights came together and organized a seven-mile march calling for an immediate stop to the raids. The march, beginning in the city of Ontario and ending in Pomona, drew an estimated 10,000 participants. The Spanish language newspaper La Opinion called it the largest demonstration in the history of the Inland Valley region (Vega, 2004: 1). Joining the march were various Latino elected officials who played a role in pressuring Asa Hutchison to stop the raids. Congress Representatives Joe Baca and Hilda Solis took the lead in securing support from members of the House Committee on the Judiciary and the Congressional Hispanic Caucus for an emergency meeting with Hutchison. In a press statement on June 13, 2004, Congresswoman Hilda Solis raised her concerns to the U. S. Border Patrol in Washington, D. C. "about recent U. S. Border Patrol activity in Southern California that has led to great fear and confusion among residents throughout the region . . . about reports that the recent Border Patrol activity in Southern California included stops on Public Streets . . . about possible racial profiling."

In a letter dated June 18, 2004, members of the House Judiciary Committee wrote to U. S. Department of Homeland Security Secretary Tom Ridge "to immediately halt these ill-considered enforcement actions and work with us on undertaking those reforms of our immigration system that our nation so badly needs."

In response to these letters, Asa Hutchison met with Southern California representatives and admitted that the raids did not follow Department of Homeland Security policy (Baca, 6/25/04).

The continued coalition efforts helped to ensure the re-election of the various representatives, including Congressman Joe Baca and Gloria Negrete-McCloud, who had been the targets of statewide and national attacks by the right wing of the Republican Party.

Other marches in the ensuing years against immigration raids and legislative proposals aimed at criminalizing undocumented immigrants and their supporters resulted in broad coalitions taking to the streets in cities all across the country. On March 25, 2006, over a million people marched in Los

Angeles against H. R. 4437, a bill that would make it a felony to reside in the U. S. as an undocumented individual. As a result of the massive protests, the bill died in the U. S. Senate. In January, 2007, in response to the Operation Return to Sender Raids, a coalition of organizations including the Labor Council for Latin American Advancement (LOCLOAA), the Latina/o Roundtable, CHIRLA, the Latino Student Union, and the National Day Labor Organizing Network came together and organized a march of hundreds calling for an immediate stop to the raids. Five months later, on May 1, 2007, a coalition of thousands of immigrants and their supporters marched throughout Southern California, including the Inland Empire, in support of a comprehensive immigration bill and against the federal government's increase in immigration raids at the workplace and in targeted communities.

RISE OF A PROACTIVE ALTERNATIVE STRATEGY TO ENFORCEMENT

In advancing an alternative to the enforcement strategies advanced by Homeland Security, the Bush Administration, and right-wing conservative groups and politicians, a proactive trend has emerged that is focusing on policies to support of the legalization of immigrant workers.

On March 31, 2005, as part of a movement to support a new direction for immigration policy, the Tomas Rivera Policy Institute brought together a broad cross-section of immigration rights leaders in Los Angeles to discuss the impacts of border enforcement on Latino communities. The speakers included University of California Professor Wayne Cornelius who argued that the increased enforcement strategy of the U. S. government has only resulted in undocumented immigrants staying longer in the U. S., a higher percentage using the services of professional "coyotes," and an increasing number who have faced physical danger and vigilante activity associated with entry into the U. S. (Cornelius, 2004). At this same conference, immigration attorney Peter Shey, Executive Director of the Center for Human Rights and Constitutional Law, proposed the need for a movement that could pressure the U. S. government in enacting a reasonable statute of limitations for immigrants already in the country. In advocating that the immigrant rights movement organize proactively rather than defensively, Shey proposed putting an end to the backlog of immigrant applications already in process. According to Shey, "we are at an all-time high of 2.6 million pending applications, 1.8 million of which are 'relative' applications (Shey, 3/31/ 2005)."

In addition to organizing farm worker marches throughout the state to protest the immigration raids that took place in 2004 and 2007, the United Farm Worker's Union has spearheaded a coalition of over four hundred organizations, representing agriculture, business, church, and immigrant advocacy organizations in support of the Agricultural Job Opportunity, Benefits, and Security Act. The AgJobs legislation would grant half a million undocumented farm workers temporary legal status if they work at least one hundred days as farm laborers over an eighteen month period. If they work in agriculture for another 360 days during the next six years, they can apply for permanent residence status.

Various other coalitions, including the Latino/a Roundtable, LCLAA, the Inland Valley Coalition for Immigrant Rights, The UCLA Labor Center, and the Coalition for Humane Immigration Rights of Los Angeles (CHIRLA) have been advancing this proactive trend by organizing citizenship/voting registration drives and sponsoring forums on legalization legislation such as the Dream Act. The Dream Act would permit undocumented immigrant students who have grown up in the U. S. the rights to receive in-state tuition in all institutions of higher education and to apply for legal status.

CONCLUSION

Although immigration laws and raids are once again being used by the U. S. government and various politicians to attack immigrants as threats to the national security, the immigrant rights movement has seen the rise of a new trend that is not just reacting to attacks by the border patrol, right wing anti-immigrant groups, and nativist legislation. The immigrant rights movement has been effective in stopping immigration raids each time that they have emerged in various localities. At the same time, the movement has been effective in building coalitions that are uniting diverse groups and communities in advancing strategies and policies aimed at turning back the post-September 11th provisions that have increased the categories of "deportable" crimes and that have further criminalized undocumented workers. This emerging trend, demanding "legalization" for the 12 million undocumented immigrants in the U. S., has shown how a united proactive response can be effective in exposing the scapegoating of immigrants, mobilizing support for pro-immigrant legislative policies, and building broad community-based coalitions to defend the civil and human rights of all immigrants and their supporters.

REFERENCES

Acuna, Rodolfo. *Occupied America: A History of Chicanos, Fourth Edition.* Menlo Park, CA: Longman, 2000.

Bernard, William S. "Immigration: History of U. S. Policy." *Immigration Reader: America in a Multidisciplinary Perspective,* edited by David Jacobson. Malden Massachusetts: Blackwell Publishers, 1998.

Baca, Joe. "U. S. Congressman Joe Baca Representing California's 43rd District Undersecretary Hutchison: Border Patrol Procedures Not Followed in Sweeps." June 25, 2004.

Barrera, Mario. *Race and Class in the Southwest: A Theory of Racial Inequality.* Notre Dame, IN: University of Notre Dame Press, 1979.

Calavita, Kitty. "Gaps and Contradictions in U. S. Immigration Policy: An Analysis of Recent Reform Efforts." *Immigration Reader: America in a Multidisciplinary Perspective,* edited by David Jacobson. Malden Massachusetts: Blackwell Publishers, 1998.

Cornelius, Wayne. "Controlling Unwanted Immigration: Lessons from the United States, 1993–2004." *CCIS Working Paper Series.* San Diego, CA: University of California San Diego Center for Comparative Immigration Studies, December, 2004.

Flaccus, Gillian. "More Than 700 Arrested in Immigration Sweep in Los Angeles Area." *Associated Press* 23 Jan. 2007.

Gonzales, Manuel G... *Mexicanos: A History of Mexicans in the U.S...* Bloomington: Indiana University Press, 1999.

Gonzalez, Juan. "Free Trade: The Final Conquest of Latin America." *Harvest of Empire.* New York: Penguin Books, 2001.

Hayes-Bautista, David E. *La Nueva California: Latinos in the Golden State.* Berkeley: University of California Press, 2004: 125–136.

Hom, Howard. "The Immigration Landscape in the Aftermath of September 11." *Los Angeles Lawyer,* September, 2002: 23–26.

Noticiero. Azteca America Channel 54, Los Angeles, CA. (10 June 2004).

Sanchez, Linda, Howard Berman, John Conyers, Jr., Sheila Jackson Lee, Maxine Waters, Robert Wexler, Adam B. Schiff. "To Secretary U. S. Department of Homeland Security Tom Ridge." 18 June 2004 Congress of the United States Committee on the Judiciary.

Shey, Peter. "Looking to the Past to Inform the Future: What Can We Learn from Past Amnesty Programs?" Immigration and U. S. Citizenship in an Era of Homeland Security Conference. The Tomas Rivera Policy Institute and School of Policy Planning and Development, University of Southern California. Omni Hotel, Los Angeles. 31 March 2005.

Solis, Hilda. "News from Congresswoman Hilda L. Solis 32nd Congressional District of California." June 13, 2004.

Sutcliffe, Bob. "Immigration and the World Economy," *Creating a New World Economy: Forces of Change & Plans for Action,* edited by Gerald Epstein, Julie Graham, and Jessica Nembhard. Philadelphia: Temple University Press: 84–107.

Sutcliffe, Bob. "Freedom to Move in the Age of Globalization." *Globalization and Progressive Economic Policy,* edited by Dean Baker, Gerald Epstein and Robert Pollin. New York: Cambridge University Press, 1998: 325–336.

Takaki, Ronald. *A Different Mirror: A History of Multicultural America.* Boston: Little, Brown, and Company, 1993.

U. S. Immigration and Customs Enforcement. "Week-long ICE Operations Targeting Criminal Aliens and Illegal Alien Fugitives in the Southland Nets Record Arrests." January 23, 2007.

Vega, Miguel Angel. "Migrantes Reclaman Justicia." *La Opinion* (14 June 2004): 1.

Chapter Fourteen

Linking Critical Democratic Pedagogy, Multiculturalism, and Service Learning to a Project-Based Approach[1]

José Zapata Calderón and Gilbert R. Cadena

As colleges become more diverse, new strategies are being developed to reflect the changing communities around them. The use of creative project-based methodologies in developing connections between critical democratic pedagogy, service learning, and multiculturalism are seen as new models for meeting the needs of a diverse student body as well as ensuring the involvement of the community in that process (Judkins & LaHurd, 1999; Wallace, 2000). This chapter provides examples of these linkages in classes taught by the authors during the academic year 2004–2005, in the diverse settings of California State Polytechnic University-Pomona (Cal Poly Pomona) and the city of Pomona.[2]

In collaborating to build connections between critical democratic pedagogy, service learning, and multiculturalism, the authors sought to apply an approach that could overcome the limits of a quarter system.[3] In this process, the authors collaborated in designing and implementing courses that celebrated the contributions of individuals and groups who have been marginalized or excluded from mainstream historical texts. At the same time, as part of these courses, the authors developed dialogue around specific readings that connected to the issues being faced by local communities. This analysis and dialogue was followed up with the application of a service-learning pedagogy that was collectively developed alongside community partners using various participatory action and research (PAR) methodologies (Mora & Diaz, 2004). Ultimately, this led to some form of action in the classroom and in the community that resulted in various community-building outcomes.

Projects that involved the students and faculty from various classes connected the classes and the class content. This project approach used the readings in the classroom to help inform the students about the work that they were carrying out in the community.[4] At the same time it allowed for collaboration between faculty, students, and community partners.

The project-based approach, as developed by Randy Stoecker in his book *Research Methods for Community Change*, develops out of a perspective of trying to understand the participants "we are working with, what is happening to them, and what they can do about the problems that are affecting them" (Stoecker, 2005, p. 5). This type of participatory research and involvement emerges from a question that comes from the participants themselves regarding a problem that they would like to resolve. In this process, the participants follow some of the basic steps that are part of the project-based approach. That is, they begin by discussing a problem, analyzing how they will deal with the problem, implementing a plan of action, carrying out the action, and evaluating the results.

Although the authors developed the intersections between these different aspects in each class, the article is divided into sections that accentuate the application of critical democratic pedagogy in relation to the *matricula* service project as part of the Ethnic Immigration and Chicano/Latino Contemporary Issues classes, the project-based research approach in the Grant Writing and Christmas Parade projects in the Community and Culture and Community Service Learning classes, and the emphasis on multiculturalism in the Agbayani and Alternative Spring Break projects as part of the Rural and Urban Social Movements and Community Service Learning classes.

CRITICAL DEMOCRATIC PEDAGOGY
AND THE MATRICULA SERVICELEARNING PROJECT

In our classes, we practice what Ira Shor, in his book *Empowering Education*, calls a critical democratic pedagogy for self and social change. This approach works to develop a student-centered classroom that involves both the teachers and students in the "habits of inquiry and critical curiosity about society, power, inequality, and change" (Shor, 1992, p. 15). At the same time, it follows with the critical-holistic paradigm that is based on empowering community participants to "help themselves by raising their level of consciousness about their problems and the societal causes and remedies available" (Wright, 2000, p. 8r6). Hence, this approach combines the creation of a democratic space for dialogue and inquiry in the classroom as part of working alongside community participants to advance models of "social action and social change for the purpose of achieving social justice" (Strand et al., 2003, p. 8). This type of service learning requires faculty to challenge their traditional control of the classroom and to have confidence that their students will empower themselves to complete their projects. With preparation and experience, faculty contributes to the structure of service-learning projects while simultaneously recognizing the role that students and community partners have in developing their specific interests and outcomes (Dardar, 2002; Horton & Freire, 1990; Shor, 1992). Although this type of pedagogy inherently includes ambiguity and uncertainty, the stress and benefits are ultimately created and shared by the students and community partners involved in the process.

In the fall quarter we taught two courses that exemplified this approach. In the courses, Ethnic Immigration (see Appendix 4.A) and Chicano/Latina Contemporary Issues, we structured our classes as "learning circles" that promoted dialogue and critical thinking about the assigned readings. We used the "critical democratic pedagogy" approach that placed topical issues and academic themes in the context of the lived experiences of the students. Simultaneously, we involved the students in choosing service-learning sites that best fit their interests and the themes of the classes. [5]

From our classes, students learned material that helped them to understand the plight of immigrant workers, which helped them to carry out their particular service-learning projects. One student, for example, reflected on the meaning of participation as tied to the ideas of Paulo Freire:

> Community involvement can be very deceiving when people do not grasp an understanding or passion for what they are doing. The important part is not to simply give your time as a form of volunteering but instead giving your thoughts and efforts into creating change within that organization or movement. I like how Paulo Freire proposed, in *Pedagogy of the Oppressed*, that the solution for the oppressed is not to "integrate" them into the structure of oppression, but to transform the structure so that they can become "beings for themselves." (Rocio Navarro, major in Gender, Ethnicity, Multicultural Studies, and Sociology)

At the same time, a group of students attended Friday morning meetings at the Pomona Day Labor Center. At these meetings, the workers and students held discussions on developing new employment opportunities and dealing with employers who refused to pay the workers. The Mexican Consulate contacted the Pomona Day Labor Center and proposed the idea of holding a consular mobile-clinic service day for the purpose of having immigrants apply for and obtain consular-approved identification cards (called *matriculas*); one of the Friday meetings was devoted to organizing this project. In this meeting, the workers and students discussed the importance of obtaining a *matricula consular* card that was officially recognized by the Mexican government and various cities and law enforcement agencies throughout the country. Further, they discussed the "need" to have a *matricu-*

la card to help them to open bank accounts, cash checks, send remittances abroad, and to defend their human rights.

From this initial meeting, our students began the process of creating a larger coalition by reaching out to community-based groups and churches in the region. Meeting at the Cal Poly Pomona Downtown Center, the coalition included students from the classes of the two authors, representatives from the Mexican Consulate, students from the Claremont Colleges, the Inland Valley/San Gabriel Valley Latino/a Roundtable, the Latino Chamber of Commerce, Our Lady of Assumption Church, Our Lady of Guadalupe Church, and the Pomona Day Labor Center.

As part of their participation, our students joined various committees where they worked alongside other members of the coalition in providing logistical support to the Mexican Consulate: writing press releases, obtaining donations, distributing leaflets at churches, and recruiting students to plan day care activities. As the organizing developed, students summarized their experiences in the classroom and implemented outreach contact to other groups on campus.

The success of the organizing effort was best exemplified by the 300 immigrants who were already standing in line at four in the morning.[6] Ultimately, out of 1,000 immigrants that showed up to apply, 550 applicants were able to obtain their *matricula* identification card on the same day. Just as impressive were the organizing efforts of the students from our classes who used the medium of art to involve the children of the immigrants in sketching, drawing, and face painting. Other students helped in creating a festival atmosphere to the service day. Eddie Cortez, mayor of Pomona, and Angela Sanbrano, director of the immigrant rights organization CARECEN, spoke on the need to build coalitions that could advance the successful legalization and integration of all immigrant families in the United States.

After the event, the workers and students evaluated the project and summarized that the organizational effort had gone beyond any of their expectations. The large turnout, they proposed, showed how hungry immigrant families were for having some type of identification that would make it easier to survive in U.S. society. Although both the students and day laborers described the day as a means of service to the immigrant community, they also characterized it as one more tool for the workers to defend themselves.

In this context, the *matricula* card took on a special significance, immigrant workers being treated as human beings. The meaning that the workers attached to the *matricula* card was one of human rights, and therefore it was viewed as a material act in the process of obtaining social justice. Nationally, although nine states are accepting the *matricula* card, there has been stated opposition to the use of the card by various political representatives, government officials, and political organizations. Nevertheless, in a vote of 222 to 177, the U.S. House of Representatives voted in September 2004 to support the use of the *matricula consular* to open bank accounts (Immigrants' Rights Update, 2004). While pro-immigrant groups support the *matricula* as a means of advancing democratic rights for new immigrants, those opposed to its use see it as one more obstacle in the battle to curtail "illegal" immigration and to ensure national security.

Overall, the *matricula* service day represented a larger struggle as to whether immigrant workers, and especially undocumented workers, will have access to some of the same basic democratic and human rights that other citizens have. The creation of a project for these basic rights began with an environment in the classroom where dialogue broke down barriers of authority between the students and professors. It was further advanced with readings that introduced students to the underlying reasons why immigrants were being forced out of their homelands to be used as cheap labor in the more developed countries. This practice was reinforced with the Friday meetings at the day labor center where day laborers raised their concerns and the students listened. In the process, the workers and students expanded a democratic space that came to include a coalition of community groups. In the end, the *matricula* service day created another democratic space for hundreds of immigrant workers who saw the *matricula* as part of one more step in gaining more equality and a voice in U.S. society.

PROJECT-BASED RESEARCH IN GRANT WRITING AND CHRISTMAS PARADE PROJECTS

In the winter academic quarter, the authors involved their students in collaborations that used aspects of the project-based research approach. This approach, part of implementing a community-based research strategy, involves students, faculty, and community members in social change projects based on finding alternative solutions to community problems (Strand et al., 1993).

In implementing this approach, Professor Calderón and a group of students met with the Pomona day laborers at one of their weekly Friday meetings to discuss the obstacles that the workers were confronting in their efforts to develop their own day laborer advocacy organization.

One of the day laborers, Samuel, explained that the workers had formed an organization of day laborers that had begun to meet on Wednesday evenings. Another worker expressed that the workers had also elected a group of four officers for the organization but that they were having difficulties in making agendas, implementing rules, ensuring minutes, and facilitating the meetings. After analyzing the problem, the workers proposed that the officers and members of the group needed more training in how to run an organization. At the same time, the workers insisted that no one had the time to get trained. They settled on the idea of finding resources for one of the day labor leaders to get trained so that he could, in turn, train the others. In the course of this discussion, Professor Calderón and the students were tapped as a resource for writing a grant proposal with the specific purpose of hiring and training a day laborer organizer. This was an example where the workers and students engaged in a discussion about a problem of significant importance to the day labor center and worked together to find a mutual solution and plan of action. Together, the workers, the professor, and the students proposed that it would be beneficial to write a proposal to hire an organizer from the ranks of the day laborers themselves. The workers proposed that this individual could be trained by IDEPSCA, a southern California popular education organization, or by the National Day Laborer Network. The process of writing a grant proposal began out of an identified need. In this process, the students carried out service-learning projects at the center, attended the weekly Friday meetings of the workers, and worked with Professor Calderón in writing a grant proposal with the input of the workers. Reflecting on the experience of writing a grant alongside the workers, one of our students commented:

> I did not know how to draft a grant, but the other students did not know either, so it was a learning process for all of us. In the grant we focused on how the services provided at the center promote social change at the level of empowering workers. It has been a great learning experience and an opportunity to realize that an individual can make a difference and be a part of social justice, not only for immigrants, but for all humanity. I have been inspired to continue work with the organization and in the future to do volunteer work overseas. I have also learned firsthand the reasons why immigrants come to this country and that the myths about immigrants are false (Analisa Alvarez, major in sociology).

By the end of the quarter, a grant proposal was written to the Liberty Hill Foundation that led to two seed grants totaling $20,000. The seed grants laid the foundation for the hiring and training of a day laborer organizer and the development of a day laborer advocacy organization. The final phase included the direct involvement of the workers in telling their stories to the foundation representatives who carried out interviews as part of the final phase of the review process.

As described through this example, the collaborative and participatory nature of project-based research does not fit into a traditional model where the purpose is primarily to serve the interests of the expert. Research as action brings the community participants to the center stage of the process by sharing their experiences, deepening the understanding of their experiences through dialogue, and reflecting on those experiences as a means of developing a plan of action for change (Stoecker, 2005). While service is part of the research process, the difference is that this type of research is "trying to create some difference in real people's lives, and the research exists in the service of that effort" (Stoecker, 2005, p. 8). In this type of research, "the outcomes of the project, not the results of the research, are most important. The research is important but only in the context of the project" (Stoecker, 2005, p. 14).

Another good example of a project that emerged out of a problem and involved all the steps in a project-based research approach was the Day Laborer Christmas Parade Project, which involved students from our classes in the fall quarter.

Panchito, a 75-year-old day laborer, brought a "research question" to a weekly meeting of the day laborers and students. After citing a letter to the editor that referred to day laborers as "criminals," he asked the day laborers and students, "Why do they hate us? We work hard and don't bother anyone, but why do they hate us?" Various workers responded from their own experiences. One worker responded that some of the parishioners at his church, although Latino, truly believed that immigrants were taking the jobs away from residents. Another worker proposed that it was the fault of the politicians who always blamed the immigrants for any downturns in the economy. A heated dialogue developed when one worker suggested that the day laborers were to blame "because you are not as smart as the white man." This last assertion was completely discounted by all the day laborers present. Eventually, the workers agreed that the media and the politicians portrayed the day laborers as taking jobs and services away from the residents. They agreed that this was contrary to their own experiences of being needed by many employers, taking the jobs that no one else wanted, and contributing much to the economy through their work and payment of taxes.

After sharing and analyzing their experiences, the workers and students discussed a plan for reaching out to the community at large. One worker proposed the idea of marching in the annual Pomona Christmas Parade. At first, the idea was laughed at by the other workers. One of the students from our classes questioned whether the action would be perceived as a protest against the parade. The mood became more serious when one of the workers, a known day-labor carpenter, responded that this was the season of Christmas and that "Jesus was a carpenter like myself." When this worker spoke, the eyes of all the other workers lit up, and one after the other offered to bring their tools. As the workers deepened their analysis for reaching out, the students joined in the excitement by volunteering to make a leaflet describing the day labor center, explaining the reasons why the day laborers were marching, and collaborating on a banner that could be carried at the front of the procession. The leaflet, passed out to thousands of spectators on the parade route, included a summary of the day laborers' conclusions as to why they were marching:

As day laborers, we are walking in the Christmas parade asking the residents of Pomona to open their hearts in the spirit of the holidays. Remembering that Joseph and Mary walked door to door at this time of year, we are walking, tools in hand, searching for an open door in the form of jobs—so that we can provide for our families. We ask you to open your hearts by providing work and we are grateful for your support.

On the day of the parade, forty-five workers turned out in their work clothes holding hammers, saws, paintbrushes, shovels, rakes, and other tools.[7] Two workers carried a banner in the front of the procession that read "Pomona Day Labor Center." Eight students divided up 4,000 leaflets and began to pass them out to the spectators as the day laborers made their way down the street. The success of the action was expressed in the applause that the workers received from the crowds gathered throughout the route of the parade. A month after the parade, when workers and students gathered to evaluate the results of the action, day laborer Eduardo Nuno summarized that the march and leafleting were very positive and had resulted in a sharp increase in the number of jobs for workers.

Similarly, a Latina first-generation student shared the positive lessons that she had learned from her participation:

I learned that when a community is united and organized, a more effective change can occur. This has helped me to appreciate my community more. The laborers that I have met and spoken with do not have an academic education or speak English. Despite their limited education, they are very wise and have proved to me their wisdom and knowledge of life and how to be a leader in the community. (Maria Guzman, major in sociology)

As shown by this action, the nontraditional character of research can emerge in forms that are nonacademic but help to advance unique bridges of civic and democratic participation. In this example, a community-based research style emerged where a problem was identified, a solution was agreed upon, a plan was implemented, and there was an evaluation of the results in the end.

MULTICULTURALISM AND THE AGBAYANI AND ALTERNATIVE SPRING BREAK PROJECTS

The challenge in our classes was also to ensure multiculturalism as a key aspect of the readings, projects, and actions. We began by finding spaces for practicing a type of multiculturalism that could involve our students in "shifting" their "center of thinking so as to include previously silenced voices" and to implement projects that could place at center stage the experiences of oppressed groups that have been historically excluded by the "power and privilege" of others (Andersen & Collins, 2004, pp. 15–17).

One project that emerged from our classes in social movements and community service learning involved 25 students learning about the role that Filipino farm workers played in the development of the United Farm Workers (UFW) Union in California. In this example, after students read about the history of Cesar Chavez and the United Farm Workers (UFW) movement, our students visited the sites and met with the leaders that they had read about. As part of an "Alternative Spring Break" in La Paz (Keene, California), the students stayed at Agbayani Village, a retirement housing complex for elderly retired Filipino farm workers, located in Delano.[8] The 60- unit village is named after Paulo Agbayani, a Filipino farm worker who died on the picket line in 1967 (Scharlin & Villanueva, 1994). The village was constructed brick by brick through the labor of students and farm workers between 1969 and 1974. At one time, 61 Filipino farm workers who had been evicted from the labor camps during the 1965 grape strike lived in the complex (Ferris & Sandoval, 1997).

Today, all the Filipinos have passed away and their new replacements are primarily Mexican-origin retired farm workers. Agbayani also has a memorial room set aside where Cesar Chavez slept during his 36-day fast in 1988. The experience of our students sleeping there was itself an education on the history of the farm worker movement and the coalitions that developed between the diverse ethnic groups. At the same time, our students had the opportunity to listen to the stories of the farm worker movement from Cesar Chavez's bodyguards, a Filipino and former mayor of Delano, a farmworker woman who had been wounded on the picket line, and the contemporary leaders of the United Farm Worker's Union. One of our students, a female Latina senior, explained that the experience of meeting these leaders had helped her to understand their "passion for what they did" and "the pitfalls that they had to face" (Andrea Serrata, major in gender, ethnicity, and multicultural studies). Another student, of mixed Asian Pacific and Latina background, reflected that the experience had taught her the significance of the farm worker's history in promoting unity among diverse groups: "One of the largest issues that arose in the Civil Rights Movement was the inability for the people to respect that the movement was not only a movement based on people of color but also included women's struggles and gay rights" (Amy Tam, major in sociology and gender, ethnicity, and multicultural studies).

In the course of carrying out service projects, our students were introduced to a room at Agbayani decorated with numerous pictures of the Filipino elderly who had lived in the complex. These pictures were not organized in any sequence and lacked any historical labeling or content. The director of the center, an elderly farm worker woman who had been a leader in the first strikes called by the UFW in the early 1970s, explained the role of the

Filipino farm workers while pointing to each picture. In an ensuing discussion with the students, the director raised the need to frame and label the pictures of the Filipino farm workers with a history of each individual's contributions to the farm worker movement. In order to implement service that came out of this need, the students measured the size of each photograph. They took the measurements back with them and developed a plan for returning and framing some of the pictures.

When the students returned to Cal Poly, they took the lead in organizing a Cesar Chavez commemoration week that included a panel on the history of the Filipino farm workers, a Cesar Chavez breakfast honoring UFW co-founder Dolores Huerta, a city proclamation, and a four-mile pilgrimage walk from Pomona city hall to Cesar Chavez park.[9] One of the Filipino students who participated in the Alternative Spring Break returned from La Paz and formed the Agbayani Organizing Committee to help follow through on the picture framing historical project. In advancing the commitments made to this project, students from our spring classes in Rural and Urban Social Movements and Community Service Learning returned to Agbayani in the spring quarter to document more stories about the Filipino elders, to frame their pictures, and to mount them on the village's walls.[10]

As shown through the Alternative Spring Break and Agbayani project, the practice of multiculturalism and participatory research can be combined out of something as tangible as the framing of pictures and the researching of the histories of those in the pictures. Other forms that followed with this included the use of skits, drumming, and "*teatro*" presentations. On the last evening of the Alternative Spring Break, the students summarized their experiences at La Paz through teatro presentations to the farm worker community. They also used the arts of drumming, music, and dance as a form of reciprocity and as a means of sharing their traditional and nontraditional multicultural talents with the larger UFW community.

CONCLUSION

Overall, this chapter has presented examples of campus and community collaborations that have resulted in the diagnosing and implementation of creative plans of action to achieve diverse forms of social justice and social change outcomes.

Through the application of the project-based approach, the authors and their students worked alongside day laborers, farm workers, and community-based organizations in defining the specific problems being confronted and implementing service-learning projects to find alternatives to those problems or issues.

In analyzing the participatory outcomes as lessons learned, the results of these projects have advanced the concept of "multiple layering": the intersection between various classes, professors, campus organizations, and community partners working on simultaneous projects. This chapter has highlighted some examples of these intersections, whose successes were achieved through the synergy of several campus entities including faculty from the Ethnic and Women's Studies Department, professional staff from the Cesar Chavez Center, students from various classes, members from the Weglyn Endowed Chair committee, and student leaders from various campus organizations. Off campus, the coalition efforts have involved collaboration with various community partners ranging from the San Gabriel/Pomona Valley Latino Roundtable and the United Farm Worker's Union to the Mexican Consulate, Park West High School, and the Pomona City Council.

In addition to creating models of social change, these collaborations with immigrant and farm workers have brought to center stage the culture and history of those that have been excluded. This has been accomplished through the consistent and conscious use of cultural productions (such as music, theater, dance, photography, signage, and banner making) to achieve social justice outcomes that have contributed to the faculty and students' passion for service learning. After being involved in many of the various projects, student Maná Guzman commented on this increased passion:

> Through my participation . . . I have also acquired leadership skills, self-confidence, political and social awareness of the injustices occurring in my communities. My commitment to my community has grown because of my knowledge and belief that anything is possible. My desire to go back and help my community stems from my passion and strength in the belief that the unity of a people, of an organized group of committed people, can fight for a common cause.

Overall, the collaborative work on common projects, as described in this chapter, has contributed to a type of dialogic democratic teaching and learning that has engaged the students and community participants in building diverse coalitions, tapping unheard voices, and creating a culture of action for social justice and social change.

NOTES

1. Copyright Acknowledgement: This chapter was previously published in the following: *Race, Poverty, and Social Justice.* Calderón (ed.) co-authored with Gilbert Cadena. Herndon, VA: Stylus Publishing, 2007.

2. Cal Poly Pomona is located about 30 miles east of Los Angeles. The city of Pomona represents some of the demographic changes taking place throughout California. The city of Pomona has grown from 131,723 in 1990 to 149,473 in the year 2000, a 13.5% change. The population changes between 1990 and 2000 have resulted in Latinos growing in numbers from

54.3% (77,776) to 64.5% (96,370), the population of Asian Pacific Islanders increasing from 6.9% (9,846) to 7.2% (10,765), African Americans decreasing from 14.4% (19,013) to 9.6% (14,398), and EuroAmericans decreasing from 25.6% (36,687) to 17% (25,348) (U.S. Bureau of the Census, 1990, 2000). Cal Poly Pomona is considered one of the most diverse campuses in the United States, with 40% Asian and Pacific Islander, 26% Latino, 4% African American, less than 1% Native American, and 30% Euro-American, Middle Eastern, and others. The mission statement of the university reflects a commitment to connect "theory and practice in all disciplines" and to prepare students "for lifelong learning, leadership, and careers in a changing multicultural world" (Cal Poly Pomona Catalog, 2003, p. 14). This campus and city setting in southern California provides an important context for creating multiethnic partnerships and projects.

3. Some of the obstacles in developing service learning classes and cultivating community partnershps in CSU campuses on the quarter system include the 10-week quarter, a high percentage of students working more than 20 hours per week, and a commuter campus environment. Faculty members also have a course load of three classes per quarter with ongoing pressure to increase their full-time equivalent (FTE). To help overcome these barriers, the Offices of Community Service Learning on each CSU campus are attempting to assist faculty, community partners, and students in institutionalizing service learning throughout the curriculum and providing needed support.

4. Some of the readings, in addition to introducing students to community-based research approaches, also included traditional methodologies for gathering and coding field notes, writing final papers, developing senior capstone projects, and presenting at service-learning and academic association conferences.

5. Students had a choice of suggested sites and projects. Ultimately, this included 12 students from the Chicano/Latino Contemporary Issues class and 12 from the Ethnic Immigration class who worked on the *matricula* service-learning project.

6. The *matricula* service day took place October 9, 2004.

7. The parade took place on December 4, 2004.

8. The Alternative Spring Break was held in La Paz and Delano, California, March 18–21, 2005.

9. Various planning meetings were held at Agbayani Village and La Paz with the students, where they made commitments to continue working in all these service-learning projects during the spring quarter.

10. Presently, students are continuing to carry out research on this history and have already returned to Delano to frame more of the remaining pictures.

REFERENCES

Andersen, M. L., & Collins, P. H. (2004). *Race, class, and gender*. Belmont, CA: Wadsworth.

Cal Poly Pomona Catalog 2003–2005. (2003). Pomona, CA: California State Polytechnic University.

Dardar, A. (2002). *Reinventing Paulo Freire: A pedagogy of love*. Boulder, CO: Westview Press.

Ferris, S., & Sandoval, R. (1997). *The fight in the fields: Cesar Chavez and the Farmworkers Movement*. Orlando, FL: Paradigm Productions.

Horton, M., & Freire, P. (1990). *We make the road by walking: Conversations on education and social change*. Philadelphia: Temple University Press.

Immigrants' Rights Update (2004, September 21). Vol. 18, No. 6.

Judkins, B. M., & LaHurd, R. A. (1999). Addressing the changing demographics of academia and society. *American Behavioral Scientist, 42*(5), 786–789.

Mora, J., & Diaz, D. R. (2004). *Latino social policy: A participatory research model*. Binghamton, NY: The Haworth Press.

Scharlin, C., & Villanueva, L. V. (1994). *Philip Vera Cruz: A personal history of Filipino immigrants and the farmworkers movement*. Los Angeles: UCLA Labor Center, Institute of Industrial Relations.

Shor, I. (1992). *Empowering education: Critical teaching for social change*. Chicago: The University of Chicago Press.

Stoecker, R. (2005). *Research methods for community change: A project-based approach*. Thousand Oaks, CA: Sage.

Strand, K., Marullo, S., Cutforth, N., Stoecker, R., & Donahue, P. (2003). *Community-based research and higher education*. San Francisco: Jossey-Bass.

U.S. Bureau of the Census. (1990, 2000). *Statistical Abstract*. Washington, DC.

Wallace, J. (2ooo). A popular education model for college in community. *American Behavioral Scientist*, 43(5), 756–766.

Wright, M. G. M. (2000). A critical-holistic paradigm for an interdependent world. *American Behavioral Scientist*, 43(5), 808–824.

Chapter Fifteen

Civic Engagement

A Tool for Building Democracy[1]

José Zapata Calderón

More than ever, there is a need to build a society that is inclusive of many voices, that allows for democratic decision making, and that opens the doors for our diverse communities to be involved in and knowledgeable about the issues they are facing. Teacher education can serve such a role, but presently, there is the reality of a top-down authoritarian trend that is being forced on our school systems. To turn this trend around will take the courage and energy of educators to promote and create prototypes of a type of learning based on creating democratic spaces of engagement in the classroom, in the community, and in the larger society.

With the growth of a global economy, there is the need for a type of educational system that promotes civic engagement as a means of building new models toward a democratic society. Our present educational system, unfortunately, is going back to the days of reproducing individuals to fit a more authoritarian philosophy. The norm is to move toward a managerial "banking" system, where the power of disseminating knowledge is being transferred to the needs of the business and political establishments. This shift fits into the early 20th-century industrial model of schools where students were socialized in assembly-like rows to be taught the status quo and not to be heard from. With the promotion of standardized tests and quantitative methods that evaluate the performances of teachers and students, there is a diminishing of the space for the creation of democratic bridges between the classroom (and what is being learned therein) and the challenges of democratic decision making in our communities. This trend is characterized by the growth of charter schools and for-profit companies who are redefining the meaning of education. Rather than tapping the passionate reason why so many college graduates become teachers, this trend vilifies teachers and forces many to turn away from the educational world as a career. Instead of an educational system where the teachers are students and the students are teachers, the trend is to position the teachers as the "experts and subjects" and the students as mere "objects" whose minds are to be filled with the wisdom of authors chosen by other and by teachers approved or ratified by top-down bureaucratic administrators, politicians, and so-called choice corporate interests.

With so many problems being faced by our society, there is the opportunity for our schools and colleges to play a role in advancing new forms of research, learning, and practice that can help engage our teachers, faculty, and students in critical thinking and problem solving to find solutions to those problems. This type of learning will help develop a citizenry and a leadership in the future that is more engaged and excited about participating in making the future society. There are all types of studies that show how much students benefit from connecting their learning in the classroom to community engagement: Not only do their grades improve, but they develop principles of collectivity that go against the grain of individualism. Such engagement also enhances their skills in working with diverse populations, taking leadership, creating new knowledge, and formulating solutions to real-world problems.

There is a tendency in our schools to focus on a type of service engagement that is separated from having students learn about the foundations of the social issues and problems they are working on. If this aspect is dominant, a type of civic engagement can be advanced that serves merely to perpetuate the inequalities that are already prevalent. Without an education that looks at the systemic and structural foundations of social problems, students are taught the symptoms of the problems, instead of understanding the character of the structure that is placing individuals in those conditions. Involving students only in charity work may have the reverse effect of creating a form of what is incorrectly called "community engagement" work that results in creating spaces that are the opposite of creating a more democratic and just society.

The type of teaching that is needed in this contemporary period is one where there is a passion for creating spaces of equity; where students are exposed to a curriculum that not just deals with the problems in the society but looks at the systemic and structural aspects of inequity; that brings to center stage the contributions of communities who have historically been excluded from our textbooks (because of poverty, racism, sexism, classism, or homophobia); and that involves students working alongside excluded communities on common projects to implement transformative social change.

Rather than a traditional monocultural education where the students learn very little about the contributions of the diverse mosaic that comprises the people of this country, our educational system needs to support a multicultural learning environment in which differences are embraced (not just tolerated). In this context, our institutions do need to appreciate our historical pluralism. But there is no getting around the reality that U.S. pluralism had its origins in laws and ideologies that were used to justify the stratification of different groups through conquest, slavery, and exploitation. If we do not absorb and appreciate this aspect of history in all its manifestations, there is the danger that we will maintain a society that blames the victim for his or her lack of social mobility.

Rather than frontally assaulting the national dilemma of restructuring the economy with policies that invest in education and development, energy has been diverted toward seeking someone to blame. In the debate over the state of our educational system, many taxpayers have been led to believe that the issue is only about the quality of our teachers and not about the structural inequities that many of our underrepresented students and their families confront every day in their communities.

As we seek to develop models of civic engagement in teacher education, it is important for us to look toward new ways of carrying out democratic forms of learning and curriculum building in our classrooms that connect to new models of building democratic participation in our communities. Our beginning to dialogue on these new models may help us to understand how the engagement of our school/campus and community partnerships can move beyond top-down bureaucratic structures of volunteerism (or charity) to a level of civic engagement that advances a more democratic and socially just culture in civil society.

NOTE

1. Copyright Acknowledgement: This chapter was previously published in the following: Teacher Education and Practice, Vol. 24, No.3, (Summer, 2011).

Chapter Sixteen

Perspective-Taking as a Tool for Building Democratic Societies[1]

José Zapata Calderón

When I came to the United States from Mexico with my parents as a seven-year-old child, I did not fit into my "English only" school system. In my new homeland, others rarely took the time to see the world through my eyes or to learn about me, my culture, and my family. They often perceived me as mute or as having physical or psychological problems. Only when a teacher, Mrs. Elder, reached out to get to know me did someone realize that I just didn't know English. Mrs. Elder took steps to learn about my world, visiting me and my grandparents in our home. Seeing that we lived in a one-room house—a converted gas station with no indoor bathroom, no appliances, and a wood stove—Mrs. Elder responded with empathy, sacrificing her afternoons to teach me English. What's more, in seeking to create a similarity between us, she began our lessons by asking me to teach her Spanish. Thus we became teacher-student and student-teacher. I am sure that if Mrs. Elder had not fostered this equitable environment, if she had not sought to see the world through my eyes, I would not be a professor at Pitzer College today.

As my experience shows, the ability to communicate one's perspective affects one's ability to participate in society, and with it, one's access to power. Certain individuals or groups have the power to define dominant culture, and therefore the power to oppress or liberate others. Power exists in language, too, where words create a foundation for understanding. In fact, many governments have used language to oppress others. When the Treaty of Guadalupe Hidalgo was signed to end the US-Mexican war, it included legal protections that Mexican-origin people living in the United States held by custom and culture, including language rights and property rights. But after 1848, the treaty was broken when Mexican-origin people faced language discrimination, resulting in losses of land and of democratic access. Thus the value of perspective-taking lies in part in its relationship not only to power, but also to democracy.

PERSPECTIVE-TAKING AND DEMOCRATIC ENGAGEMENT

In *The Drama of Diversity and Democracy*, the Association of American Colleges and Universities brought these two terms—power and democracy—together. The publication defined democracy as "the ideal that all human beings have equal value, deserve equal respect, and should be given equal opportunity to fully participate in the life and direction of the society" (1995, 9). It also proposed that "when diversity is characterized by patterned inequity and the marginalization of specific groups," it "can signify unequal access to political, economic, social, and cultural power" (9).

Barack Obama began to question this very relationship between democracy and power when pondering what to do after college. As he read about the sacrifices ordinary people made during the civil rights movement, he imagined himself in their place, as a Student Nonviolent Coordinating Committee worker "convincing a family of sharecroppers to register to vote," or as an organizer of the Montgomery bus boycott (Obama 2004, 134). In doing so, he formed a commitment beyond himself: a commitment to listening to the perspectives of others (134–35). When he became an organizer and placed himself in others' worlds, he deepened this commitment, empowering himself to empower others.

When his fellow community organizers became tired, Obama had them look out of their office windows while asking, "What do you suppose is going to happen to those boys out there?. . . . You say you're tired, the same way most folks out here are tired. . . . Who's going to make sure [those boys] get a fair shot?" (Obama 2004, 171–72). He challenged the organizers to place themselves in others' worlds. It was no coincidence that storytelling and listening to the stories of others later became cornerstones of Obama's presidential campaign. Through storytelling, campaign organizers recruited thousands of new leaders whom they trained to use their life histories and those of their communities to reach out to the voting public.

By learning to understand others' perspectives, language, and culture, Barack Obama not only improved democratic participation, but also became better able to understand himself, his family's history, and the languages, cultures, and perspectives of community members with whom he worked. His experience became a lesson for campaign organizers in the value of understanding the language and culture of those they sought to recruit. It is also a lesson for those of us who are connecting our classrooms with social change efforts in diverse communities. Through perspective-taking, we can better comprehend and appreciate each other's differences in order to find our commonalities.

PERSPECTIVE-TAKING AND LEADERSHIP

Perceiving the similarities between their own experiences and those of others led Rosa Park to sit at the front of a bus, Martin Luther King to advocate for sanitation workers in Memphis, and Cesar Chavez to live with farm workers in the San Joaquin Valley. It led writer Gloria Anzaldúa to perceive sexism and homophobia in American culture and in her own border culture, and it led psychologists Mamie and Kenneth Clark to understand why black children saw black dolls as ugly and white dolls as beautiful.

Perceiving similarities transformed Mahatma Gandhi from a simple lawyer to a great leader. As his granddaughter, Arun Gandhi, noted:

> Ironically if it had not been for the experience of racism and prejudice, he may have been just another successful lawyer who had made a lot of money. But because of prejudice in Southern Africa, he was subjected to humiliation within a week of his arrival. He was thrown off a train because of the color of his skin. . . . His first response was anger. . . . The second response was to want to go back to India and live among his own people in dignity. . . . And that's when the third response dawned on him—the response of nonviolent action. From that point onwards, he developed the philosophy of nonviolence and practiced it in his life as well as in his search for justice in South Africa. He ended up staying in that country for twenty-two years—and then he went and led the movement of India (Covey 2004, 187–88).

Perceiving similarities led Myles Horton, like John Dewey, to critique the mechanistic practices that traditionally dominated American education. While building an alternative school called the Highlander Center to empower working-class people in rural Tennessee, Horton came to see that his students "were usually quiet around strangers or people they considered 'well-spoken,' meaning educated." But once the school's staff surpassed that barrier and came to understand their students, they saw that traditional top-down approaches to teaching would be ineffective. By working instead toward "mutual learning," the staff and students "could and did learn from each other, each respecting the individual character of the other." Horton underscored the importance of perspective-taking when he said: "Insofar as I have learned to listen to people and to honor and respect them as individuals, I have been a good teacher. When I have failed to do this my teaching has failed" (Adams 1975, 46–47).

PERSPECTIVE-TAKING AND EDUCATION

All these examples suggest how perspective-taking can function as part of an empowering education. Ira Shor describes an empowering education as a "critical-democratic pedagogy for self and social change . . . a student-centered program for multicultural democracy in school and society . . . that approaches individual growth as an active, cooperative, and social process, because the self and society create each other" (Shor 1992, 15). If we faculty engage both ourselves and our students in perspective-taking as a component of empowering education, we can use our classrooms to practice creating an equitable democratic society.

Our classrooms are microcosms of society. They can be structured in a top-down fashion with the professor in command and students quiet and passive, as Myles Horton described his students when he met them. Or they can be, as Ira Shor proposes, places where students and teachers have relatively equal status as colearners and coeducators. Shor claims that inequalities in society at large result from the distribution of power in these microcosmic settings. He suggests that classroom cultures that support debate and critical study are necessary to advance a more democratic society.

Thus the way we faculty run our classrooms and the way we connect those classrooms to our communities can truly affect whether our teaching and learning practices advance a more diverse, socially just, and democratic culture. Providing time for students to learn about the professor's life and for the professor to conversely learn about the lives of students is essential to building students' capacity for perspective-taking. To succeed in fostering this capacity, faculty need to create environments where students are comfortable questioning the perspectives of others—of the authors whose works they read, of the professor, of others in the class.

PERSPECTIVE-TAKING AND COMMUNITY

In my classes, I connect assigned readings directly to challenges facing our local and global economies. These challenges affect both students' lives and the lives of the community members with whom they come in contact. I use the course readings as media for enhancing critical dialogue on the possibilities for new models of democratic engagement and collaboration. To make the readings concrete, I give my students the opportunity to work alongside new immigrants in a Pomona day labor center, day laborers on the street corners of Rancho Cucamonga, farm workers in the San Joaquin Valley, and labor and community organizers in diverse coalitions throughout the region. The readings and our class discussions become "real" when students meet with these day laborers and community organizers to work on common projects that emerge from their dialogue. Just as in the classroom, students advance to new levels of collaboration and civic engagement by practicing democratic exchange.

Having identified problems that are relevant to the workers, students use participatory community-based research and action to locate solutions. Drawing on their discussions with workers, students organize various projects that push for social change. Students and workers have collaborated to implement English classes, health workshops, and immigration rights research projects. Students have also organized petition drives, researched the constitutionality of checkpoints, marched to protest immigration raids, and campaigned to ensure continued funding for the local day labor center. To combat negative portrayals of new immigrants, students and day laborers have organized community-wide art and pictorial life history presentations. Thus the workers and students join in raising their voices and ensuring that they are heard. In all these projects, students come to accept the day laborers as teachers. With the help of the Center for Community Engagement and funding from alumna Susan Hanson, the college hosts weekly *Encuentros* (Encounters) lunches where day laborers share their life stories and converse in Spanish with students and faculty. Students also perform *teatro* (activist theater) in various communities during their spring break.

Through the projects and class readings, students become more equipped to understand contemporary debates over immigration, free trade, globalization, and the many myths that circulate about farm laborers, union organizers, and immigrant workers. By learning to respect each other's perspectives and by pursuing specific outcomes that benefit both campus constituents and workers, students and workers have developed a genuine trust over the years. In this way, the practice of perspective-taking becomes a useful tool in understanding the diverse experiences that intersect in the "border culture" between academia and the world beyond. Students learn to value the perspective of the "other": the poor, the worker, the oppressed, the immigrant, or the person of another color, class, gender, or sexuality. Similarly, workers and community organizers grow to respect classrooms as places where ideas can become deeds that advance their efforts to be heard.

Ultimately, perspective-taking cannot occur without addressing questions of power. But academia can follow emerging trends and break down structures that separate it from the larger community. This is what C. Otto Sharmer promotes as *prescencing*, the opening of "our minds, our hearts, and our intentions or wills" to "view things from the source . . . to develop a sense of the future that wants to emerge" (2009, 62). A wide range of perspectives about the plight of immigrants, people of color, women, LGBT communities, and the working class can exist in and outside of the classroom. Faculty can draw on these perspectives to make their classrooms places where students and community members work together to create a better world: one with higher levels of perspective-taking, social engagement, and leadership toward personal and social responsibility.

NOTE

1. Copyright Acknowledgement: Reprinted with permission from "Perspective-Taking as a Tool for Building Democratic Societies," *Diversity & Democracy,* vol. 14, no. 1. Copyright 2011 by the Association of American Colleges and Universities.

REFERENCES

Adams, Frank. 1975. *Unearthing Seeds of Fire: The Idea of Highlander.* With Myles Horton. Winston-Salem, NC: John F. Blair Publishing.
Association of American Colleges and Universities. 1995. *The Drama of Diversity and Democracy.* Washington, DC: Association of American Colleges and Universities.
Covey, Stephen R. 2004. *The 8th Habit: From Effectiveness to Greatness.* New York: Free Press.
Obama, Barack. 2004. *Dreams from My Father.* New York: Three Rivers Press. First published 1995 by Times Books.
Sharmer, C. Otto. 2009. *Theory U: Leading from the Future as It Emerges.* San Francisco: 2009.
Shor, Ira. 1992. *Empowering Education: Critical Teaching for Social Change.* Chicago: University of Chicago Press.

Chapter Seventeen

Latin@s and Social Movements in the Obama Years[1]

José Zapata Calderón

The significance of the election of Barack Obama in 2008 was in the rising of a social movement of Latinos and broad-based coalitions that advanced a vision for changing the direction of the country and whose interests were served.

The victory by Barack Obama in 2008 represented a transformative social movement that built multi-racial alliances and coalitions which transcended the mythical Black and Brown divide, galvanized new voters, and united hundreds of thousands around a "social change" agenda of issues. In moving large numbers of people around the ideas of equity and full participation in the life and direction of U.S. society, this social movement had the particularity of bringing diverse communities of people together in seeking new answers to their issues and the structural systemic problems being faced by the entire country.

It fit into the ingredients of a social movement where large numbers of ordinary people, disillusioned by the failings of the George Bush Administration, came together around "'collective and joint actions' with change-oriented goals to assert their rights and to demand a drastic change in the status quo (Snow, Sule, and Kriesi 1–13)." The particularity of this activity was that it was manifested in the electoral arena through the use of internet technologies, house meetings, and training of organizers. It had the characteristics of "deep pluralism," as presented by Phil Thomson in his book *Double Trouble*, where large numbers of multi-racial alliances emerge in search of a "deeper democracy" to overcome differences, "to achieve power in competitive struggles with other groups," and to strive "for a politics of common (cross-racial) good" (Thompson 22–27).

I was part of this social movement. As an academic and community organizer, I was part of a coalition of Latino community leaders and organizations who, very early on in the primary election, developed Viva Obama clubs throughout California (Wall). In the primary election, key pro-immigrant leaders in the Latino community were divided in where they would place their vote. Los Angeles Mayor Antonio Villaraigosa and United Farm Worker's co-founder Dolores Huerta supported Hillary Clinton while Angelica Salas from the Coalition for Human Immigrant Rights (CHIRLA) and Maria Elena Durazo, Executive Secretary-Treasurer of the Los Angeles County Federation of Labor, supported Barack Obama. I was part of a coalition of Latino and African American leaders who came together in the Inland Empire region of Southern California and organized widely publicized press conferences, voter registration campaigns, educational community forums, and get-out-the-vote efforts in support of Barack Obama (Wall). Some of our supporters and organizers traveled to the states of Arizona, Nevada, and Colorado to get out the vote.

What drove the unity of our coalition, as similar to other alliances throughout the country, was Obama's history in identifying with the causes of oppressed communities and his campaign promises to support immigrant rights, to improve the quality of education, health care, and employment, and to rebuild the type of alliances and partnerships that would be necessary to meet the challenges of a global economy. We were united on the significance of the election as being about the election of a person of color on the one hand, and the possibilities for building a new social movement that would genuinely unite people from diverse backgrounds in advancing a public policy agenda on how the country should be run and whose interests it should serve.

OBAMA'S HISTORY WITH OPPRESSED COMMUNITIES

A number of us, who were part of the national coalition to elect Obama, came out of a history as community organizers. Hence, Obama's stories in his two books and in his speeches throughout the country resonated with the trials and tribulations that many of us had faced or were facing.

In particular, his stories about moving from a student to a community organizer appealed to social movement organizers who often cited his memoir *Dreams from My Father* where Obama placed himself in the world of the organizer and the unorganized in seeking solutions to poverty, polluted water, and gang violence. These stories that were often also part of Obama's speeches throughout the country, fit with the experiences of many who came out of the civil rights generation and many others involved in contemporary regional equity movements (Pastor, Benner, Matsuoka 216–218).

It was the issue of "inequity," for example, in our social system that Barack Obama began to question when he was pondering what to do after graduating from college. It was by placing himself in the image of the "other" through his readings, the image of the SNCC workers "convincing a family of sharecroppers to register to vote" or the images of everyday people organizing the Montgomery bus boycott that led to his commitment beyond the individual to listen to the perspectives of others (Obama 2004: 134, 135). It was by placing himself in the world of the organizer and the unorganized that deepened his commitment that empowered him to empower others. In carrying out interviews in the poor communities of Chicago, he reflected "The more interviews I did, the more I began to hear recurring themes. The people I talked to, had some fond memories of that self-contained world, but they also remembered the absence of heat and light and space to breathe—that, and the sight of their parents grinding out life in physical labor" (Obama 2004: 155). As Obama listened to these stories, they reminded him of his family, their migration, their hardships, and the tenacity to build a better life.

When the community organizers he was working with got tired, he looked out the window and asked the organizers to look with him: "What do you suppose is going to happen to those boys out there?" . . . "You say you're tired, the same way most folks out here are tired. So I'm just trying to figure out what's going to happen to those boys. Who's going to make sure they get a fair shot?" (Obama 2004: 171, 172). In asking these questions and challenging those around him, he was asking the organizers to place themselves in those worlds. In the process, he took the time to listen to others and, in his book *Dreams from My Father,* provided examples of how he came to move "toward the center of people's lives" in his community.

> And it was this realization, I think, that finally allowed me to share more of myself with the people I was working with, to break out of the larger isolation that I had carried with me to Chicago. . . . As time passed, I found that these stories, taken together, had helped me bind my world together, that they gave me the sense of place and purpose I'd been looking for. There was always a community there if you dug deep enough. There was poetry as well—a luminous world always present beneath the surface, a world that people might offer up as a gift to me, if I only remembered to ask (Obama 2004: 190).

It was no accident then that the strategy of "story-telling" and listening to the stories of others on a one-to-one basis became a cornerstone of the campaign. More than the successful use of new technologies, this strategy worked in recruiting thousands of new leaders through door-to-door contact in neighborhoods and training them in using their life histories, and those of the communities they worked with, as a basis to reach out to the voting public.

REACHING OUT

This outreach strategy gave rise to an advancement of hundreds of multi-racial collective efforts on a local, regional, and national level comprised of all ethnic/racial groups, hailing mostly from cities and suburbs, largely younger than 30, and among all income classes. With young voters comprising one-quarter of the 44 million eligible voters, the Obama campaign recruited thousands of volunteers between the ages of 18 and 29 (Dreier). The magnitude of this campaign was exemplified by the field operation in Florida that included 19,000 neighborhood teams led by 500 paid organizers (Stirland). Using the "organizing approach," these organizers used personal narratives, a website, and weekend training programs to recruit and train one million volunteers (Burke). This multi-racial coalition that used the internet, cell phones, house meetings, and door-to-door eye contact with the voting public to find and train teams of community leaders was the foundation of the incredible voter registration and voter turn-out statistics in the primary and on Election Day.

Significantly, as part of this movement, there were 2 million more blacks, 2 million more Latinos, and 338,000 more Asian Pacific Americans that cast votes in 2008 than in the 2004 presidential election (Lopez & Taylor).

THE SIGNIFICANCE OF THE LATINO VOTE

In the primary election, there was a question as to whether Obama could build the type of coalition that it would take to win. In terms of the Latino vote, Hillary Clinton got 63% of the Latino vote, including 67% of the vote in Arizona and California (William C. Velasquez Institute). Some journalists attributed this lack of Latino support for Obama in the primary to the Black/Brown divide and to the changing urban landscape where Latino immigrants were moving into inner-city neighborhoods and competing with African Americans for jobs, housing, services, and for positions in local governments. Similar to the research in the edited volume *Neither Enemies Nor Friends: Latinos, Blacks, Afro-Latinos,* others attributed the divide to prejudices shaped in Latin America where darker-skinned indigenous people are looked down upon by those with lighter skin and a Spanish heritage. Earl Hutchison, author of the "Ethnic Presidency: How Race Decides the Race to the White House" proposed before the election that "The tensions between blacks and Latinos and negative perceptions that have marred relations between these groups for so long unfortunately still resonate." He shared his concern that "there will still be reluctance among many Latinos to vote for an African-American candidate. . . . When you've got competing ethnic groups at the bottom level, you're going to have friction because of the jockeying just to preserve their niche" (Reno).

Although Hillary Clinton was more well-known than Obama in the Latino community, Obama was able to increase the number of Latinos who voted for him by distinguishing himself from Clinton right before the primary in three key areas: "support of drivers' licenses for undocumented immigrants, a promise to take up immigration reform in his first year in office, and his background as the son of an immigrant (his father was Kenyan) and a community organizer in Chicago (Lochhead)." According to a poll and analysis by the William C. Velasquez Institute, "This shift in campaign strategy seemed to correlate with undecided voters choosing Obama as their candidate of choice in the last week of the primary campaign" (William C. Velazquez Institute).

After the primary, the question was whether Obama would get the Hillary Clinton vote or whether it would be divided and alienated. Obama's ability to retain an overwhelming majority of Clinton supporters was a key factor in his victory over McCain. Among Democratic voters who wanted Clinton to win the Democratic nomination, 82% supported Obama. The Latino vote sided with Obama and the Black/Brown division, that the media and conservative pundits had advanced as a given, never became a reality. At the same time, the coalition that had supported Clinton, made up of Latinos, union households, low income voters, and white women, was able to be united on Election Day. Obama won the Latino vote by 66% to 31%, union households by 58% to 40%, and the low income (below 50,000) voters by 60% to 38% (CNN).

With Latinos turning out to vote for Obama, they shattered the myth of a Black/Latino divide. Two thirds of Latinos voted for Obama. More voted Democratic than in any presidential election since 1996 (Lopez). Like voters nationwide, the majority of Latino voters said they had one concern above all others: the economy. This went along with the data that broke down foreclosures by race where Latinos were more than twice as likely as whites to get a high-cost loan, making them particularly vulnerable to foreclosures (Ruggeri).

While the Republicans tried to advance a strategy of using "morality" issues, such as same-sex marriage and abortion, to influence the Latino vote in much the same way that Bush had used these issues in 2004, the use of these "wedge" issues was overshadowed by concerns over the economy, health care, education and immigration.

In contrast to McCain, the Obama campaign was able to motivate and galvanize a broad-based coalition by presenting himself as a symbol of the concerns of a working public that was being affected by a deepening economic crisis. A CNN poll in September 2008, for example, pointed out that McCain exhibited a gap in "connectedness," and that the voting public by a

62–32 percentage margin, thought that Obama was "more in touch with the needs and problems" of working families (Silver). This connectedness was attributed to a number of key factors including his promises to cut taxes for ninety five percent of working families and his position to withdraw troops from Iraq. Nevertheless, while his position on the war initially placed him ahead in his campaign against McCain, he benefited even more from voter concerns over the crisis in the economy. Although polls showed that half of all voters thought that the economy was in poor condition and were worried about how the economic crisis would hurt them financially, McCain made the serious mistake of minimizing the significance of the economic crisis. While 60% of the voting public said that the economy was the most important problem that the new president would have to focus on, McCain focused on the issue of terrorism, a concern that only 9 percent of the voters saw as their major concern (Ververs). This allowed for Obama to further his argument that the election of McCain would only be a continuance of the policies of the Bush Administration. Although McCain tried, he could not separate himself from the negative feelings that the voting public had toward Bush. About half of all voters came to believe that McCain would continue Bush's policies and 75 percent said that the country was on the wrong track.

For those of us organizing in Latino communities, the election victory of Barack Obama proved what many of us had been saying all along: that the marches that many of us had helped lead against the criminalization of immigrants in 2006, and in support for the legalization of the 12 million immigrants in this country, would eventually turn into voting power. Indeed, the theme of the massive marches in 2006, "Today We March—Tomorrow We Vote," resulted in the galvanizing of immigrants and in their application for citizenship in record numbers. As part of this movement, after 2006, numerous community-based church and community organizations held citizenship and naturalization clinics throughout the country. Hence, the number of individuals naturalized in the U. S. went from 660,477 in 2007 to 1,046,539 in 2008. The Department of Homeland Security Office of Immigration Statistics not only attributed this increase to organized responses to proposed fee application increases but, most importantly, "to special efforts to encourage eligible applicants to apply for U.S. citizenship (Lee & Rytina)." Not only did this movement advance citizenship drives, but also spurred voter registration efforts that resulted in over 500,000 new citizen voters. The We Are America Alliance, alone, registered over 83,000 new voters in Florida, 35,000 in Pennsylvania, 52,000 in Nevada, and nearly 40,000 in New Mexico. The large number of newly registered voters bypassed the record 64% of eligible voters which last turned out in the 1960 election.

While there was a tendency to say that the immigration issue was placed in the back-burner in the election results, it was on the minds of our Latino communities and played a role in the galvanizing of the Latino vote. In an

NDN/Bendixen poll right before the election that asked Latinos "How important is the immigration issue to you and your family?" Between 74% and 86% of Latinos in the states of Florida, Colorado, New Mexico, and Nevada responded that it was very important (America's Voice). Some Latino voters, who had supported Bush in the last presidential election, were now polled as being disaffected by the Republican stance on immigration. Since 2006, Republicans in Congress had consistently supported immigration bills, such as the Sensenbrenner bill, that criminalized all undocumented immigrants and anyone who would support them. It was no accident that the Obama people understood the impact of such a divisive policy and flooded Latino districts with Spanish-language ads and campaign literature.

OBSTACLES IN CONTINUING THE SOCIAL MOVEMENT

After the election, the ingredients of a social movement that helped to elect Barack Obama went by the wayside. While the Obama Administration was forced to focus on the crisis state of the economy, this was not the only factor that thwarted some of its initiatives. Consequently, a number of the key policy commitments made before the election faced legislative hurdles in an environment where the corporate lobbies, defense contractors, drug companies, and conservative special interest groups staked their ground.

On the economy, Obama's mortgage payment plan promised to help millions of homeowners by creating incentives for lenders to renegotiate the terms of subprime loans. It also promised to help millions of households by paying off their mortgages and by lifting restrictions on financing. Before the election, Obama also promised a 90-day moratorium on foreclosures by banks and companies that receive any kind of government aid. However, while the stimulus package helped various bank and mortgage lenders to survive, there have been no solid guarantees to renegotiate loans or to help anyone who had already lost their home. Meanwhile, some of the companies who were bailed out a year ago, were giving bonuses to their executives. Morgan Stanley, for example set aside $3.9 billion for this purpose while Lehman Brothers Holdings Inc. reported record profits of $3.4 billion in the second quarter and bonuses "that would yield a record-setting average payout of $770,000 per employee if sustained the rest of the year (Hamilton, 2009: B1, B2). The Obama Administration's calls to stop the abuse of overseas tax loopholes, to develop a Consumer Financial Protection Agency, and to give more power to the government to regulate Wall Street have been blocked by the banking industry, the Financial Services Roundtable, and the U.S. Chamber of Commerce (Pazzanghera 2009a: B1, B3; Pazzanghera 2009b: B1, B6).

On the closing of Guantanamo Bay, Obama promised that he would close Guantanamo bay by January 2009, and that his administration would develop a task force to review existing detention policies and the lawful disposition of detainees in the U.S. custody. However, in May of 2009, the Senate by a vote of 90 to 6 voted to block the transfer of detainees to the U.S. and denied the Obama Administration $81 million that it had requested to close Guantanamo. Presently, Obama has caved in to the contention of legislators in both the House and the Senate that their constituents were afraid of placing detainees on U.S. soil and possibly placing U.S. citizens in danger.

Before the election, Obama had criticized the Bush Administration for not being transparent and keeping the truth from the American public. However, the Obama Administration's position on state secrets doctrines in urging a federal judge to toss out a law suit by former CIA detainees was questioned as being no different than the Bush Administration's position in using state secrets privilege to dismiss entire law suits before there could be any proceedings.

Although Obama has consistently stressed the need for advancing a strategy of bipartisan cooperation between Democrats and Republicans in Congress, his activist governance stance has been horrendously criticized by the likes of such conservative commentators as Glenn Beck, Lou Dobbs, and Rush Limbaugh. The conservatives in the Republican Party, who are now in a position of being the minority party, have thwarted Obama's strategy of bipartisanship. In his book *The Audacity of Hope*, Obama proposed that a genuine bipartisanship strategy would work if there was "an honest process of give-and-take" and if "the quality of the compromises" served "some agreed-upon goal" (Obama 2006: 131).

However, the debate over health care reform revealed the pitfalls in this strategy with conservative groups putting aside what was written in Obama's health care proposals and claiming that his proposals included unlimited coverage for undocumented immigrants, death panels and euthanasia for the elderly, socialized medical rationing, and planned reductions in Medicare benefits. As in some of Obama's other policy initiatives, the promise that universal health care in America would become a reality "by the end of his first term as president" was blocked by the organized force of these right-wing groups, Republican congressional representatives, and the health insurance industry. Obama's support for a more affordable "public option," as an alternative to the status quo proposals of the insurance and pharmaceutical companies, has now been put aside with a requirement that all people buy health insurance with some help from federal subsidies to help those who cannot afford it (Levey 2009b: A-1, A-16).

Rather than the broad multi-racial movement that helped to elect Obama, there is an increase in another type of movement that promotes racism and scapegoats immigrants, underrepresented communities, women, people of color, and working people for the economic problems in this country.

This was especially evident when thousands of conservative protesters, many of them Republican, took to the streets in Washington D.C. questioning Obama's citizenship status and his administration's policies with signs that read: "Is this Russia?" "Traitors Terrorists Run Our Government." "Don't Blame me, I voted for The American" (Barabak A1, A17). The open attacks on the president's character in this demonstration and the outburst by Representative Joe Wilson's (R-S.C.) of "You Lie" in the middle of Obama's address to Congress precipitated such responses as former President Carter's that: "an overwhelming portion of the intensely demonstrated animosity toward President Barack Obama is based on the fact that he is a black man" (Abcarian A1, A16).

At the same time, during the election campaign, Obama proposed that immigration workplace raids were ineffective, and called for an alternative that could bring the 12 million undocumented immigrants in the country out of the shadows. Until recently, when the Obama Administration has supported prosecutorial discretion and deferred action policies, there has been an implementation of enforcement policies that have resulted in increased immigration raids, audits of employee paperwork at hundreds of businesses, expanded a program to verify worker immigration status that has been widely criticized as flawed, and bolstered a program of cooperation between federal and local law enforcement agencies. With former Arizona Governor Grace Napolitano at the head of the Department of Homeland Security, the Obama Administration, after 2008, moved forward in authorizing as many as sixty-six law enforcement agencies to work with Homeland Security in identifying "illegal immigrants and process them for possible deportation under a program known as 287(g)" (Gorman A1, A9). Under this administration's immigration policies, deportations reached record levels rising to an annual average of nearly 400,000 since 2009, about 30% higher than the annual average during the second term of the Bush Administration and about double the annual average during George W. Bush's first term. Under this administration, the 287(g) and Secure Communities programs used local law enforcement officers to carry out the screening of people, that should have been the work of federal officers. Under the pretext that these policies were meant to arrest hard core criminals, the policies led to arbitrary arrests for minor offenses and violated the due process rights of both citizens and non-citizens. Since 2008, the Obama Administration also expanded the use of E-Verify, an existing program of employee immigration-status verification that has been criticized for using a database that contains thousands of errors and has led to as many as 19,000 people (of 6.4 million checked) that have been mistakenly identified as being deportable. Up until recently, the Obama Administration called for these programs, especially Secure Communities, to be expanded to every one of the nation's 3,100 state and local jails by 2013 although these programs have been shown to be fundamentally flawed, incompetently administered, and prone to target, not only immigrants, but Latino citizens.

This focus on enforcement, rather than legalization, was steadily eroding the strong support among Latino organizations that Obama had right before and after the election.

In a national survey of 1,220 Latino adults aged 18 and older (between November 9 and December 7, 2011) the Pew Research Center found that, by a ratio of more than two-to-one (59% versus 27%), Latinos disapproved of the way the Obama Administration was handling deportations of undocumented immigrants. This study found that more than three quarters (77%) of those who were aware of Obama's enforcement policies, strongly disagreed with these policies (December 28, 2011, "As Deportations Rise to Record Levels, Most Latinos Oppose Obama's Policy" by Mark Hugo Lopez, Ana Gonzalez-Barrera & Seth Motel).

Globally, according to a Pew Hispanic Research Center survey, approval of Obama's policies had "declined significantly since he first took office, while overall confidence in him and attitudes toward the U.S. had slipped modestly as a consequence" (Pew Global Attitudes Project).

Hence, it was no accident that the Obama Administration, reading the writing on the wall, approved a policy of "prosecutorial discretion" in August, 2011 directing ICE officials to focus on primarily apprehending hardcore criminals and not on low-priority undocumented immigrants such as those with children who are U.S. citizens, those who came to the country as minors, or those who served in the military. However, the program was deemed a failure when Transactional Records Access Clearinghouse at Syracuse University reported that "of the 298,173 cases that were pending at the end of September, 2012—only 4,585 had been closed under the program by the end of May, 2012." Hence, a program aimed at reducing nearly 300,000 pending immigration cases, only 1.5% of the backlogged cases were closed.

With the election nearing and with a national campaign by the Dream action network, the Obama Administration, on June 12, 2012, announced a policy to grant "deferred action status" to undocumented persons who fit certain criteria. This policy came at the height of a national campaign by Dream students, where they presented 11,000 signatures calling on President Obama to issue an executive order halting the deportation of Dream-eligible young people. It also came days after Dream students held a series of sit-ins inside of Obama campaign offices across the country.

While this policy does provide a two-year temporary relief to successful immigrant applicants, immigrant advocate organizations are concerned about due process problems that have been a mainstay of the previous prosecutorial discretion policies including that: there will be no impartial adjudicator, no right to meaningful review of faulty decisions, and no formalized way to present and evaluate evidence or legal arguments. Immigrant rights advocates point out that similar discretionary policies have done little to stop the increase of deportations under the Obama Administration and that, since there is no right to appeal, that erroneous decisions may lead to the deportation of qualified applicants. Still, tens of thousands of Dreamers have been standing in lines or attending workshops in recent days to receive help in completing application forms. With an estimated 1.8 million eligible applicants, the potential of a mass movement has been unleashed and there is no turning back in its mobilization potential.

The conditions are prevalent for rebuilding the type of social movement that was built before the 2008 elections in the electoral arena. However, one of the problems has been the dominance of a strategy that has not relied on the transformative alliances that were harnessed before the last two elections. This follows with a type of disenchantment that Professor Phil Thompson analyzes in his study of African American mayors and their efforts to find solutions to urban decline. In his research, Thompson analyzes how the initial excitement of electing Black mayors was diminished among the electorate when many of these elected officials adopted a traditional "pro-growth" urban policy that ultimately ended up serving the real estate and developer interests. At the same time, as the economies in urban areas moved from manufacturing to service industry employment, these mayors were blamed for the resulting urban problems. When the conditions did not change, it resulted in less political engagement by the black poor and middle class and a strengthening of conservative domination (Thompson 4, 5). Only in a few cases are there examples where Mayors bucked the system and, by relying on the base that elected them, implemented "alternative models of community building and economic development" that addressed urban poverty and made their policies accountable to the public (Thompson 41, 42).

In order for Latino organizations, such as the one that I have worked with, to have the same passion and to build the types of coalitions that existed before, it would take Obama's continuing support of the type of organizing and advancement of a social movement that took place during the election. Public intellectuals Peter Dreier and Marshall Ganz, in their article *We Have the Hope, Now Where's the Audacity,* while criticizing the Obama networks for turning to a marketing strategy of "politics as usual," proposed that the existence of such a mobilization of communities (such as we experienced before 2008) today would take the advancement of a strategy that focuses on movement-building:

> The White House and its allies forgot that success requires more than proposing legislation, negotiating with Congress and polite lobbying. It demands movement-building of the kind that propelled Obama's long-shot candidacy to an almost landslide victory. And it must be rooted in the moral energy that can transform people's anger, frustrations and hopes into focused public action,

creating a sense of urgency equal to the crises facing the country (Dreier & Ganz).

Although Obama has put a progressive and transformative strategy of movement-building to the side, this does not mean that the building of a movement should not be on the agenda of social movements and activists. Rather than allowing for a trend that wants to take the country back before the civil rights movement—that seeks to control the economy for the upper 1%—that thrives on creating fear and divisions among working people and—that uses their genuine concerns to blame immigrants for the economic problems in this country—there is the capacity to build another trend at the grassroots. This trend is seeking to control the excesses of profit by a few—and build more spaces of equity—examples of democracy—examples of a new economy—with the types of alliances and partnerships that are necessary to meet the challenges of a global economy.

In California, various community-based coalitions have arisen to challenge the federal government's immigration enforcement policies by organizing and passing legislation allowing undocumented students, not only to go to college, but to receive financial aid. I, and my students, have been part of the Pomona Habla coalition's efforts in changing the Pomona city council policies that discriminated against undocumented immigrants and were part of a larger movement resulting in the passage of a statewide bill allowing anyone stopped at a checkpoint without a driver's license to have someone come and pick up their car. This will kill the millions of dollars being made by the tow truck and impoundment companies. The governor, as a result of these movements, also signed a bill that called for "neither California nor any of its cities, counties, or special districts require an employer to use E-Verify as a condition of receiving a government contract, applying for or maintaining a business license, or as a penalty for violating licensing or other similar laws."

Now, these coalitions are moving forward in organizing to enact a new law that gives qualified undocumented immigrants the right to a driver's license.

CONCLUSION

In conclusion, the significance of the election of Barack Obama was not just in the individual but in the rising of a new social movement that united people from diverse backgrounds in advancing a vision for change in the way this country is run and whose interests it serves. While Barack Obama's exceptional history as a community organizer, lawyer, and state senator placed him in a position of mainstream credibility, it was the social movement of broad-based multi-racial alliances that put him over the top. The movement that developed before the election was one for jobs, health, education, security and equality. It was about the very foundations of local, national, and international democracy with a vision of ensuring the resource capacity of diverse local and global communities to survive. Unfortunately, the promises of the Obama Administration, that moved so many, have not been kept. The issues are still there after the election but, in spite of their collective impact, the social movements that were built on a common ground of defending the right of all people to be treated with dignity and equality were thwarted by the policies of the Obama Administration that ultimately served the power of the corporate monopolies and monied interests. However, the ingredients of a progressive social movement are still visible but the strategies have shifted to local organizing efforts that, in California, have resulted in legislation supporting: cities opting out of E-Verify, the right of AB540 students to attend college with financial aid, and the right of people without a driver's license to stop the impounding of their cars. These progressive social movements on the local level are based on defending the rights of immigrants, decriminalizing the labor of the undocumented, and challenging the federal government's enforcement policies. At the same time, the local organizing efforts are based on the long-term premise of making the Obama Administration accountable for the policies promised and the policies being implemented.

NOTE

1. Copyright Acknowledgement: This chapter was previously published in the following: *Camino Real Journal*, vol. 5, no. 8 (2013).

REFERENCES

Abcarian, R. & K. Linthicum. "Conservatives Say it's Their Turn for Empowerment." *Los Angeles Times*, 17 September 2009: A-1, A-16. Print.

America's Voice. "The Power of the Immigrant and Latino Vote in the 2008 Election." 14 October 2008. Web.

Barabak, M. Z. "Tensions Rise over Afghan Strategy." *Los Angeles Times*, 16 October 2009: A-1, A-17. Print.

Burke, J. "Marshall Ganz: Traditional Approach vs. Organizing Approach." *Organizing For America*, 9 November 2008. Print.

CNN. "Obama's Election Redraws American Electoral Divide." 05 November 2008. Web.

Dreier, P. "Millenials Could Be Key Voters in Swing States." *The Nation*, 15 September 2008. Print.

———. & M. Ganz. "We have the Hop. Where's the Audacity?" *The Washington Post,* 30 August 2009. Web.

Gorman, A. "Tough Rules on Policing Migrants." *Los Angeles Times*, 14 October 2009: A-1, A9. Print.

Hamilton, W. "Crisis Has Not Altered Wall Street. *Los Angeles Times*, 14 September 2009: B-1, B-2. Print.

Hugo-Lopez, M., A. Gonzalez-Barrera & S. Motel. "Deportations Rise to Record Levels, Most Latinos Oppose Obama's Policy." Pew Hispanic Research Center. 28 December 2011. Print.

Lee, J. & N. Rytina. "Naturalizations in the United States: 2008. DHS Office Of Immigration Statistics." March 2009. Web.

Levey, N. "A Key Health Goal is Elusive." *Los Angeles Times*, 13 October 2009: A-1, A-2. Print.

———. & J. Oliphant. "Health Bill Passes with 1 GOP Vote." *Los Angeles Times*, 14 October 2009: A-1, A-16. Print.

Lochhead, C. "Obama Takes Big Risk on Driver's License Issue." *San Francisco Chronicle*, 28 January 08: A-1. Print.

Lopez, M. H. "The Hispanic Vote in the 2008 Election." Pew Hispanic Center. 07 November 2008. Print.

———. & Paul Taylor. "Dissecting the 2008 Electorate: Most Diverse in U.S. History." Washington, D. C.: Pew Hispanic Center. 30 April 2009. Print.

Obama, B. *The Audacity of Hope*. New York: Crown Publishers, 2006. Print.

———. *Dreams from My Father*. New York: Three Rivers Press, 2004. Print.

Parsons, C. "Tensions Rise over Afghan Strategy." *Los Angeles Times*, 16 October 2009: A-1, A-17. Print.

Pastor, M., C. Benner & M. Masuoka. *This Could Be the Start of Something Big*. Ithaca, NY: Cornell University Press, 2009. Print.

Pazzanghera, J. "Reform Plan is Likely to Get Rewrite." *Los Angeles Times*, 24 September 2009: B-1, B-3. Print.

———. "Obama Slams Plan Opponents." *Los Angeles Times*, 10 October 2009: B-1, B-6. Print.

Pew Hispanic Research Center. "Pew Global Attitudes Project." 13 June 2012. Print.

Reno, J. "Black-Brown Divide." *Newsweek*, 26 January 2008. Web.

Ruggeri, A. "Behind Obama's Victory: A Major Swing by Latino Voters: Back to The Democratic Fold." *U.S. News and World Report*, 06 November 2008. Print.

Silver, N. "Why Voters Thought Obama Won." *Five Thirty Eight*. 27 September 2008. Web.

Snow, D. A., S. A. Soule & H. Kriesi. "Mapping the Terrain" *The Blackwell Companion to Social Movements*. D. A. Snow, S. A. Soule & H. Kriesi (Eds.) Malden, MA: Blackwell Publishing: 2004: 1–13. Print.

Stirland, S. Lai. "Obama's Secret Weapons: Internet Databases and Psychology." *Wired*. 29 October 2008. Print.

Transactional Access Clearing House. "Drop in Ice Deportation Filings in Immigration Court." 30 July 2012. Web.

Thompson, J. P. *Double Trouble: Black Mayors, Black Communities, and the Call For a Deep Democracy*. New York: Oxford University Press, 2006. Print.

Ververs, V. "A Mandate for Change." CBSNews. 05 November 2008. Web.

Wall, S. "Political Coalition Hopes to Unify, Harness Latino Vote." *San Bernardino Sun*, 17 January 2008. Print.

———. "Latino Vote Crucial for Presidential Hopefuls." *San Bernardino Sun*, 01 February 2008. Print.

William C. Velasquez Institute. "The Latino Super Tuesday: Underneath the Numbers." Los Angeles, CA. 2 July 2008. Print.

Chapter Eighteen

One Activist Intellectual's Experience in Surviving and Transforming the Academy[1]

José Zapata Calderón

My survival in higher education has its roots in the connections between my lived experience as the immigrant son of farm worker parents and the lessons learned in overcoming systemic obstacles as a community organizer and intellectual activist. Whenever the road in academia got rough and I had to face another hurdle, I always remembered the difficulties that my immigrant farm worker family had to face. In this way, the problems I encountered in academia appeared smaller and more manageable. My struggles with learning English and growing up in a poor immigrant farm worker family became the foundations of language, labor, and immigration issues that I passionately took up in my organizing, teaching, and research as an activist intellectual in academia.

I have survived the ivory tower by being proactive in both finding and creating spaces that bridge the gaps between the academic world and community-based projects for action and social change. This has included organizing not only in the community, but organizing on the campus to validate the significance of the carpentry that it takes to build such spaces. In his article "College in the Community," sociologist John Wallace provides a glimpse of "what college education could be" if such spaces were created "with reality, with diverse disciplines, with a community of co-learners, with true self, and with purposes larger than the self" (2000: 762). For intellectual activists or organic public intellectuals who are tenacious in constructing such spaces in higher education, the obstacles are immense. It does mean creating a balance between the personal and political to advance ongoing educational and societal structural changes that recognize the significance of teaching and learning outside the traditional walls of academia.

The immensity of this endeavor has been recognized by the American Sociological Association (ASA). Through the efforts of 2004 president Michael Burawoy, a Task Force on Institutionalizing Public Sociologies (2005: 2) acknowledged that "despite the long-standing tradition of American public sociology going back to the nineteenth century, the work of public sociologists traditionally has not been recognized, rewarded, or encouraged in many of our sociology departments." A step in this direction is the task force's call to academia to recognize, validate, evaluate, and reward public sociology as both an applied and scholarly enterprise.

Public sociology has particular salience for historically excluded individuals from diverse racial, class, gender, and sexuality backgrounds, for whom the educational experience can be both an alienating and empowering experience. This chapter chronicles my journey in public sociology. It is a narrative about finding one's passion in one's lived experience as a foundation for overcoming obstacles in academia, connecting an engaged pedagogy to social activism, and advancing social change practices through learning, teaching, and research transformations.

EARLY FOUNDATIONS OF ACADEMIC SURVIVAL

As an immigrant who arrived in the United States at the age of seven, I did not know any English. I experienced the discrimination that many non-English-speaking students faced in the schools. My first six months in first grade were spent not understanding a word the teachers said. Everyone thought something was wrong with me. I learned how to organize every hour of my day at school so that I could make it through the day without speaking to anyone. I ensured that my bathroom breaks were after classes. To avoid interaction with anyone, I always ran home at noon for lunch. However, there were times during the winter when I was forced to bring my sack lunch to school. This practice stopped when a group of students made fun of the bean tacos my mother had made for me. After this experience, when the winter snows kept me inside, I quietly slipped away and hid in another room while my classmates ate their lunches.

I learned English with the help of a teacher who realized that there was nothing wrong with my ability to speak. She realized that I was silent most of the time because I did not understand the language. This teacher, Mrs. Elder, began to stay with me after school. She began by pretending to want to learn Spanish. In the process, she learned some Spanish and I learned to speak English. A half-dozen other Mexican students who were part of my first grade class eventually dropped out. They were not provided the same opportunity since, structurally, bilingual education had not been established at the time. Later, when I was a student at the University of Colorado, I went back and carried out research on these students, many of whom were working in low-paying jobs as waiters, truck drivers, and farm laborers. When I wrote a paper on these students, I realized that many of them had never learned English.

My research revealed the price I had had to pay for "making" it through the school system.[2] The school promoted assimilation, calling me the "good Spanish boy." Those who dropped out were called "Mexican." In my school, being called "Mexican" was a fighting word. The teachers had created a culture where being "Spanish" was acceptable and "Mexican" was not.

Unbeknownst to the teachers, I kept my Mexican culture, including the Spanish language, because of the persistence of my parents. They continued to emphasize that I was Mexican, that I should be proud of it, and that I should know my language. Knowledge of the Spanish language became a means of survival for me economically and academically. When I was in junior high school, I contributed to my family's finances by working as an interpreter in a local clothing store. In tenth grade, when everyone was required to take another language, I shined in Spanish classes and got straight A's. For the first time in my life, the Euro-American students were coming and asking me for help. My Spanish also helped me survive graduate school. When I was at the last steps of finishing my PhD, one of the requirements at UCLA was that one had to take a sociology exam in another language. The test required one to read excerpts from various sociology journals and answer multiple-choice questions based on the content. Many of these articles were difficult to understand in English, let alone in another language. I was able to whisk through the exam because of my Spanish.

EARLY CONNECTIONS BETWEEN THE ACADEMY AND SOCIAL CHANGE

Encouraged by a high school counselor to succeed in sports, I attended Northeastern Junior College in Sterling, Colorado, on a track scholarship. By my second year, I got involved in student government and decided to focus on my studies. I worked alongside other students in questioning why a meat-packing plant across from the library created such a bad odor that permeated the whole city. Some of us began to research the plant and found that the company had been cited for polluting a stream near the plant site. We took our research and turned it into action by organizing a demonstration that resulted in the closing of the plant until it dealt with its pollution problems. The significance of this first organizing experience is that I began to learn about the potential for turning research data into action for social change.

Motivated by this discovery, I applied and was accepted to the University of Colorado (CU) as a major in communications.

At the University of Colorado, I survived by continuing to connect the classroom to social issues and by continuing my involvement in student government. I took various sociology and political science courses that introduced me to the debates that were going on about the war in Vietnam. In one sociology course, I challenged a professor who said that he had two positions on the war: one was his personal position and the other was his "institutional" position. My questioning led to a panel debate on the meaning of the word "integrity" in the class. Little by little, my convictions deepened my commitment to the antiwar movement. Subsequently, as vice president of the student government, I joined the antiwar movement on campus and helped organize a rally of ten thousand students in support of a national student strike against the war in 1970. Instead of completely shutting down the university, we turned this action into a learning moment during the last two weeks of the spring quarter. By working collectively with dozens of students and faculty, I learned about the power of popular education and how it could be implemented in opening a new university that connected classes in the various disciplines with study and debate on the educational system and how it was affected by an unjust war. Subsequently, we had media students writing columns and letters to the newspaper, engineering students building peace domes, and art students creating murals and posters on the effects of the war. One of our efforts included placing various billboards throughout the city depicting a young dead soldier on the ground with an inscription reading "Dear Mom and Dad Your Silence is Killing Me in Vietnam."

During my involvement in the antiwar movement, between 1968 and 1971, I also became active in the struggles to get more students of color on campus. I joined the United Mexican American Students in asking for funds to develop summer programs to prepare Chicano/a students to go to college. We occupied a building on campus when Board of Regents representative Joe Coors took a position that minority students were less qualified than other students to attend the university and that no funds should be used for their recruitment. The first summer programs were developed after we were able to show that there were dozens of qualified Chicano/a students who could be admitted to the university but who lacked the necessary resources to survive. Out of those summer programs, I met students who eventually went on to become social workers, teachers, lawyers, doctors, community organizers, and political leaders.

While organizing on campus, I met various students who were involved with a farm worker support group on the campus. In addition to getting the student senate to allocate funds for the group, I joined them in traveling to Center, Colorado, and joining striking lettuce workers on the picket line. It also led me to make connections between the farm worker movement and the antiwar movement. For one of my classes at CU, I wrote a paper called "Rhetoric of the Chicano Movement." In looking at the persuasion strategies of leaders in the Chicano/a movement, I was most impressed with the strategies of Cesar Chavez. In carrying out the research, I was shocked to find that the Defense Department, under the Nixon administration, was buying tons of grapes when the farm workers were on strike (Del Castillo and Garcia 1995: 92). This really affected me since I had witnessed the burial of various friends who had died in the war. On the one hand, the labor of the farm workers was being used to increase the profits and power of large agribusiness corporations (Barger and Reza 1994: 22–25). On the other, the sons of these farm workers were being drafted in disproportionate numbers, representing 20 percent of those who died on the front lines (Gonzalez 1999: 211–213).

Feeling that I could do something about these injustices, I decided to go and learn firsthand about Cesar Chavez's union. With only $57 in my pocket, I caught a Greyhound bus that took me to Delano, California, where I observed the organizing strategies of Cesar Chavez and the violence being waged by the growers against the farm workers. I also heard a speech by Cesar Chavez that changed my life. In challenging the young students volunteering with the union, Cesar proposed that "we have only one life to live" and that "the highest level of using your life is in service to others." It was after this experience that I made the decision to return to northern Colorado and to use my education to organize against systemic injustices that had kept farm worker and immigrant communities at the lowest levels of the economic ladder. The sacrifices of farm worker organizers, including Cesar Chavez, who received only five dollars a week for their organizing efforts, inspired me in this direction.

CONNECTING POPULAR EDUCATION TO COMMUNITY ORGANIZING

Galvanized by my experience with the farm workers, I returned to Ault, Colorado, where I had grown up, and began my organizing efforts. I first developed a community center out of a garage in my parents' backyard. Remembering the difficulties I had faced in not knowing English at an early age, I used the methods of Paulo Freire in teaching young Mexican children to speak English.[3] These educational strategies would later become a part of my teaching methods in the college classroom. I also used the research skills that I had obtained from my undergraduate education to discover that eight out of ten Mexican children who started in the first grade in Ault eventually dropped out of school. After learning this information, the students and their parents collectively used this research to appear before the school board to demand that bilingual education be instituted in the school district. The response of one school board member was that if we wanted bilingual education, we could "return to Mexico." This response led to a seventy-mile protest march from Ault to the state capital in Denver. Our efforts, coupled with organized student walkouts, led to an ongoing social movement in the region that resulted in the establishment of bilingual education programs and the hiring of bilingual teachers and administrators in many Weld County schools.

As a result of these organizing efforts in the next few years, I was asked to teach a class called "The Community" at Aims Junior College. The class was my first major experience in having students connect the classroom to community service and social change issues. Hearing about the successes of the class, the Sociology Department chair at the University of Northern Colorado asked me to teach a similar class there. Before long, without a master's degree, I was teaching as much as a full-time professor (on part-time pay). The experience of teaching sociology classes strengthened my affinity for the field of sociology. Simultaneously, it allowed me to experiment with various forms of using critical pedagogy and research by having students conduct research on migrant housing through the Colorado Migrant Council and volunteer at a community center that we developed in the north side of Greeley, Colorado. I did not know it then, but these organizing efforts laid the foundation I needed to complete my PhD and be a teacher and researcher at the college level. Like other activists of this time period. I began my teaching at the university without a PhD (Ichioka 2006: 281).

For the next twelve years, I survived on little income, but I was sustained by the spirit and passion of the farm worker, immigrant, student, and poor communities that I collaborated with. Working with various national organizations, such as the Workers Viewpoint, I was motivated to look beyond issues of race to working-class issues that affected low-income people from all racial/ethnic backgrounds. The unity of multiracial leaders who turned away from luxury to devote their lives to building a more just and equal society energized me.

CHALLENGES TO ECONOMIC AND ACTIVIST SURVIVAL

In 1984, after marrying and having children, I faced the reality of looking for a long-term career that would allow me to meet my responsibilities to my family as well as allow me to continue my commitment to community organizing and social change. After coming across an announcement for a graduate fellowship at UCLA, I filled out an application and obtained recommendation letters from my former undergraduate professors. In June of 1984, I was accepted to UCLA. Although saddened at the prospect of leaving our friends and their families, my wife, Rose, and I agreed that that we could no longer survive on part-time jobs in the Greeley area and that we had to plan for the long term.

After saying goodbye to friends, we drove to Los Angeles in a U-Haul truck with our two young boys in the front and our belongings packed in the back. Rose obtained employment as an administrative assistant with the Mexican American Legal Defense and Education Fund, and I obtained a part-time job as a counselor with the Optimist Boy's Home in Highland Park. This highly demanding job involved implementing counseling projects to advance teamwork and leadership skills among one hundred young men who were primarily referrals from the County Department of Probation. My life consisted of managing the freeway from our apartment in El Sereno to classes at UCLA, working at the Boy's Home, studying at the library, and juggling home and day-care chores with Rose.

Unhappy with this new life, I longed to return to my life of community organizing in rural Colorado. At UCLA, I became part of a graduate student cohort group that focused on comparative and historical sociology. While enthralled by the readings. I was frustrated by the lack of connections between the classroom and community-based issues. I had envisioned UCLA's sociology graduate school program as one that was engaged with the urban problems faced by the mosaic of diverse communities in Los Angeles, but my classes focused primarily on historical comparisons and theory that lacked grounding in participatory transformative social change. My involvement in various study groups and my teaching experience in Colorado had provided me with some understanding of the theories of power and conflict, particularly Marxism. I used this understanding to critique the arguments in the assigned readings. Rather than simply analyzing the authors' data, my arguments centered on whether the theories would be useful as agents of social change. The discussions in the class appeared to be polemical—so I made them polemical.

At the time, I didn't fully understand why the professors and some students would roll their eyes when I spoke. In the ensuing months, I learned that the task was to find "holes" in the authors' arguments regardless of what significance their arguments had to our lived experiences and practices in social justice organizing. It is this connection between intellectual activity and "the experience of human beings in a specific community at a certain moment in history . . . a social interaction involving both thought and feeling" that is often missing in the academic classroom (Shor 1992: 22). By the second semester, when I had begun to figure out what the professors wanted, I was already making plans to complete my master's degree and quit the PhD program to work in a union.

In the Optimist Boy's Home, I also faced the frustration of having to do "therapy sessions" with dozens of Latino and African American teenagers without any room to empower them or to create structural changes in the institution. Tired of the bureaucracy, I went to the campus employment office and found an internship with the city manager's office in the city of Monterey Park.

CONNECTING RESEARCH WITH COMMUNITY ORGANIZING

This internship led to my involvement in the city and fostered my survival in the PhD program. In the mid-1980s, Monterey Park was going through a dramatic demographic transformation that reflected the larger changes taking place in California. Monterey Park's population had gone from 85 percent Euro-American, 3 percent Asian and 12 percent Latino/a in 1960 to 56 percent Asian American, 31.3 percent Latino/a, and 11.7 percent Euro-American in 1990. When I started working in the city manager's office, Monterey Park had just received a national designation as an "All-America City" for its innovative volunteer programs that reached out to new Chinese immigrants. At the same time, an organized backlash against the unbridled growth policies of the city council had begun. As part of blaming the "growth" problems on the new Chinese immigrants, an all-White city council passed an "English only" ordinance making English the official language of the city, calling for the local police to cooperate with the Immigration and Naturalization Service, and giving nonsupport to any city that advocated sanctuary for immigrants. As an intern in the city manager's office, I was assigned to carry out research on the passage of a similar ordinance in the city of Fillmore. I was almost fired by the city manager when I used the research to criticize the city council, at one of their open meetings, for passing such a racist measure. By the time my internship was coming to an end, I was already involved as a community organizer, resident, and co-chair of a coalition to defeat the English-only initiative.

In 1988 and 1990, I complemented my organizing activities in the community by working as a researcher with Professor John Horton of the UCLA Department of Sociology and a seven-member local research team in a study of the politics of conflict and cooperation in Monterey Park.[4] My research, as part of the study of demographic transformations taking place in Los Angeles County, where racial minorities and new immigrants are becoming the majority, focused on the changing ethnic and class alliances between Latinos/us, old residents, and new Asian Pacific immigrants.

The Monterey Park research project brought together what I had been looking for in the academic world: a concrete connection between sociological theories and the lived experiences of diverse communities in an urban setting. The project also created a space for my passion as a former immigrant, an activist, and a researcher working for social change. The experience strengthened my commitment to finish my dissertation and provided a glimpse of how I could connect the academic world with community-based participatory research, teaching, and learning.

Rather than perpetuating the traditional idea that researchers should not participate in the organizations they study, the project allowed for my involvement as an organizer and researcher in the community. My data was gathered from field notes written from my lived experience as a resident in the community and from my participation in numerous community-based organizations.[5] I remained conscious throughout the process of representing the meanings and actions of the participants without discounting my own perspectives as a participant. After my thesis proposal was reviewed and accepted. I learned that the time between the proposal and the actual writing of the dissertation is crucial in finishing the PhD. I applied some of the recommendations from David Sternberg's (1981) *How to Complete and Survive a Doctoral Dissertation* for my own academic survival, including prioritizing my commitments to ensure a focus on the task at hand, ensuring a balance between my academic and family responsibilities, putting aside at least three hours a day to writing, organizing a personal file system, developing a support network, and finding employment with a flexible environment. My support network included employment as a graduate research assistant with the Chicano Studies Research Center and involvement with other Latino/a graduate students through the Raza Grad Student Organization. We organized the latter group to bring students together to share, socialize, mentor, and to survive the academy. We developed our own newsletter and at one point organized a demonstration to advocate for our rights as graduate students. To this day, I have close ties with many of these friends who are now colleagues in various colleges throughout the country.

In addition to these networks of support, there were various professors, such as John Horton, David Lopez, David Hayes-Bautista, and Edna Bonacich, who took the time to mentor me and other Latino/a students. They encouraged me to utilize my ability to tell stories as a vehicle for ethnographic research.[6] Another professor, Richard Berk, saved me from drowning in a required two-quarter statistics course by creatively integrating storytelling in his assignments. Rather than writing endless formulas from the textbooks on the board and moving ahead before we could explain our confusion, this professor connected statistical theories and formulas to data that involved compelling issues in our lives. Analyzing historical data on the death penalty taught us the meaning of "longitudinal concepts." I remember the excitement I felt when he complimented my analysis of statistical data on the economic conditions of farm workers in the United States.[7]

I survived the dissertation process, graduated from UCLA in 1991, and landed a position in sociology and Chicano Studies at Pitzer College in Claremont, California.[8] I had planned with my family to return to Colorado, but there were no jobs available there in my field at the time. Nevertheless, I was drawn to Pitzer by its ethos of advancing intercultural and interdisciplinary understanding in the context of social responsibility. It was the type of place that fit with my passion of connecting the academic world with social change.

For six years, I had driven twenty-five miles west from Monterey Park to UCLA. Now, I drove thirty miles east from Monterey Park to Pitzer in Claremont. The distance added to the difficulties of finding a balance between my teaching and committee work on campus and my family and organizing activities in the community. The only way I could do all this and still find time to conduct research was to continue to develop creative ways of connecting the classroom with the community and to write about it.

CONNECTING TEACHING AND RESEARCH
TO SCHOOL TRANSFORMATIONS

When a series of fights erupted between Latino and Chinese American students at a high school that my son attended, I joined with other parents in organizing a coalition, the Multi-Cultural Community Association, to resolve these conflicts. After numerous meetings between the leaders in the Latino/a and Asian Pacific communities, we successfully pressured school administrators to establish an official advisory group to the school board, the Alhambra School District Human Relations Advisory Committee.

In this committee, I worked in the dual roles of researcher and committee chair. As a researcher, I worked alongside the community representatives to counter the views of some administrators who blamed the conflicts on the "hormones" of the students. The survey showed that 86 percent of the students at Mark Keppel High School and a majority of the students at all three high schools in the district perceived racial tensions as a big problem.

At the same time, at Pitzer I collaborated with sociology professor Betty Farrell in developing a conflict-resolution service learning class. In addition to encouraging students to conduct research on a multicultural curriculum and ethnic conflict-resolution programs, this class provided students with a unique opportunity to help the Alhambra School District assess the effectiveness of its policies for dealing with racial and ethnic conflict (Calderón and Farrell 1996). The foundation of the program was the training the students received in ethnographic research and the literature related to ethnic conflict resolution. The students' research included the gathering of census data and information from the district's schools (e.g., ethnic makeup, dropout and expulsions rates, etc.) and interviews with students, teachers, and administrators that identified issues confronting ethnic/racial groups in the district.

Ultimately, the Alhambra School District's Human Relations Advisory Committee utilized the collaborative research of the coalition and Pitzer students to develop a policy on hate-motivated behavior and to implement a racial/ethnic sensitivity program for all teachers. As part of this policy, the school district institutionalized conflict-resolution classes as part of the curriculum and gave students the option of mediation as an alternative to expulsion (Calderón 1995).

CONNECTING SERVICE LEARNING
TO THE FARM WORKER AND DAY LABORER EXPERIENCE

In reflecting on my lived experience as a farm worker and the impact that Cesar Chavez had on my life, I sought to develop a class that would have the same influence that the farm worker social movement had on my life. Out of this passion and with the help of various farm worker contacts, I developed another service learning class called Rural and Urban Ethnic Movements. In this class, now in its seventeenth year, students learn about community-based organizing theories and how they apply to the civil rights, farm worker, immigrant, and contemporary social movements (Barger and Reza 1994; Broyles-Gonzales 1994; Bulosan 1984; Buss 1993; Del Castillo and Garcia 1995; Edid 1994; Ferris and Sandoval 1997; Ganz 2009; Rose 1990; Ross 1989; Scharlin and Villanueva 2006; Shaw 2008; Weber 1994; Wells 1996; Zavella 1987).

During the spring break, the class visits the historical sites of the United Farm Workers Union in La Paz (Keene, California) and Delano. The students learn from farm worker leaders about the history of the movement, particularly the strategies that the union has used to survive. In return, the students implement service projects based on the union's needs. In the first alternative spring break in 1994, alongside Filipino American leader Pete Velasco, the students planted one hundred roses at the gravesite of Cesar Chavez. In the following year they helped to clean up after a flood hit the community. Seven years ago the students carried rocks from a nearby creek to help build the foundation for a Cesar Chavez Memorial. That experience involved students from Vina Danks Middle School, located in the nearby city of Ontario, and day laborers from the Pomona Day Labor Center. This collaboration resulted in the painting of two murals, one at Vina Danks and one at the day labor center, led by community-based artist Paul Botello. More recently, the students traveled to Delano and began framing the pictures of sixty Filipino farm workers who, because of antimiscegenation laws in California, never married and passed away in an elderly farm worker village, Agbayani Village (Calderón and Cadena 2007).

When I began the service learning project with the farm workers, another opportunity for a service learning site came forward when the city of Pomona passed a resolution in 1996 that anyone caught on a corner asking for jobs could be fined $1,000 and spend six months in jail. The ordinance was clearly aimed at the community's growing day laborer population. I was teaching a class, Restructuring Communities, when immigrant rights activist and Pitzer student Fabian Nunez organized a coalition of students, day laborers, and community supporters to pack city hall. When the city council argued that it could not fund a center for undocumented workers, the students gathered research showing that many of the day laborers were also permanent residents. In 1998, these efforts led to the establishment of a nonprofit day labor center, $50,000 in funding from the Pomona city council, and an advisory board that included Pitzer students and faculty. Fabian Nunez, the nonprofit's first board chair, eventually ran for the California state assembly and became one of the most influential Latinos when he was elected as the speaker in Sacramento. [9]

Since the center opened in 1998, students from my classes have joined in collaborative programs with the day laborers in developing employment training programs, health referral networks, immigration rights counseling, and biweekly organizational meetings. In addition to holding language and computer classes every morning, the students have been instrumental in ensuring worker representation on the organization's board. Rather than allowing city officials or consultant "experts" to control the decision-making process, we have organized biweekly meetings to build the collective voice of the workers in running the center. As a result, two day laborers were employed as coordinators and the son of another day laborer is serving as an office administrator. In further advancing the historical partnership between Pitzer College and the day laborers, one of my former students, Suzanne Foster, was hired as the center's director.

In response to the city council's decision to minimally fund the day labor center in the future, we have utilized surveys, questionnaires, and focus groups to establish the amount of resources that the workers have and how they can be maximized. [10] Our collaborative research with the workers has resulted in the writing of various grant proposals to area foundations. One grant helped pay for a day laborer organizer and allowed us to develop a health referral program for the day laborers and their families. Another grant assisted in expanding language, computer, and job-training programs.

SURVIVING PROMOTION
THROUGH CREATING TRANSFORMATIVE SPACES

I survived the joint appointment pressures and both my tenure and full professor reviews by relying on the support of collective action and by ensuring
structural change in my lived environment. Flowing from the vivid examples
presented to us by various union organizers in the region, I worked alongside
my family, day laborers, students, faculty, and community friends to develop
democratic "spaces" that exemplified the type of society we would like to
live in. In our home, Rose and I created a culture where we all shared in
carrying out the household chores. In the day labor center, the day laborers
and students went beyond "charity" services to collaborating in organizing
pilgrimage marches in support of driver's licenses for immigrants, pickets of
employers who refused to pay, and community "fiestas" to build broad coalitions of support for immigrant rights.

One lesson I have learned in creating a democratic classroom and having
students think critically about the social issues around them is that the students' growing conscience and engagement often lead to collective action.
This was the case when some students at Pitzer, motivated by their experiences of working in service learning projects with unions, day laborers, and
farm workers, joined the college's cafeteria workers in their efforts to obtain
higher wages and better health benefits. As early as 1991, when I began as a
professor at Pitzer, a collaboration developed between the cafeteria workers
and various faculty and student leaders to address worker grievances. One
student, Juan de Lara, who later became Pitzer's first Rhodes Scholar, met
with cafeteria supervisors when the workers faced problems. This practice
continued throughout the years until students and workers agreed that the
grievances could be handled more efficiently through a union. After vocal
demonstrations by the workers and students, the workers joined the Hotel
Employees and Restaurant Employees (HERE) union.

The beauty of having a critical pedagogy turn into practical examples of
social change can be exhilarating. On the other hand, it can affect the evaluation process when one comes up for tenure or promotion.

As a junior faculty member, I had to figure out how to publish enough
work to ensure tenure. I did this by writing throughout the process of the
service learning projects I designed. As a result, I published a number of
articles based on my organizing work in Monterey Park, the Alhambra
School District, the United Farm Workers Union, and the Pomona Day Labor
Center (Calderón 2004b). I also joined a dialogue in the Pitzer Faculty Executive Committee to change the faculty handbook so that it was more inclusive of the teaching, research, and service activities of a public intellectual. [11]
Today's faculty handbook includes sections recognizing the contributions in
this realm as part of the contract renewal, promotion, and evaluation process:

effectiveness inside and outside the classroom, sponsorship of internships and other non-traditional means of teaching and learning, the supervising of student participation in research projects, evidence of applied research and/or action research, service to the wider community, and acting as an intellectual resource for colleagues, students, and the community (Pitzer College Faculty Personnel Policies and Procedures 2009, Section V-A).

The changes in the faculty handbook, together with the development of a core of faculty who supported service learning initiatives, ultimately helped me to obtain tenure and full professor status. Although numerous professors supported me in this process, there were struggles along the way. My ongoing support of the cafeteria workers' unionizing efforts resulted in a letter from the administration questioning my involvement as an employee of the college. When I argued for an increase in the number of underrepresented faculty at one faculty meeting, I was stunned to hear a professor who considered himself progressive argue that affirmative action "discriminated against White males." When some students questioned why various art murals had been painted over, I stood with the students in their efforts to ensure that designated spaces were made available on college walls and columns for student-created art pieces. Mindful that the negativity in these conflicts was stirred by a small number of individuals, the collaborative governance structure at Pitzer responded by developing an art committee that included the voice of the students and changed the faculty handbook in support of specified affirmative action goals. [12]

In 2004, after overcoming the "full professor" promotion hurdles, I jumped at the opportunity to apply for a newly created revolving chair position, the Michi and Walter Weglyn Endowed Chair in Multicultural Studies, at Cal Poly Pomona University. I was drawn to the position by the rich diversity among students on the campus, the requisite that one had to only teach one class per quarter, and the reality that I would have more time and resources for my service learning and participatory research work in the community. [13]

MOVING TO HIGHER LEVELS IN APPLYING PARTICIPATORY SERVICE, TEACHING, AND RESEARCH

This two-year position expanded my history of connecting academic teaching and research with community organizing and social change initiatives. Michi and Walter Weglyn, for whom the endowed chair position was named, were examples of individuals who used their lives to carry out research and to use that research in service to the community and to advance social change policies. They were examples not only in the academic sense (with Michi Weglyn producing a book *Years of Infamy: The Untold Story of America's*

Concentration Camps [1976]), but also in the participatory action sense. Hence, Michi Weglyn's book and efforts helped advance a movement that eventually led to reparations for more than eighty thousand interned Japanese Americans and exposed the kidnappings of thousands of Japanese Latin Americans who were forcibly held as prisoners of war during World War II.

Since I was the inaugural chair for the position, I had the opportunity to develop a plan and implement it in the context of the Weglyns' visionary commitment to turning learning, teaching, and research into civic engagement. Although I had been implementing aspects of critical pedagogy, multiculturalism, service learning, and participatory research in my academic work, the endowed chair position gave me the time and space to deepen my understanding of these concepts and their integration. [14] Working alongside Professor Gilbert Cadena, professors from the Ethnic and Women's Studies Department, and the Center for Community Service, we developed a faculty learning circle that met every other Friday. [15] The faculty learning circle was a foundation for deepening my study of the project-based approach as described by Randy Stoecker in *Research Methods for Community Change* (2005). It was also a catalyst for working with a diverse group of faculty and students at Cal Poly in developing various interdisciplinary projects at the Pomona Day Labor Center and organizing a campus-wide conference on service learning and participatory research. [16]

In connecting the reading materials in the classroom to the history of local communities, I also had the opportunity to experiment with service learning and participatory research projects that included the contributions of groups that our educational system has had a tendency to marginalize or exclude. As a Civic Scholar with Campus Compact, a national organization of colleges devoted to civic engagement, I had the opportunity to participate in a dialogue with other national scholars on how to make the classroom more a part of the civic realm and to encourage students' skepticism of traditional historical documents.

In this chapter, I have chosen to tell selected stories from my lived experience that include the lessons learned in surviving the educational system by making learning, teaching, research, and organizing part of a lifelong commitment to advancing social change and social justice. To survive, I have found my passion from reflecting on the "individual issues" that affected my family and working with others in linking these issues to what other oppressed groups have faced historically, placing these issues in a larger context, and implementing strategies for change through nontraditional forms of campus and community engagement. [17]

Along the way, I have had various mentors and teachers who helped me in overcoming academic obstacles: from the support of my family and Raza Graduate Students to various professors in graduate school who helped me make the positive connections between my activism and participatory research.

From graduate school to the present, I have steadily deepened my understanding and implementation of these connections. Through my involvement in the Monterey Park project, I was introduced to the use of ethnographic methodology. As a professor at Pitzer College, I learned to collaborate with other students and professors in applying both service learning and participatory research techniques in implementing solutions to racial conflicts in the schools. Through my work with the United Farm Workers Union and the Pomona Day Labor Center, I learned the importance of making a long-term commitment to a particular site and how service learning and participatory research could move beyond charity to social change and leadership empowerment initiatives. As an endowed chair at Cal Poly Pomona, I had the opportunity and time to work with a diverse group of students and professors in applying aspects of the project-based approach.

As my story has shown, there are spaces in the academy for those who connect their teaching, learning, and research with their passion for social justice. The creation of such democratic spaces takes the organized collective support of family, mentors, colleagues, and community activists who are supporters and participants in transforming the educational system to transform society. The application of a transformative pedagogy, rooted in a passion for overcoming systemic and historical injustices, can determine whether historically excluded individuals and groups can survive the traditional walls of the academy and can play a role in advancing long-term structural changes in the larger society.

NOTES

1. Copyright Acknowledgement: This chapter was previously published in the following: *Transforming the Ivory Tower: Challenging Racism Sexism, and Homophobia, in the Academy*, edited by Mary Danico and Brett Stockdill, Honolulu, Hawaii: University of Hawaii Press, 2012.

2. For a more developed account of this life experience tied to Chicano history see Calderón 2004a.

3. I used Freire's *Pedagogy of the Oppressed* (2000) in implementing a style of teaching that asked students to express the words that best reflected the day-to-day experiences in their lives. I would write their words on square sheets made from cardboard boxes. On one side, their word was written in English and on the other in Spanish. Eventually, each student owned a box that included dozens of their "own" words. As the students shared each other's words, they began to develop a dialogue in English.

4. One result of this collective project was a book, *The Politics of Diversity* (Horton 1995), and a PBS film, *America Becoming*. Additionally, two other books connected to this project included Leland Saito's *Race and Politics: Asian Americans, Latinos, and Whites in a Los Angeles Suburb* (1998) and Mary Pardo's *Mexican American Women Activists: Identity and Resistance in Two Los Angeles Communities* (1998).

5. At the time, our research team used the ethnographic methodology as prescribed by John and Lyn Lofland in *Analyzing Social Settings: A Guide to Qualitative Observations and Analy-*

sis (1984). At the same time, Linda Shaw trained our team using materials from a book that she would later coauthor with Robert Emerson and Rachel Fretz, *Writing Ethnographic Field Note.*

6. I have always been good at telling stories. I grew up hearing stories about the history of Mexico through the lived experiences described by my mother. I resonated with author Gloria Anzaldúa's stories, in *Borderlands* (1987), about how her grandmother and father used *cuentos*, much like the indigenous people, to connect the "artistic" with "everyday life."

7. This moment of survival reminded me of another teacher in high school who saw that I was having problems understanding the sine, the cosine (cosecant), and tangent in a geometry class. Rather than ridiculing me in the class, he took me outside with another student and showed me how to measure between buildings. To this day, I have not forgotten those terms and their meanings. In later years, it also taught me the significance of "doing" sociology.

8. The thesis, "Mexican Americans in a Multi-Ethnic Community," was completed in the spring of 1991.

9. The early history of the center is documented in an article, "Organizing Immigrant Workers: Action Research Strategies in the Pomona Day Labor Center," published in the book *Latino Los Angeles* (2006) and written with the collaboration of two former Pitzer College students, Suzanne Foster and Silvia Rodriguez.

10. A dozen students have written their senior theses on the topic of the informal economy, while others have made presentations at the National Association of Chicana and Chicano Studies (NACCS), the American Sociological Association, the American Association of Higher Education, and the Pitzer College Undergraduate Research Conference.

11. Sociology professor Michael Burawoy, when he was president of the American Sociological Association, helped to bring to the forefront the need to appreciate a public sociology "that seeks to bring sociology to publics beyond the academy, promoting dialogues about issues that affect the fate of society" (2004: 104). In August 2004, the Task Force of Institutionalizing Public Sociologies (2005: 2) was developed by the American Sociological Association to develop proposals "for the recognition and validation of public sociology, incentive and rewards for doing public sociology, and evaluating public sociology."

12. Pitzer College adopted an affirmative action policy with the goal "of increasing, during the period 2001–2015, the overall size of the faculty and the proportion of women and persons from the underrepresented minorities on the continuing Pitzer faculty from the 1994 31 percent of women faculty members to 50 percent or more, and from 1994 19 percent of faculty members from underrepresented minorities to 50 percent or more" (Pitzer College Faculty Personnel Policies and Procedures 2001). These goals were met and new goals are being formulated for adoption in the academic year 2010–2011.

13. The endowed chair position allowed me to experiment with carrying out community-based teaching, research, and organizing without the tremendous workload exacted by being in a joint appointment. Most of the faculty of color at the Claremont Colleges, up until 2010 when the policy was changed, was hired in joint appointments that divided their teaching load with three-fifths in a primary discipline and two-fifths in a five-college department (Black Studies. Chicano Studies, Gender and Feminist Studies, or Asian American Studies). Ultimately, the many responsibilities of serving on many committees and having advisees from all five campuses cut into the amount of time that professors could devote to community-based research and service learning. The professors who do carry out these types of pedagogy in the community usually do it out of a deep commitment to the benefits of applied learning. At the same time, they do it with an understanding that this work is not valued as much as traditional academic activities and that it often has to be done above and beyond all the other typical responsibilities of a faculty member.

14. Over the years, I had invested many hours in studying the literature on these methodologies advancing from traditional ethnography to critical pedagogy, action research, participatory research, community-based research, and project-based research. The result has been an ongoing learning process of implementation and collaboration with others in what Randy Stoecker's project-based approach describes as a cycle of diagnosis, prescription, implementation, and evaluation.

15. The faculty learning circle held discussions on such books as *Empowering Education* (Shor 1992) and *Community-Based Research in Higher Education* (Strand et al. 2003).

16. Our version of implementing the project-based approach is described in Calderón and Cadena 2007.

17. C. Wright Mills, in the *Sociological Imagination*, wrote that many personal troubles cannot be solved merely as such, but must be understood in terms of public issues—and in terms of the problems of history making. Within that range the life of the individual and the making of societies occur, and within that range the sociological imagination has its chance to make a difference in the quality of human life in our time (Mills 1959: 226).

Chapter Nineteen

The Commonalities in Our Past Transform Pedagogy for the Future[1]

José Zapata Calderón

As I embark on a journey to retirement and work to create new models of alternative forms of teaching and learning, I write this chapter as a culmination of observations and reflections on the climate of how the "other" is being treated and how our classrooms can become prototypes of "the future as it is emerging." The concept of "leading from the future as it emerges" appears in the book *Theory U: Leading from the future as it emerges* by Sharmer (2009), and is based on the idea of breaking "the patterns of the past [as we] tune into our highest future possibility—and to begin to operate from that place" (p. 4).

In this context, then, it is important to begin with the trends that are affecting teaching and learning, which will eventually lead me to focus on specific examples of critical service-learning engagements with students and community partners. There are two trends developing nationally—one that is about the future as it is emerging and one that wants to take us back to a time before the Civil Rights Movement. On the one hand, the first trend has been seeking to establish unity among this society's diverse groups by building the types of alliances and partnerships that are necessary to meet the challenges of a global economy. The second stated trend is one that is thriving on creating fear and divisions among working people by using their genuine concerns to blame immigrants, women, poor people, and people of color for the economic problems in this country.

These two trends are manifested in the many debates taking place on college campuses today over the direction of the curriculum and the types of pedagogies that should be used as part of teaching and learning inside class-rooms. The latter trend, based in stereotyping and scapegoating tactics, has reached our classrooms where, for instance, in Arizona there have been open attacks against Ethnic Studies programs that seek to include the histories of underrepresented and oppressed communities in the curricula.

It is in this context that we, as public and activist intellectuals, need to analyze how our classes can advance a trend that is democratic, brings to center stage the histories of those who have been historically excluded, and connects what is being learned in classrooms to community-based research, critical service-learning initiatives, and action for social change.

BRINGING TO CENTER STAGE
THOSE WHO HAVE BEEN EXCLUDED

In terms of bringing to center stage those who have been historically excluded, Anderson and Collins (1995) propose that this type of "reconstructing knowledge" requires moving from an exclusionary perspective to one that shifts "the center" to include "the experiences of groups who have formerly been excluded (p. 2)." Such an inclusive perspective, one that puts at the forefront the experiences of those who have been historically excluded, has been the foundation of Ethnic Studies. Having emerged out of the movements of the 1960's and having been the basis for the establishment of Ethnic Studies, this trend is one that promotes the particular histories of individuals as part of appreciating the cultures and histories of the many people who make up this country. The outlook is that, in understanding our historical differences, there is a foundation to genuinely understand what unites us. At the same time, to meet the challenges of an increasingly global society, there is a need for students to learn about the contributions of the diverse mosaic that comprises the various people of the world. There are many examples in our history of individuals who belong at the center stage of our teaching and learning. These are individuals who have used their knowledge to point out injustices and who used their skills and abilities to empower their communities.

One of these individuals is Cesar Chavez whose birthday, March 31, is celebrated in California as a state holiday. Many of my students, particularly those who come to the United States as immigrants or who are farm workers in the fields, can identify with Cesar Chavez. In particular, many of my students identify with how Chavez's views on nonviolence and morality were influenced by his mother and his grandmother. They identify with his struggles with racism in his school years when Euro-American children called him "dirty Mexican" (Griswold del Castillo and Garcia, 1995, pp. 5–6). Others identify with the story of how the Chavez family was stopped by immigration officials when they came to California from Arizona in the 1930's on the suspicion that they were undocumented immigrants. They identify with Chavez's life of fighting racism in all its forms and his consistent practice of building multi-racial coalitions to fight injustice. Additionally, many of my students identify with how Chavez resisted various forms of injustice by boycotting, marching, fasting, and engaging in community-based organizing strategies, which ultimately contributed to the building of the United Farm Worker's Union.

We have many other examples of individuals in our history that our students are often not taught about—examples who made a choice to use their skills and abilities as a means of service to the community, as a means of advancing spaces of equality in our communities. Two examples of such individuals are Michi and Walter Weglyn, in whose name I held an endowed chair position at Cal Poly Pomona for two years. They were examples of individuals who used their lives to conduct research and to use that research in service to the community and to advance social change policies.

They were examples, not only in the academic sense (with Michi Weglyn producing a book, *Tears of Infamy: The Untold Story of America's Concentration Camps)* but also in the participatory action sense. Hence, Michi Weglyn's book and efforts helped advance a movement that eventually led to reparations for more than 80,000 Japanese Americans interned during World War II and exposed the kidnappings of thousands of Japanese Latin Americans who were forced to serve as prisoners of war during that time.

Similarly, in the last decade, we have had a number of leaders pass away who, like Michi and Walter Weglyn, unconditionally paved the way in frontier areas of service, research, and action in our communities. We have the example of Kenneth Clarke who, along with his wife Mamie Clarke, studied the responses of more than 200 Black children who were asked to choose between a white or a brown doll. Their findings, which showed a preference of the children for white dolls, led to a conclusion that segregation was psychologically damaging and played a pivotal role in the *Brown vs. Board of Education* Supreme Court decision that outlawed segregated education. In recent years, we had the passing of Gloria Anzaldua whose book, *Borderlands,* courageously critiqued both sexism and homophobia in the dominant culture as well as in her own culture.

With these examples, we should also remember Fred Korematsu, who was awarded the Presidential Medal of Freedom and other honors for his courageous spirit in arguing before the Supreme Court that incarcerating Americans without charge, evidence, or trial was unconstitutional. Alongside these examples of bringing to center stage individuals who created a pedagogy for social change is Martin Luther King, Jr. Not many of our students are taught that King was more than a community organizer. He entered Morehouse College at the age of 15 years old and graduated with a bachelors degree in sociology. Then, he enrolled in Crozer Theoological Seminary and eventually received a doctoral degree from Boston University in systematic theology in 1955. King was a writer, a philosoper, a poet, an author, an activist, and the youngest individual to be awarded the Nobel Peace Prize.

Nevertheless, one of King's distinctions was that he put his studies, philosophies, principles, and values into practice for social change. Too often, this society tends to diminish the contributions of such individuals who dare to challenge the status quo and who dare to use both their intellectual and activist skills (against all odds) to fight injustice.

While it is important to bring to center stage the leadership of Martin Luther King, Jr., it is equally important to commemorate the thousands of people involved in the Montgomery Bus Boycott between 1955 and 1956, the Greensboro sit-in of 1960, and the marches for civil rights (e.g., the Selma to Montgomery, Alabama marches of 1965, etc.). It is also important to recognize the tenacity of the Montgomery Improvement Association to desegregate buses (a event that made Martin Luther King a nationally known figure). In recognizing the association, one must also acknowledge the courage of Rosa Parks, a seamstress by profession and a secretary for the Montgomery chapter of the NAACP, who refused to move to the back of the bus. It is also necessary to remember fifteen-year-old Claudette Colvin who, before Rosa Parks, was the first African American woman arrested (1955) for refusing to give up her seat (see Branch, 1988).

The actions in Montgomery, Alabama served as examples of a social movement involving a diversity of community-based organizers. For months, the African American community, with some support from other communities, responded to the arrest of Rosa Parks (as well as other discriminatory acts) by developing their own system of carpools—many used cycling and walking as alternatives to riding the bus. Their tenacity led to a November 13, 1956 Supreme Court ruling that Alabama's racial segregation laws for buses were unconstitutional (Branch, 1988).

Like Martin Luther King, Jr. and Rosa Parks, there are many other examples of everyday individuals who dreamed, who had a vision, and who used their skills and abilities to organize, to empower others, and to turn injustice on its head. Recently, I have asked students in my classes if they know these individuals. Many of my students don't know them. This is similar to recent studies that show that many college students know about the existence of a Cesar Chavez holiday, or a Martin Luther King, Jr. holiday, but know very little about the individuals themselves or the specific roles they played in the social movements that opened the doors to historically excluded groups in this country.

BUILDING CONNECTIONS OF KNOWLEDGE AND PRACTICE

We not only need to teach and learn about the history of these individuals whose contributions are often diminished by the larger society, but we also need to advance the connections between what we learn intellectually and what we practice in our teaching, research, and organizing in the pursuit of building a more just and united society. This involves researching and identifying our commonalities. As a first generation Mexican-origin immigrant, I know the many commonalities that we have had. Similar to African Americans, before the 1960s, we too faced segregation in schools, in colleges, in stores, and in the workplace. The case of "Mendez vs. Westminster" was important in putting a halt to the segregation that Chicano children were facing in public schools (Acuna, 2000). This case was part of the long road of struggle that led to the historic *Brown vs. Board of Education* decision in 1954. The unity of our struggles at that time was exemplified by the role of Thurgood Marshal, a young attorney who helped write the brief for the Mendez case.

Encompassed in this reality is the growing number of immigrants in cities across the United States. The demographics of the largest twenty cities are now majority Black, Brown, and Asian. In New York City, three-fifths of those residing in the city are foreign born with the majority not being able to vote. At the same time, they do pay taxes. This means that the places where immigrants live are highly overrepresented, yet immigrants are structurally excluded.

With their growing numbers and potential political power, immigrants become easy targets for both exploitation and scapegoating. This is an issue of race relations and is one that is both critical and a challenge to those of us who are part of the social justice and immigrant rights movements. Although the social justice and immigrant rights movements have distinct roots, they also share a common ground. The immigrant issue is not a new issue, but it is the newest version of a long existing use of laws to create an exploitable class of exploitable labor. Unfortunately and throughout history, every time ethnic and racial groups in this country have advanced social justice efforts to unite around common issues and struggles, there have been attempts by those in power to keep this from happening.

CITIZENSHIP FOR DIVISION OR UNITY

One of the issues that has been used to divide the various ethnic and racial groups in this country is citizenship. With the rise of the immigrant rights movement in recent years, the issue of citizenship has come to the forefront. There has been a tendency by conservatives to define citizenship primarily as a legal construct with distinct rights and privileges attached, often conferred by one's country of birth and/or one's parentage. Groups such as the Minute Men have used the constitution to claim that all undocumented immigrants are "criminals" and need to be deported since they are not legal citizens. Like the conservative politicians, the right wing groups use the legal definition of citizenship as a means of attacking immigrants.

While all working class people in the United States do not have full citizenship in terms of guaranteed employment, health care, and education, the issue is how the right to citizenship has been constructed. As early as 1790, Congress passed a law that defined American citizenship as being only for "free" white immigrants resulting in "non-white immigrants" not being allowed to be naturalized until the Walter-McCarren Act of 1952.

Both Latino and African American experiences are examples of where legal citizenship has not insulated a group from socioeconomic exploitation. In the case of many Latinos, although they were considered citizens of the U. S. after 1848, this did not insulate them from the use of laws to take their land. In the case of many African Americans, although supposedly freed from slavery, the reality is that they continued to be used as cheap labor without full rights. Legal citizenship, in this context, is a hollow promise that creates citizens "in name only."

If legal citizenship is going to be more than an empty victory, then there must be a vision of full citizenship that is both legal and social in nature. True citizenship goes beyond narrow legal definitions to include equality in all spheres. It is in this struggle to achieve full citizenship where there is a common ground.

Despite differences in legal citizenship, skin color, country of origin, religious affiliations, language, and region, African Americans and Latinos, for example, share historical experiences where laws, social practices, and race-based ideologies combined to create a caste-like society that benefited a few at the expense of the many. The systems of slavery and colonization served as tools to ensure the Western European elite's access to the raw materials and human labor found in Africa, Asia, Latin America, and the Caribbean. These systems of slavery and colonization institutionalized a form of structural violence that used laws to ignore a group's basic human rights.

One manifestation of this denial of human rights has existed in the perpetuation of a divisive relationship that African Americans and Latinos have to formal citizenship.

In the case of African Americans and Latinos, race was used to keep them in the lower levels of the economic ladder and to use them as a cheap labor force. Black people were brought from Africa to the United States as slaves to have their labor fully used. They were also brought to Mexico and Latin American countries for the same purpose. Very early on, race was used in

Mexico to separate Black people or those who married Black people. Hence, Mulatos were placed at the very bottom, which was similar to what happened in the U. S. The separation of people based on race and skin tone was an attempt to maintain the power of the ruling, or dominant, Spanish people in Mexico and the English elites in United States.

This aspect of history included African Americans being defined as non-persons who could be bought, sold, and traded like commodities; defined as partial persons by the Constitution which counted slaves as three-fifths of a person; and denied true citizenship through Jim Crow laws that punished and killed those who dared to exercise their constitutional rights to vote.

Similarly, approximately 75,000 Mexicans woke up on February 2, 1848 to learn they now resided in the U. S. rather than Mexico (McWilliams: 1968). The Treaty of Guadalupe Hidalgo ceded almost half of Mexico's territory to the U. S. Although the treaty assured citizenship rights to the Mexican people and the protection of customs, languages, law, and culture, the treaty was later broken. Instead, they were faced with discrimination in all spheres of life, including loss of land and democratic rights.

There was a commonality here in terms of migration. When the African slaves were freed, they became part of the working class and moved north. "Like most Mexicans, African Americans were following the jobs. By 1930, some two million African Americans had migrated to the cities of the North. Nevertheless, they were historically and structurally excluded from every vehicle that would allow them to have social mobility: homesteading, union jobs, disability, social security and unemployment insurance, suburban housing, jobs and schools, access to higher education.

Similarly, as Mexican laborers lost their land, they too became workers in ranching and agriculture. At the same time, they also found themselves as conditional friends: welcomed when there was a labor shortage and deported when it was economically and politically advantageous. When the economy went downward during the depression of the 1930s, for example, the U. S. Government gave consular offices the charge of deporting anyone who might add to the "public charge" rolls (Bernard: 1998). During this period, at least half a million people of Mexican origin were put on trains and deported (Acuna: 2000; Gonzales, 1999). In the early years of the depression, any Mexican-origin person who applied for welfare, unemployment, or any type of social service was forced to leave the country under the U.S. government category of "voluntary repatriation." Approximately half of those deported were U.S. citizens, a clear violation of both their civil and human rights.

In the recent decades, thousands of Latino immigrants from Guatemala, El Salvador, and other Central American countries have crossed into the U. S. for economic survival and as part of a legacy of a cold war strategy that engaged in proxy wars throughout Latin America. Changes in immigration laws and regional economic restructuring are also credited for this migration and the ultimate stratifying of Latin Americans in the low-wage and low-skill service sector. The passage of the Hart-Cellar Act in 1965 increased the total number of immigrants to be admitted to the U. S. and inadvertently gave opportunities to approximately five million immigrants in the service sector based on low-wage workers and an informal economy (Waldinger and Bozorgmehr, 1996).

THE SIGNIFICANCE OF KNOWING IN BUILDING UNITY

In this context, in order to develop unity among different communities, it is important to understand why immigrants come here, why they risk life and limb for a meager existence in the shadows of our laws? In large part, U. S. policies, with international support, have continued the dominance of global corporations in the so-called developing world. The new globalization operates via trade agreements, such as the North American Free Trade Act, and decision-making bodies such as the World Trade Organization. The "free trade agreement" as it is called, has removed existing trade barriers, eliminated tariffs left on American imports, allowed U. S. corporations full ownership of companies in Mexico, and granted U. S. financial services greater access to Mexican markets. The system of high subsidy payments paid to U. S. farmers by the government has allowed for the exporting of poultry, beans, and corn that serve to undercut the small farmers and farm workers in Mexico. Forced to move to the cities and finding no employment there, these sojourners travel to the U. S.-Mexico border where they either find employment in the maquiladora industry or join the thousands of undocumented immigrants who join low-wage economy in the U. S. Any talk of benefits to the Mexican people becomes questionable when one looks at the dismal results of the "maquiladora" industry all along the Mexican side of the border. These corporations, which have runaway from the U. S. in search of cheap labor and less regulation, have not been able to hide the costs of their social and environmental destruction. Not only have they been caught polluting the air and water, but they have also had a profound effect on the cohesion of the Mexican family. It is commonplace for these plants to primarily hire women and children. No compensation is made for the hidden costs of profit: familial disintegration and inadequate housing, healthcare, and childcare.

BRINGING TO CENTER STAGE:
OUR HISTORICAL COMMONALITIES

In bringing to center stage this slighted history of commonalities, it is important to analyze what we can do in our classrooms today in implementing a type of teaching and learning that advances the creation of a democratic culture both on university campuses and in the surrounding communities. In this process, it is important to begin by questioning the content of the curriculum and questioning the dominant traditional style of teaching in the classroom that often has left out, or marginalized, diverse voices. If we are serious about creating a diverse and engaged democracy, we have to begin where we have the most influence. Our classrooms can be examples of top-down bureaucratic decision-making or they can be spaces where we advance a critical pedagogy, where we can question the traditional literature, and use research methodologies that can be carried out alongside historically marginalized, underrepresented communities.

In many of our institutions, there is still a tendency to separate the content of the curricula from the connections that can be made within local communities. Yet the best type of learning is where the reading materials in the classroom help students to learn about the history of the communities in which they are working and/or living. The type of learning where there is a separation of curricula from community issues ignores the rich promise of multicultural classrooms and multicultural communities; it also reiterates the exclusion of the history of marginalized people from different nationalities, genders, and sexualities.

As a way to not engage in the aforementioned type of learning, we should examine history and historical documents inside our teaching and have learning objectives that situate those documents in an analysis of the particular period in which they were written. This means connecting that analysis to an engaged pedagogy that is collectively developed alongside community partners, using various methodologies (e.g., quantitative, qualitative, and action research; the use of reflections; etc.), and using forms of implementation (e.g., role-playing, journals, teatro, essay writing) that lead to meaningful outcomes. This work begins with the premise that history provides a kind of situated knowledge that is necessary for understanding and participating in the civic realm. In using hands-on research to find creative solutions to compelling problems, these kinds of experiences have helped my students to develop as participant translators. By making connections between the university and the community, my students and I have been involved in translating silence into critical consciousness (see Lorde, 1980).

In applying connections between civic knowledge and civic engagement, students in my classes have been transformed as learners through studying history in combination with service learning and community-based participatory research. In one of my classes, "Rural and Urban Social Movements," for example, students spend the first half of the semester learning about Cesar Chavez, the history of farm workers dating back to the early 1900s, and contemporary efforts to build unions. During their spring break, the students travel to the headquarters of the United Farm Workers to carry out service projects, to work alongside some of the historic figures they have read about in their books, and to listen to stories spoken in the workers' own language. Throughout the semester, students gather field notes and write final research papers based on these experiences. Some of these students have used their research as foundations for community grant proposals, as presentations at undergraduate conferences and national associations, and as thesis papers and projects.

As an example of connecting history to concrete lived experience, I have been taking students to Delano, California (the birthplace of the farm worker's movement) to learn about the history of the Filipino farm workers, individuals who prominently are left out of U.S. history books. In the first years of our visits, students were able to hear firsthand accounts about the hardships of many Filipinos from those who were still alive. In our first year, a diverse group of students worked alongside Pete Velasco, the former president of the United Farm Worker's union, to plant a hundred roses at the gravesite of Cesar Chavez. In the process, Velasco shared many stories as to why some Filipinos became disconnected from their families. It is the story of many immigrants who come to this country looking for the American Dream, not finding it, and creating stories to their loved ones abroad as to why the relatives should not visit them. Ultimately, as a result of being caught in the lowest levels of the stratification structure with no way to get out, they lose all contact with their homeland. This was the case of many Filipino farm workers who grew old and, when it came time for them to retire, had no place to go. It was out of this reality that the United Farm Worker's union, with the help of many college students, constructed a retirement home, Agbayani Village, for the elderly Filipinos.

When my students visited Agbayani Village, listened to these important stories, and planted roses alongside Velasco, they decided that the stories needed to be told to other students and faculty. Realizing that they needed funds for this purpose, the students applied for an "academic scholars" grant. Although Velasco did not have an academic background, the students argued that his experiential knowledge offered an insight into the history of Filipino workers—an insight that is often excluded from academia. Subsequently, a "scholar's proposal" was funded that allowed both Pete and Dolores Velasco to spend a week sharing their stories in the classrooms at Pitzer College. In addition to "teaching" students about the history of the farm workers and the role that the Filipinos played in that movement, the Velascos moved the students into action. Noticing that the grapes that were being served in the college dining hall were non-union, Pete challenged the students to put their "learning into action." Subsequently, by the middle of the week, the students called for a boycott of the cafeteria and passed out leaflets to students at all the entrances. After two days of this action, the Aramark Corporation called for a meeting with the students and, with Pete sitting in, agreed to sign an agreement that prohibited the serving of grapes until they were unionized.

This successful action by the students was exemplary in many ways. First, the students brought to "center stage" a farm worker leader who shared the history of Filipino farm workers, a history that is often left out of our history books. Secondly, the act of treating Pete Velasco as a scholar helped to preserve a history in the process of students actually learning about this history. Third, the academic knowledge that students were learning from their books was transformed into a direct form of engagement that resulted in outcomes that simultaneously informed the campus community about the farm worker social movement and advanced an outcome that directly aided striking farm workers in the fields.

It was also an example of building an empathy that would be the basis for building the strength of a future partnership. When Pete Velasco left campus, he wrote a twenty-seven page letter to the students and thanked them for treating him, not just as a farm worker organizer, but as a scholar. Subsequently, in the following year, when he died from terminal cancer, the students were invited to help carry his casket and to participate in holding flags at an all-night vigil in La Paz (Keene, CA). To commemorate this beginning partnership, the farm workers donated a dozen union roses that the students took back and planted in a designated section of Pitzer College's community garden. In the following year, a farm worker carpenter, who learned about the garden, made a sign that is still there today and reads "farm worker garden." In addition to the roses and the sign, the garden includes a bench with wording on a plaque that commemorates "the La Paz Alternative Spring Break, Brother Pete, Cesar Chavez, Linda Chavez Rodriguez, and all those who have inspired our lives."

The garden is still there today as a symbol of the historical partnership that has developed over the years between the farm workers and the students. Also, after twenty-one years of this annual Spring Break experience with the farm workers, Dolores Velasco still greets the students every year at the entrance to La Paz (Keene, CA) and she is always the last one to bid them farewell. Our Spring Break always ends with a circle ceremony and quotes from Pete Velasco at his gravesite. Over the years, the partnership with this site has been strengthened and has allowed students to both carry out service learning projects as well as carry out community-based research. The partnership has also been exemplary in redefining the meaning of "service learning" to include social change organizing where students organize actions in support of farm workers issues. In recent years, the social change learning has included the making and distribution of leaflets, posters, banners, flags, and press releases for various types of public actions. In Bakersfield, it has been a tradition to rally on the four corners of a mall and carry out advocacy education in support of unionization campaigns in the fields, a Cesar Chavez national holiday, AgJobs, card check legislation, stopping the use of harmful pesticides, and ensuring water and shade for all farm workers in the fields.

Another action that can be considered "service" but takes on a social change character of presenting outcomes and raising consciousness is the use of the methodology of "teatro," once used by the UFW and Teatro Campesino as a means of training new leadership. When students first arrive at La Paz, they are divided into various groups and informed that they should collectively document all their experiences because, on the last day of their visit, they will present a summary of what they have learned in the form of a "teatro." The final outcomes, with at least five teatros presented to dozens of UFW workers and staff members in La Paz, have always resulted in "moving" and "emotional" presentations that invigorate all the participants.

This spirit of creating social change continues when students return to the Pitzer College campus and join in organizing various activities including: organizing a breakfast/luncheon to honor community leaders who represent the values of Cesar Chavez, and arranging a pilgrimage march to promote civic engagement, non-violence, and selfless acts of empowering others. The character of this learning is "social change" because the outcome is one that is consciously designed to go beyond charity projects that often disempower the participants. This is the same type of learning that has taken place in Rancho Cucamonga where workers gather each morning looking for jobs. Initially through my Restructuring Communities class, students began teaching ESL classes right on the street and began holding meetings with the workers every week. The classes and meetings allowed the workers to collaborate with students and join together in defending their civil rights. One of these workers, Fernando Pedraza, a Mexican immigrant father of five daughters and a grandfather of seven, took the city of Rancho Cucamonga to court in 2002 when they tried to get the workers off the street with a no loitering ordinance. Pedraza won the case that allowed for workers to seek employment on the corner as long as they did not block traffic.

Again, like the example with Pete Velasco, Pedraza became a leader to the students. When students organized an art/pictorial display, Pedraza was invited to be the keynote speaker. This was the same time period when the Minute Men and the Ku Klux Klan had been protesting on the corner. On Cinco de Mayo, 2007, a spontaneous demonstration by the Minute Men against day laborers in Rancho Cucamonga ended with the death of day laborer leader Jose Fernando Pedraza when an SUV, that hit a car in the intersection, rolled onto the sidewalk where the day laborers were gathered. On any other day, the day laborers would have left by the noon hour. On this day, they stayed because the Minute Men showed up to protest the day laborer corner.

During the months before his death, Pedraza had attended several meetings of the Rancho Cucamonga city council to support his fellow day laborers so that they could have a job center where they could be safe from hate-based attacks and traffic accidents. Hence, it was no accident that the Minute Men chose Cinco de Mayo as a day to protest the day laborers. It is important to note that as part of the civil rights movement in the late 1960's, Cinco de Mayo was celebrated in the Southwest as a day when the French colonizers in Mexico were defeated and as a day of consciousness raising about the violation of human rights of the Mexican-origin people in the United States.

In this example, the use of ESL classes and community meetings with the workers led to their empowerment. As students carried out service projects, social justice issues emerged that moved the character of organizing to a level of social change organizing. Today, that character has not changed as students have continued to organize weekly meetings, a soccer team, and a yearly day laborer mass at Saint Carmel, a local community church. The inspiration of Pedraza's life led the day laborer workers, with the help of day laborer organizer Eddie Gonzalez and graduate student Junko Ihrke, to orga-nize a soccer team that, although having few resources, took first place in a soccer tournament at the Rose Bowl. The bishop from the San Bernardino diocese, so deeply moved by the achievements of the Rancho day laborers, held a mass in their honor at Mt. Carmel. At a packed church service, the Rancho day laborers carried their five foot trophy to the front altar and had it blessed by the Bishop. In his sermon, the Bishop urged the parishioners to support the day laborers and all immigrants in their efforts to obtain full democratic rights. This tradition has now expanded to include a yearly me-morial to commemorate the life of Pedraza and all day laborers who have given their lives in efforts to advance immigrant rights, locally and globally. The yearly memorial, led by the Fernando Pedraza Memorial coalition, has included participation from the Bishop, the faith-based organization CLUE, the student organization Latino Student Union, the Dream network of AB-540 students, and the community-based organizations of the National Day Labor Organizing Network and the Latina/o Roundtable. Today, this ongoing organizing effort has become an example of bringing to center stage those community leaders who traditionally have been left out of history. At the same time, in continuing to create a space of "sanctuary" in Rancho Cuca-monga, students and day laborers have created an example of building a type of multi-racial collaboration that is steeped in the future possibility of obtain-ing legalization for the 12 million undocumented immigrants in the U. S.

BRINGING COMMONALITIES TO THE CENTER: CONCLUSIONS

This essay has addressed two emerging national trends: one that is focused on scapegoating immigrants, working people, and people of color for the contradictions in the economic system, and another that is seeking to bring to center stage the social change histories and organizing examples of those who have been historically excluded. Without classrooms that bring to center stage the common histories of those who have been labeled as "other," there is the danger of advancing a type of traditional education that separates students from the reality of problems that their communities are confronting. If this trend becomes dominant, a type of civic engagement can be advanced that serves merely to perpetuate the inequalities that are already prevalent. Without an education that looks at the systemic and structural foundations of social problems, students will be taught the symptoms of the problems instead of understanding the character of the structure that is placing individuals in those conditions.

The type of teaching, learning, and engagement that is promoted in this essay is one where: there is a passion for creating spaces of equity; where students are exposed to a curriculum that looks at the systemic and structural aspects of inequity; that brings to center stage the contributions of communities who—because of poverty, racism, sexism, classism, or homophobia—have historically been excluded from textbooks; and that involves students in working alongside historically marginalized communities on service-learning projects grounded in a pedagogy of engagement that includes transformative, democratic examples of connecting the past to the present and the future.

NOTE

1. Copyright Acknowledgement: This chapter was previously published in the following: *The Pitzer College 50th Anniversary Engaged Faculty Collection.* Ed. Tessa Hicks Peterson. Claremont, CA: Pitzer College Community Engagement Center, 2014: 85–93.

REFERENCES

Acuna, R. (2000). *Occupied America.* Wesley Longman, Incorporated. 279–280.
Anderson, Margaret L., Patricia Hill Collins (2006). *Race, Class, and Gender.* Wadsworth Publishing Company.
Anzaldua, Gloria. *Borderlands/La Frontera: The New Mestiza (1987).* San Francisco, CA: Spinsters/Aunt Lute Book Company.
Branch, T. (1988). *Parting the Waters: America in the King Years.* Simon & Schuster, Incorporated. 120–123.
Del Castillo, Richard Griswold and Richard A. Garcia (1995). *Cesar Chavez: A Triumph Spirit,* Norman, OK: University of Oklahoma Press.
Gonzales, Manuel G. (1999). *Mexicanos: A History of Mexicans in the U. S.* Bloomington: Indiana University Press, 1999.
Lorde, A. (1980). *The cancer journals.* San Francisco: Spinster, Ink.
Sharmer, C.O. (2009). *Theory U: Leading from the future as it emerges.* San Francisco: Berrett-Koehler Publishers.
Waldinger, Roger and Mehdi Bozorgmehr (1996). "The Making of a Multicultural Metropolis." In Ethnic Los Angeles, edited by Allen J. Scott and Edward W. Soja. 3–38. New York: The Russell Sage Foundation.

Weglyn, Michi(1976). *Years of Infamy: The Untold Story of America's Concentration Camps.* New York: Morrow.